Love as always,
Kurt

Love as always, Kurt

Vonnegut as I Knew Him

LOREE RACKSTRAW

DA CAPO PRESS

A Member of the Perseus Books Group

Photos on pages xviii, 24, 114, courtesy of the author; the author
gratefully acknowledges the following for use of additional photos:

Chapter 3, page 42, Joe Petro III; Chapter 4, page 70, Marc Rae;
Chapter 5, page 96, Joe Petro III; Chapter 7, page 130, Joe Petro III;
Chapter 9, page 174, Leslie Wilson; Afterword, page 262, Peter Reed

Design and composition in Garamond by Cindy Young.

Library of Congress Cataloging-in-Publication Data
Rackstraw, Loree, 1931–
    Love as always, Kurt: Vonnegut as I knew him / Loree Rackstraw.
        p. cm.—Includes index.
    ISBN 978-0-306-81803-5
    1. Vonnegut, Kurt.   2. Novelists, American—20th century—
Biography.   I. Title.
PS3572.O5Z798 2009
813'.54—dc22
[B]

                              2008053660

Published by Da Capo Press
A Member of the Perseus Books Group
www.dacapopress.com

Da Capo Press books are available at special discounts for bulk purchases
in the U.S. by corporations, institutions, and other organizations. For more
information, please contact the Special Markets Department at the Perseus
Books Group, 2300 Chestnut Street, Suite 200, Philadelphia, PA 19103,
or call (800) 810-4145, ext. 5000, or e-mail
special.markets@perseusbooks.com.

10 9 8 7 6 5 4 3 2 1

This book is lovingly dedicated to the memory of my late husband, Richard Rackstraw, a gifted poet whose vision burned brighter than even his beautiful voice could carry, and in celebration of our children, Leslie and Rob Wilson, and Kevin, Geoffrey, and Didi Rackstraw.

CONTENTS

LIST OF ILLUSTRATIONS

ACKNOWLEDGMENTS

I wish to thank my longtime friend and colleague, Peter Reed, who not only read the first draft of this book, but unfailingly provided needed counsel and information until its completion. It was his advice and that of my son-in-law, Kevin Lynch, which led eventually to my agent, Joy Tutela—a literary angel without whose editorial skills and faith this story would not have made it into print. She was ably assisted by her gifted intern, Jenny Davis, herself a writer.

And Joy was right about the talented expertise and wisdom of my Da Capo editor, Renee Sedliar, who took us the rest of the way.

I'm especially grateful to my friend, Tom Thompson, for his unfailing emergency house calls to supply digital counsel, and to David Wood for explaining how computers work and doing magic with mine. I'm also beholden to Sid Huttner, director of the Special Collections Library at the University of Iowa, for his generous guidance, appraisals, and security for precious books and documents.

My dear friends and fellow writers Alice Swensen and Tina Bourjaily were readily available for caring advice when I needed it. Local healers Linda, Pam, and Kent provided sustaining energy and balance, as did my yoga instructors. Supportive phone calls from Joe Petro III, always arrived when I most needed his friendly voice and cheer.

And finally I thank my dear family and friends for their continuing inspiration and loyalty. Leslie and Rob Wilson were with me from the beginning and continue to be an important part of this story. Their encouragement and faith are powerful sustenance. My sister Lois has been a loyal backup whenever I needed to talk. The trust of Nanny Vonnegut was a gift welcome beyond words. My three Rackstraw step-kids were faithful cheerleaders from opposite sides of the country, and the loyalty of my longtime local "sistahs" continues to be a source of strength and inspiration.

Last but not least, I thank the School of Music at the University of Northern Iowa and the Waterloo-Cedar Falls Symphony Orchestra whose music never fails to restore. As Kurt always said, "No matter how bad things get, the music will still be wonderful."

He was right about that, and a lot more. . . .

PREFACE

It was a hot September afternoon in 1965 when I joined other writing students in our Quonset hut classroom at the University of Iowa. This was my second year of graduate work at the Iowa Writers' Workshop, and I was torn between anger and anxiety about the new person who'd be teaching our fiction writing section this semester.

I was a single mom with two kids and the usual pressures of limited time and money. My former mentor, the novelist Verlin Cassill, who'd approved my admission into the writing program the year before, had rather abruptly accepted another position after a disagreement about the Workshop's administration. We former students had only recently received announcement of his replacement, and so far I'd not found anyone who'd heard of Kurt Vonnegut, Jr. I had found a copy of a novel he had published a couple years earlier called *Cat's Cradle* and had given it a fast read. It was compelling but far removed from books and stories I'd been studying the past year. Henry James he was not.

So it was with considerable apprehension that I trudged across Madison Street from my half-time job at the University of Iowa's public relations office, to the Workshop Quonsets for the first meeting with our new writing coach. What none of us knew was that Kurt Vonnegut was as apprehensive as we were. He'd been trained in the sciences and had done graduate work in anthropology. And he'd never taken, never mind taught, a college course in fiction writing.

I took a seat next to Andre Dubus—a dear friend who'd played second dad to my son the previous spring when he'd been roughed up by a third-grade bully. He had news about our new guru: Vonnegut and his teenaged daughter had moved into the big house on Van Buren

Street next door to the Dubus family. So Andre had already met him and assured me he was "a great guy; lots of laughs."

Just then Mr. Vonnegut came through the door, ducking his head to enter the sultry room, dressed in chinos, a somewhat rumpled short-sleeved shirt, and scruffy, tan sneakers. He sat atop the desk at the front of the room and faced us. Conversations quieted abruptly.

He was a great bear of a man with an elongated boyish face, cropped hair, and almost-protruding hazel-blue eyes. He surveyed the room of young writers, myself the exception in my mid-thirties. I saw lots of smile lines around his eyes and a nice grin. He ground out a cigarette and pulled another from the Pall Mall pack in his shirt pocket. His hands were those of a pianist, with unusually long fingers. Lighting the cigarette, he told a joke and laughed profusely through the smoke, coughing just as much. A couple of students glanced at each other with rolled eyes. He would say later that "following Verlin Cassill in front of this audience was like following Judy Garland."

His message that day was not profound, but it was clear: He hadn't been educated in an English department, but he knew the most important thing a writer had to remember was the reader. He drew some murmurs when he said he didn't see any reason for working on a story unless you wanted to sell it. (Some of us still considered financial reward beneath one's dignity.)

But his was another take on the craft: "What do you need to be a writer in America? An audience! You don't need to supply useless information. Readers don't need to know how many freckles are on a lady's thigh and what she had for breakfast!"

And writers must provide enough props so readers are comfortable and don't get lost. "It's OK to let them know right away where your character's going to end up. But then make your character clearly want something so your readers will have to find out how the character gets there."

By the time he was finished, I was quietly impressed. Since I'd been supporting myself and two kids for several years as a journalist and public relations writer, I knew the value of keeping the reader reading to the end. And it didn't hurt that he had a sense of humor.

I hoped the first story I handed in a few weeks later met some of Mr. Vonnegut's expectations. I was nervous but looking forward to our appointment. His tiny office in the Quonsets was furnished with a wooden desk and chair plus a shabby, upholstered recliner where he sat reading my manuscript, cigarette in hand. A typewriter rested atop an upside-down wastebasket next to him.

He had a cheerful way of disarming apprehension and appearing to be intensely interested. Primed for his reactions, instead I blurted out worries about my work—and found myself revealing the disaster of the novel manuscript I'd abandoned the previous month.

That past summer, when my two children had been away to visit their father, I'd devoted every available moment of that rare time to my own writing. With forty pages of a novel completed that might qualify toward a required thesis for the Master of Fine Arts degree, I rewarded myself to a night out at a newly released movie. To my dismay, the film's plot became increasingly recognizable.

Soon after, my manuscript received a ritual cremation in my charcoal grill.

So now, I told Mr. Vonnegut, I had less than a year to finish a new novel or a book-length collection of stories in order to graduate by the end of next summer. And I *had* to graduate! Another year here was not financially possible.

I stopped for breath. He would think I was an idiot.

Without cracking a smile, he said, "You could have written *Madame Bovary* and tried to publish that, if you really wanted to get in trouble." And somehow I was able to laugh instead of cry.

That was how it began—the semester and a friendship that grew in richness and value over the next forty years, until his death in the spring of 2007. Our relationship was mostly sustained by hundreds of letters and phone calls, with only occasional meetings. It granted me the opportunity to follow his career with unusual if distant intimacy through his spectacular tenure as one of the most significant and beloved writers in America and abroad.

To "understand" our friendship was not something I gave a lot of time to. We broke a couple of taboos that first year, something Kurt alluded to near the end of Chapter 1 in *Slaughterhouse-Five*, about teaching at "the famous Writers' Workshop." I was a participant in the "beautiful trouble" he got into and got out of again. That "trouble" evolved into a bond unique in my life's experience. From the beginning, it defied analysis, so I simply accepted it and came to trust it.

Naïve though it may seem, that *was* our relationship—simple, unquestioning, trusting, generous—and richly profound. It was not to be feared or doubted or heaped with expectations. It simply existed. It felt right. I believe he agreed. What became much more important was that Kurt continued to be my friend and mentor until the time of his death.

His was the most richly complex mind I have ever known. I was a willing listener when he wanted to vent or celebrate—or share a funny story. I took his fiction seriously and wrote a number of reviews and scholarly articles exploring it. I believed he was a creative genius. I still do.

Because our friendship was sustained mostly by the U.S. Postal Service, over the years I filled several drawers of a file cabinet with his letters and copies of his essays, speeches, page proofs, and reviews. As he began taking his visual artistic talents seriously, examples of his "colorful doodles" decorated the walls of my home. And as my sense of his work's significance and its humanizing effect on American culture grew, I came to believe I must give serious effort to share the insights I felt I had gained during our relationship. I began to write what would become this memoir. About two years before he died, I told him what I was attempting. He immediately asked if I planned "to include the time [back in 1975] when we damn near swamped our boat off Key West in a one-foot chop?" When my reply was "yes," he said, "Hurrah!"

I completed the first draft of this book a few days before he died.

I miss him a lot. We all do.

Kurt Vonnegut in his Quonset hut office, 1965.

The Writers' "Gang" in Iowa, 1965–1966
God Bless You, Mr. Rosewater

A few days after my disastrous confessional meeting, I stopped at Kurt's office again, this time to actually discuss the story I'd handed in. Coming from a figure drawing course, I was hauling some quite awful one-minute charcoal sketches I'd done. He insisted on looking at them and listened to my frustration about having to sketch so fast. I confessed, I was a plodder.

He didn't reveal his own artistic talents, but I'd noticed some intricate doodles on his desk. He said his daughter Edith was interested in art and pretty good at it. He was planning to meet her at the Union next door for the peace rally later that afternoon. "That guy who burned his draft card last weekend, Steve Smith? He's going to speak today. I've talked with him a little. Did you know he was teaching at a Mississippi grade school last year, a segregated school? The father of one of his students got dragged behind a car and killed." He shook his head, and said quietly, "*There's* a story."

Then he smiled and handed me my story manuscript. We talked about intentions, and he playfully wondered if perhaps too much early detail in my story might be hampering where I wanted it to go. It seemed to him the story was about a married couple on a collision course.

"How would you feel about throwing away the first two or three pages? Begin the story by saying that?"

"What do you mean?"

"Just that: 'Rachel and Bill were on a collision course.'" He lit a cigarette from one smoldering in his hand, exhaled, and leaned forward in the raggedy recliner with a little grin. "That would get my attention."

I pondered a bit and said I'd give it a try.

"Good. Now—you really want the story to be set at Christmastime?"

I nodded.

"So any way you could make that a little more—I mean, with Rachel pregnant in this god-awful town—no place at the Inn and all . . . ?"

Of course. Somehow I hadn't even thought of the significance. "But I don't want it to be obvious. . . . I'm afraid it's already too sentimental."

"I was thinking more of parody," he grinned.

I took a deep breath and thought for a while. Wow. It had possibilities. "I see what you mean."

He handed me the manuscript. "I think it's a little gem just lying there waiting."

"I'll give it another shot," I said.

"Good. See how it goes. And then we'll put it on the worksheet and try it out on the others."

I gulped. "I don't know—do you think it's ready for that?"

He looked at me expectantly and grew suddenly serious. "How many stories have you had on the worksheet?" he asked quietly.

I winced. Cassill had never put one of my stories up for discussion. I'd thought he was probably just being kind, and besides, I was secretly glad not to have to face the feedback critiques, most of them from men. And several had already published, like my friend Andre Dubus. Very few women were in the program, and those who were, like Joy Williams, were so good they were ready to publish now.

Kurt said earnestly, "You're a good writer, you know." He lit another cigarette. "So how about a Coke? My daughter will be at the Union in about half an hour. She'll like you."

We walked next door.

He wanted to know more about the Engles. Since Paul Engle, the Workshop director, was on leave in Europe that semester, he hadn't met him. Instead, Kurt's friend George Starbuck, in the Poetry Workshop, had offered him the job. "Paul himself probably invited Nelson Algren and José Donoso."

"You're in pretty good company," I teased, though I admitted I hadn't read Donoso yet. He was a Chilean who had only a couple novels available in translation.

"Algren hasn't read him, either," he chuckled. "The first week here we were all going up the steps to the English Department, and Algren said to Donoso. . . ." He interrupted himself with laughter—"Algren says, 'It must be nice to live in a country so long and narrow.'" His laugh and wheezing cough were inevitably infectious, and I never could help joining him.

I told Kurt how kind Paul and his wife, Mary, had been to me and my kids the past year, even including us for meals. Their Stone City summer home had been destroyed by fire two years earlier, and I'd toured its stark remains, overlooking the area's rolling, forested hills and stone quarries.

"So it's still there, the ruins?" Kurt asked.

"Just the rubble of limestone slabs and a couple of standing fireplace chimneys. It's only about an hour's drive."

He looked past me to wave at someone. "There's Edie."

"Hey, Pops!" Edith was a sixteen-year-old darling with a sparkle in her eyes. She was ready to take on the CIA and defend draft dodgers to the death.

Outside a crowd had already gathered around a platform between the Workshop Quonsets and the Union when we joined them. A student speaker, just finishing to cheers, introduced an elderly faculty member. Kurt nodded toward several men in suits moving about the perimeter of the gathering.

"FBI," he said. "They're probably taking pictures."

Edie tugged at my arm. "Let's pose for them." Kurt was engrossed with the speaker. Edie and I sidled toward the observers. When two of them got closer, we faced them in an obvious pose with arms across each other's shoulders. The one taking notes stepped toward us.

"C'mon," I whispered to Edie, yielding to her adolescence. "We can lose them."

We wheeled up the back stairs into the Union. The guy was actually following us! I dragged Edie up two flights through the door of the ballroom. It was pitch black inside.

"Just feel your way along the wall. There's another door over this way."

"Wait'll I tell Dad," she chortled, as we made our way out and back to the rally.

That autumn protest was the first of many that year as sentiment against Vietnam involvement grew in Iowa City and across the nation. Along with it came increasing concerns about voter registration and civil rights in the South.

* * *

One Saturday, Kurt called to ask if I wanted to help pack food to be sent to Mississippi and Alabama in support of the voter registration drive there. After packing the food, we stopped for a beer. Inevitably, the Vietnam conflict came up.

"When I was in college," I told him, "about half the guys in our senior class went off to Korea during Christmas break. That was called a conflict, too. At least a *real* War was declared for yours."

I knew Kurt had been in the Infantry during World War II and captured during the Battle of the Bulge.

"I've been trying to write *my* version of that war for years," he said. "Problem is I've blanked out some of the most important stuff. None of the survivors I've found can remember much. Have *you* ever heard of the Dresden fire-bombing?"

I hadn't.

"Well, I was there. Dresden was beautiful—an open city—and it really happened. A hundred and thirty-thousand Germans died—incendiaries alternating with high explosives for hours, dropped by the RAF and our own air force. And nobody in the States even knew it happened."

He explained how he'd tried to locate old war buddies once he started writing, and how all of them had vague recollections about the horrific event.

My memories of the war were pretty blurry, too, being nine years Kurt's junior. That was before TV, and back then, timely war news was sparse. I remembered headlines from countries I'd hardly heard of, along with short clips in movie theaters prior to feature films.

"They were always followed by the 'Star Spangled Banner,'" I told Kurt, "and then the audience would stand and sing."

I was surprised how interested he seemed to hear my descriptions about troop trains passing through on the Minneapolis & St. Louis Railway near my house. And how my teen-aged girlfriends and I would bake cookies and then rush, giggling, to hold up trays so the young recruits could grab them as they rolled past. And how our school had War Stamp drives and victory gardens to supplement rationing. He was especially interested in how my father, a World War I veteran, grimly insisted on silence every evening at five o'clock when he listened to H. V. Kaltenborn's daily war news on the radio.

But when Kurt began talking about his war recollections, his voice lowered to almost a half-whisper as he said abruptly, "My mother died before we even disembarked." And then, more softly, "She took pills."

His recounting of her Mother's Day suicide in 1944, when he was home on furlough prior to being shipped to the European front, was stunning. I hardly knew how to respond, except with something inane, like "How *awful.*" I felt a pained look on my face as he continued, almost in a matter-of-fact way.

"Six months later with my infantry battalion—we ended up at the Battle of the Bulge. We had a big howitzer. But one of our guys got hit, and pretty soon we couldn't catch up." That's when he was captured, in November of 1944.

I know I reached across the table to take his hand. I can't recall details, but I remember feeling almost shocked at his manner. It was as though he was forcing himself to whisper this important information.

He asked if my parents were still living and told me his father had died eight years earlier. His voice again had an almost wistful tone when he said quietly, "I'm an orphan now."

Ordinarily he had a rather short attention span and was quickly bored with small talk, but this more solemn mood was substantially different from his usual upbeat manner. It was like his frame of mind on another occasion, when he told me about the death of his sister, in the awed voice of an unbelieving observer.

"Allie died of cancer the day after her husband was killed in a horrendous railroad bridge accident." The more stories he told, the more I realized how much his life had been shaped by untimely death or by violent accidents.

Kurt rarely spoke of his wife, Jane, who was back in Barnstable on Cape Cod with Nanny, his nine-year-old, "the last of our children at home," Kurt said.

The same age as my daughter, Leslie. I presumed early on that Kurt and Jane were estranged, but I didn't want to intrude and figured he'd tell me if he was conflicted about what felt to me like our growing affection.

One night, however, he stopped by my apartment for a late dessert. Eventually, our conversation about the challenges of kids led him to the incredible story about how he and Jane had taken in three of his sister's sons when they were orphaned. It didn't quite register with me then how recently that had been—only seven years earlier. He recounted a strange story of how Jane had gone through what he called an actual schizophrenic experience during the time his sister Alice had been fighting cancer.

"I'd been to visit Allie and returned home to find Jane hallucinating: She'd been taking food out to our barn for 'refugees' who she thought were secretly hiding there. It was astonishing. Of course, there *were* no refugees." He went on to explain the even more amazing thing: "On the very day my sister died, Jane dramatically recovered."

When I marveled at how difficult this abrupt family expansion of three additional sons must have been for her, Kurt's understated response was meant as a serious compliment: "She washed a lot of diapers."

Jane's remarkable story about this experience would eventually be published (posthumously) in 1987, long after the Vonneguts had divorced and she had married Adam Yarmolinsky. Her moving narration in *Angels without Wings* makes clear the challenges that must have drained both her and Kurt, to say nothing of their bank account. Indeed, her characterization of the "schizophrenic experience," while she later recognized it as verging on insanity, had nonetheless been seen by her then as a spiritual premonition: The "refugees in the barn" were the orphaned children who soon *did* arrive at their doorstep in 1958.

Neither Jane nor Kurt would have been idle during those years. Looking back, their children marvel at how their mother managed to feed half the kids in the neighborhood and still provide supervised space for games and competitions. If Kurt's publication record suggests they were without financial concerns, however, read Jane's book. Big money was not available then for published novels, especially for unknown writers. Kurt told me his *Sirens of Titan* paperback original in 1959 earned him "a flat $3,000 minus 10% for the agent."

During the seven years since the Vonneguts had acquired those three new "sons," and Kurt's arrival in Iowa City, he had completed and/or published three new novels: *Mother Night* in 1961, *Cat's Cradle* in 1963, and *God Bless You, Mr. Rosewater*, finished only the previous spring.

Now in the fall of 1965, their son Mark was in college and the three older nephews had left home and were scattered. With Nanny and Jane living in Massachusetts, and Edie and Kurt in Iowa City, somehow it seemed intrusive to push Kurt about his estrangement or whatever it was. But of course, I wondered. I recall only one time that he expressed anything resembling marital discord. It had to do with his feeling that Jane was living her life through him and was too intimately subject to his ups and downs.

One Saturday that fall, we were sitting on the porch steps of the big house at the dead end of Van Buren Street in Iowa City where he and Edie lived, waiting to go over to Andre and Pat Dubus's house next door to watch *Batman*. This comical new TV series was a favorite that Kurt, Edie, and the Dubuses hardly ever missed on Saturday afternoons. My children were playing in the yard with the three Dubus kids, Andre III, Jeb, and Nicole.

While we were waiting for *Batman*, Kurt had shown me a copy of *The Bell Jar*, Sylvia Plath's autobiographical novel published following her suicide, and asked if I had read it. I'd seen some of her poetry and knew of her struggle with depression and her death, but I didn't actually read *The Bell Jar* until several years later. At the time, however, I briefly wondered why he would be reading something as dreary as Plath. He was usually such a clown that he often had people around him laughing uproariously. It stayed on my mind that he urged me to read it, but I just didn't have time then for unassigned downers.

I wasn't alone in believing Kurt was a born comic, though when I first met him it was sometimes difficult to tell when or whether he really was being serious. I wasn't used to satire, which was standard in much of his conversation, even in commenting on a story. I knew several Workshop students who swore he dropped LSD regularly in Iowa City. I knew he didn't. Yet certainly one of the reasons we all came to love being with him so much was because he was such hilarious fun.

Increasingly, I came to realize that Kurt's frenetic energy and impatience with tedium were somewhat relieved by his joviality and satire. Mostly, he seemed in fine fettle, with melancholy rarely in evidence. Especially when he was watching the amateurish heroism of Batman as he sailed through the air to rescue an innocent victim from evildoers, and comic-book sound effects that appeared on the screen— "BAM! POW! WHAM-O!"—punctuated by our laughter and cheers.

* * *

It was a chilly day in early November when Kurt and I drove to Stone City in his Volkswagen Bug to visit the remains of the Engle summer home. The overgrowth in the wooded hills surrounding the farm fields and distant quarry seemed denser than I had remembered, so much so that I wasn't sure I could find the Engle site. A familiar landmark was the old limestone church across the gravel road from the ruins. A dirt lane led up a rise. The site was abandoned, covered with matted grass and shin-high leaves. But then we saw the stark fireplace chimneys in a bit of a clearing. Kurt parked the car, and we walked around the limestone foundation, peering into the shaded opening that was either a cellar or had been the first of a two-story dwelling. The stone had come from the limestone quarries, probably the one visible through the trees from here. It was eerie and magical.

An undamaged smaller outbuilding near the ruins was probably the milk house. We pushed through the creaky door. Petite, painted images were faintly visible on the walls—intricate figures of farm animals and a field with haystacks and buildings.

"They say Grant Wood did these," I told him. It was like a secret shrine.

"Astonishing," he said quietly. "It's a museum."

On a slope beyond the house, surrounded by trees and growth, was a covered gazebo-like structure, with benches around the sides. We climbed the steps and sat there having a smoke and talking for a long while. As it grew chilly, Kurt put his coat around my shoulders, touched my face, and then held me close. Except for the sound of a few birds and the rustle of leaves in the breeze, the stillness of that wooded grove surrounded us like a blessing.

It was some time later that we heard the startling call of a strange bird. It seemed to celebrate the changed significance in our relationship that afternoon, a wildly cheerful cry, something I never forgot.

"Is it a whippoorwill?" I asked. "I've never heard one before."

"An epiphany!" he said with a big smile.

"What a strange sound!"

"He's celebrating!" said Kurt. "Come on, it's getting cold."

It was about a decade later that I read his new "autobiographical" novel *Slapstick*, so called because it was "what life feels like" to him. It was a story about a twin brother and sister born grotesquely retarded and hidden away in a deserted mansion located in an Eden-like forest of apple trees. But Wilbur and Eliza eventually discovered a spectacular single intelligence when they "put their heads together" in an orgiastic epiphany. The unusual union of these twins was always celebrated by the cry of a "Nocturnal Goatsucker," along with their brilliant new insights.

But as for Kurt and me, back in the ruined forest mansion of Stone City, the autumn shadows were indeed growing frigid. We walked to the car, hand in hand. Kurt reached for a bottle on the back seat, "To take off the chill." Opening the glove compartment, he found an old china mug with coins in it, one of those thick cups you see in diners. He dumped out the coins—"It's good, clean money"—and poured in some scotch, offering me the first swallow. It was deliciously warming.

The drive back to Iowa City was a journey into a reality subtly transformed. When we reached my apartment, he insisted I keep the cup.

As the season changed into winter, I saw him more frequently: I'd stop at his office for a quick chat, a question about a manuscript or one of the drawings I was working on. Sometimes he'd pop in at my apartment unannounced, usually in late evening after my kids were in bed, for cookies and milk, or to tell a funny story. I loved our intimacy, our conversations, our laughs. Sometimes he'd unexpectedly show up with a little gift and then leave abruptly—a recording of bird songs or the new Modern Jazz Quartet album. Or maybe a sack of plump artichokes.

I was living at an accelerating pace, my energy level boosted by a Dexedrine prescription from a sympathetic doctor, and really didn't have time to wonder about the future. The occasional private moments we shared were sweet luxuries.

Once Kurt surprised me with a Saturday morning visit when I was in the midst of making changes in the graph I'd created to track my novel's plot line. I'd used a long roll of shelf paper to diagram the narrative of my characters with different colored lines, indicating crossed paths and rising or falling action. Somehow it helped me keep everything in mind to see the visual image.

Kurt seemed amused by my strategy, and I was a bit miffed that he seemed to find it playful. Perhaps he may instead have found it ironic: I later learned he had used a somewhat similar strategy in the grad thesis proposal he'd recently sent to the University of Chicago. He'd hoped it would finally earn him his long-delayed master's degree in anthropology. Instead of mapping characters, his graphs illustrated how differing plot lines of stories reflected distinctions among ethnic cultures.

It didn't immediately get him that elusive degree, but it did evolve into a popular chalk talk device he later used to conclude his public speeches. He claimed to illustrate differences between "good news and bad news" among familiar stories, beginning with "Cinderella," whose rising plot line goes off the top of the blackboard "when the shoe fits." His conclusion powerfully illustrated how the *level* plot line of truly great literature, like Shakespeare's *Hamlet*, achieves its profound truth: real life provides us with neither good news nor bad news, but rather leaves us in limbo.

Of course writing was central to everyone in the Workshop, but there was time for fun, too. Everyone dined like kings when Vance Bourjaily and his wife, Tina, hosted their annual Workshop pig roast out at their Red Bird Farm, a large wooded acreage. This was a first for most of the Workshop children and a momentous event for everyone's appetites. Their wonderful hospitality included a dammed-up pond where everybody could swim—nirvana for children and parents alike. Kurt obviously enjoyed Vance's company and occasionally hunted pheasants with him or played clarinet in pickup jam sessions at Vance's country schoolhouse studio.

Music was something that kept Kurt going no matter how difficult things became. One night we drove to a Cedar Rapids club to hear a jazz combo play old standards we both loved. Quite unexpectedly, part of the show included a rather tasteful transvestite performance— several exotic female impersonators—something I hadn't seen before.

I marveled at their beauty and didn't realize for some time they were men. Kurt seemed moved by their performance, commenting quietly that they did "good, honest work." At the time I thought how sensitive he was compared to most of the Workshop men, many of them unabashedly homophobic.

Among those less gentle souls was Nelson Algren. Like all of us, Kurt had considerable respect for Algren, a somewhat incorrigible addition to the staff, although surely the most famous that year. His previous and well-known affair with Simone de Beauvoir had only recently ended. Nelson soon earned a reputation at an ongoing high stakes poker game in town, and according to scuttlebutt, had not had very good luck. In fact, it was rumored that he'd lost his entire Workshop salary in a game.

The first time I'd seen him was actually before classes began that fall—when I had accompanied a woman registered for his Workshop section to a pre-class conference with him. The lasting impression of that experience was not a pleasant one.

She had explained, with exaggerated reverence, how she'd come from Idaho just to work with Algren, "the most important living writer in this country." She'd mailed him her novel manuscript prior to her arrival, and he'd agreed to meet with her. She was nervous about their appointment and asked if I'd walk with her to the Union coffee shop the next day when she was to meet him.

We spotted him sitting at a table by the windows overlooking the Iowa River, a slight, balding man, staring expressionless and smoking a cigarette. A black folder, apparently containing her manuscript, rested on the table before him. She squeezed my arm with cold fingers and said, "Wish me luck."

She approached the table and stood, waiting for him to look up. I couldn't hear what he was saying, but then, he put his hand on her manuscript and slowly slid it to the floor. She didn't move for a few seconds, then stooped to pick it up, and raced for the door. I followed her down the hall and into the women's john.

"What happened?" She was sobbing silently, with her hand over her mouth. "What?" I demanded. "What did he say?"

She shook her head, devastated. "He said, 'I don't get paid to read shit like this.'" She wheeled about and entered one of the cubicles, slamming the door behind her. I never saw her again.

On some later occasion, I recounted this episode to Kurt, but afterward wished I hadn't done so. When I finished my account, he said nothing at all, and I felt ashamed to have revealed this side of the man. Kurt was rarely critical of others, unless, perhaps, they were in high political or corporate office. One afternoon later, Kurt and I were walking through the Union lounge where students often gathered to study or nap. We noticed, over in a shadowed corner, a reading lamp illuminating Algren's prone body on a couch. One hand dangled to the floor to rest on a book splayed open, face down. It was Truman Capote's *In Cold Blood*, his new innovative, nonfiction novel. Algren shared Kurt's regard for the controversial book, spurned by some literary purists at the University.

"There ought to be an endowed retirement center for writers somewhere in this country to take care of people like Algren," Kurt said quietly.

There may be such a place, but if not, Kurt created a fictional one called Xanadu in his last novel, *Timequake*, in 1997. It was a wonderful residential center where his favorite character, Kilgore Trout, could retire with heroic status. Many years later, when I visited Kurt and his second wife at their summer home in the Hamptons, Kurt introduced me to Gloria Jones, the generous widow of author James Jones. She had become a kind of personal "retirement center" who watched out for Algren in his last years. A delightful Earth Mother, she took me to the Parkland Cemetery in Sag Harbor where he was buried. It was nice to think Algren's powerful talents had been comforted with kindness and warmth in his waning days.

Algren's sharp tongue had rather intimidated me, and I never took a course from him, but we became friends over our mutual admiration of the Armenian American novelist and playwright, William Saroyan. One late May evening at my apartment when I was hosting a farewell gathering for Workshop friends, Algren showed up. He regaled my children with funny stories and was in splendid form, when he launched into Saroyan anecdotes and aphorisms for my benefit. Before he left, he scrawled a self tribute across several pages of my paperback copy of his novel, *A Walk on the Wild Side*:

> For Lori [*sic*] Wilson—This may be the biggest shocker of my writing generation. This well may be one of the most powerful talents now protesting in Americka. Not only that but I am *very* well dressed. With all best wishes to Lori from Nelson
>
> *Iowa City, May 30, 1966*

Writers like Algren were just one of the many fascinating characters in our Workshop community that made the challenge of parenting easier for me, while enriching my kids' lives, as well. Both Leslie and my son Robbie liked playing with the Dubus kids, especially after their new baby sister arrived. Pat Dubus was a wonder of a mom and sweetly caring with my children. She and Andre, like many grad students, supplemented their groceries with what were called government "subsidies," a pre food-stamp program. Peanut butter was an excessively supplied subsidy and amply shared by Pat for sandwiches my kids loved. She mothered any number of Workshop children, always with a smile and her New Orleans accent.

The Dubuses also gave great parties. One particularly memorable was Andre's birthday party. Pat had made a huge cake for the occasion. The celebration included a spontaneous emergence of a favorite Workshop entertainment: literary quotation challenges. A competitor might begin with something easy: "Do not ask for whom the bell tolls . . . ," and his opponent would return: "It tolls for thee." Losers failing to complete a quote had to chug their drink. Hemingway was a favorite, but so was Shakespeare. And Flaubert. The party that night was growing tumultuous, and Andre was mercilessly winning. Not only was he the single student among us who had sold a novel, but he also had a great memory. Finally, he challenged with "For Emma Bovary, 'life was as cold as . . .' *come on!*—'as cold as an attic with . . . ?'" He howled with laughter at his opponent's defeated shrug, and shouted: "'*as cold as an attic WITH A WINDOW LOOKING TO*

THE NORTH!' Drink up!!" His loser moaned, and Andre gave him a hug, chugging along with him.

He couldn't lose that night and proceeded to grow more and more impressed with his stature. I noticed Pat sensing things might be getting out of hand. It was time to wind things down with dessert. She got a firm grasp on the tray that held her gorgeous cake with its abundant pink frosting, and made her way smiling toward Andre just as he was shouting: "To make war all you need is intelligence. But to *win* you need . . . ?"

Andre saw her coming and beamed, "HA! To win you need—*a woman with tits as gorgeous as Pat's!*"

His triumph resulted in the most spectacular demonstration of wifely affront I had ever witnessed: The cake landed squarely in Andre's face and chest, nearly knocking him down.

Andre recovered to howls of laughter. With jovial poise he redeemed himself by feeding the remains of the cake to everyone with hugs and kisses, including a particularly sticky one for Pat.

* * *

Another great asset in Iowa City was easy access to the arts. My daughter, Leslie, was thriving on ballet lessons from Marcia Thayer at the university. Robbie wanted to take trumpet lessons, which I couldn't quite afford until Kurt generously insisted on supplementing the lesson fee. One Saturday morning, Kurt showed up at our apartment with an old tuba.

"Found it at a rummage sale for a buck!" he announced triumphantly. "The mouthpiece alone is worth five!"

It became a major trophy for Robbie with his pals. The Beatles were just coming into their own, and my kids did their best to help me appreciate their music, a trade-off for mom taking them to free university concerts and art shows.

Springtime did have some challenges, however. My fatigue level was taxed by an extracurricular job that I needed for the money—writing the Iowa section of a travel book that Paul Engle had generously passed on to me. A major test was the need to smuggle books out of the

Historical Library (which didn't have a loan policy) so I could work at night, and then smuggle them back in the next morning. I was also pursuing job interviews in teaching and in advertising. With my kids, my job at the university, two Workshop courses, a lit course mid-semester exam coming up, and all with my Dexedrine dosage running thin, stress was at an all-time high. I was also writing a special PR story for the reissue in hard cover of Kurt's original paperback of *Player Piano* that April, which I wanted to be perfect, so I focused a lot of my energy on that.

This book, his first novel, was a fictionalized critique of how mechanized mass production was leading to dehumanization, the first "automation novel" ever published. By then I had also re-read *Cat's Cradle* with a stronger appreciation of its powerful social satire than I'd first realized in my quick read. But I was most moved by *Mother Night*, a paperback original published in 1961, also about to be reissued by Harper in hard cover. It portrayed the complexity of war through the author's view that "We are what we pretend to be, so we must be careful about what we pretend to be." It was clear why critics were saying he was "the best, least-read novelist in America." I was almost as eager as he was to see *God Bless You, Mr. Rosewater*, the book he'd finished before coming to Iowa, which would also be out that spring.

I was spending whatever time I could with Kurt, with growing enthusiasm about his burgeoning success and intrigue about his hope to move more toward theater "where the action is." He'd confided he was "crazy about it, the excitement and drama, you know? I want to get a piece of the ball right on the sweet part of the bat and smash it—kapow!—right out of the ball park."

So I was totally taken aback, when he phoned one evening to tell me that his wife Jane and daughter Nanny would be arriving from Massachusetts the next day.

I was speechless. The next day! I think I said something like, "Oh." And hung up. Stunned, I simply could not comprehend why he hadn't told me this was a possibility, or at least given me more time to adjust or discuss it. He *must* have known Jane would be coming to Iowa long before.

I was in shock. Finally I phoned my teenaged sitter and then drove around out in the country to be alone for a while, down by the river where it was quiet. I needed to stop my racing mind and think more clearly. In the distance was a tiny symphony of early spring frogs. There was a bright moon. No whippoorwill.

I couldn't shake it—the pain felt like betrayal, even though I realized I had no real right to feel that. It grew into guilt: heavy and dulling and stifling.

By the next day, after a sleepless night, I knew I needed some help, and had the good sense to get myself an appointment with a very nice psychiatrist at University Hospitals to discuss how tantalized I'd been with the luring enticement of the sparkling Iowa River the night before. A dear Workshop couple came to stay over the weekend with my kids so I could move into their apartment to sleep and get my head straight and body back to normal. It worked, and eventually I figured out how to never let myself ever become that vulnerable again. Or to take Dexedrine.

*   *   *

Kurt's wife and daughter did arrive that next day, well in time to celebrate a few weeks later the triumphant reissue of those two early novels, with early positive reviews already appearing in major journals and papers for *God Bless You, Mr. Rosewater*. It looked like Kurt's work was finally taking him beyond the cult recognition that had barely sustained him and his family for more than a decade.

Of course I was nervous about meeting Jane, but when I did, the origins of Edie's puckish energy were evident. She reminded me of a winged creature bouncing from flower to flower, in delight with life itself, but never quite sure of where she was landing in space and time. There was such a childlike innocence about her that I had the crazy impulse to hug her in the wonder of how she had survived not only the needs of her own three children and husband, but also of those suddenly orphaned nephews. Yet, a bright intelligence glowed behind her apparent naïveté that seemed to keep her from foundering. We became immediate friends.

I felt she had some sense of my earlier relationship with Kurt, but she and Kurt had not discussed anything specific so far as I knew. Nor had Kurt and I, either, at any length. It was evident to me he was loyal to Jane, so I was too. I wasn't naïve, I was realistic. Besides that, I liked her.

My Workshop friends probably had sensed Kurt's and my closeness, and had seen us together at various times before Jane's arrival, but I had never been aware of anyone's concern. I'd learned early on that "the Workshop" was its own unique family culture that respected privacy and loved loving without criticism. We knew we were all in this thing together. I've never experienced anything like it before or since.

So Jane was an enthusiastic participant in plans for the May surprise party to honor the new publications of Kurt's novels. By then, just about everybody in the Workshop had read and was crazy about Kurt Vonnegut and his work. All had welcomed Jane into the Workshop family and were pleased she had arrived in time to be part of the celebration.

The party became a major event. Several fellow students turned up at the Dubuses that Saturday afternoon to craft, under Edie's direction, huge posters replicating the covers of all of Kurt's books, including the new reissues. Jane's part in the collusion was to arrange a theater date with English professor Bob Scholes and his wife Joan, which would take the Vonneguts away from their house by 7:30 that night. (By then Bob had become one of the early scholarly critics of Kurt's work and saw him as a leading "fabulist" in American letters.) I had garnered student contributions to purchase a Workshop gift of an HO gauge electric train, something Kurt had earlier confided his love for as a kid. His youthful romance with real steam engines as well as miniatures continued well into his later life.

A select decorating committee was secretly waiting that evening at the Dubus house, as the Vonneguts pulled away for the theater. On signal, we rushed over to adorn the walls with posters and hook up the train tracks in the middle of the dining room table. An ice-filled farm tank for cooling beer soon appeared outside the back door.

Workshop students and faculty couples began arriving by the dozens, secretly parking their cars on nearby streets. My children, who had by then become buddies with both Nanny and Edie, joined in the breathless wait for *the surprise*. Everything was in readiness in the darkened house by the time the Vonneguts and Scholeses arrived for their presumably quiet evening nightcap.

To everyone's delight, it truly was a surprise.

The innocent charm of that evening was a celebration of the downright joy we all felt about the long-awaited recognition Kurt had finally achieved with the hardcover reissue of *Mother Night*. Coupled with the reissued *Player Piano* and with the new *God Bless You, Mr. Rosewater*, it was a sign that his time as a significant novelist had finally arrived.

Andre Dubus had the honor of presenting the gift by lifting the cloth covering the train, as someone plugged it in to begin its action to the cheers of the crowd pressed around the table. Kurt was speechless with delight, but his appreciation was evident and somehow radiated most fully in his shy grin as he watched the little train making its rounds. Then Andre raised his hand for silence and shouted, "To the author of *Mother Night*, God bless him—and Rosewater, too!" He planted a big kiss on Kurt's cheek, and started the chant: "Hip hip, HOORAY."

It was a sweet moment, a love fest that lasted most of the night. My kids were put somewhere to bed with Nanny. The crowd eventually dwindled, and grinning, Kurt silently took my hand and led me into the darkened living room where we danced to the music of an old ballad playing on the phonograph: "There's a small hotel. . . ." We didn't speak. It was as though the movie scene had shifted without transition, and somehow I knew everything was going to be all right. Years later, I wondered whether we all had somehow adapted to Kurt's nonlinear time sensibility. Tralfamadore appearing in the middle of Iowa City was just part of the whole life picture. Not to worry. Somehow, there was a magic there we could all trust. Not to worry . . .

When I drove over to the Vonneguts the next morning to pick up my kids, it looked like another party was underway in the backyard.

Edie was hauling cans of V-8 juice to mix with beer, "the hair of the dog that bit you." The Vonnegut's sheepdog, Sandy, was scurrying happily from person to person for treats, the only creature there not hung over. Kurt, haggard but smiling, was standing barefoot listening to Andre dramatize an important hangover cure from his marine days that had something to do with raw fish caught fresh from the Pacific.

It was just about the most down-to-earth, middle-America family gathering one might imagine, except that the central passion of everyone there, with the possible exception of Sandy, was the crafting of creative ideas and the artistic discourse to express them. All of us would consciously or unconsciously work to shape into some literary form what we had come to sense and know from and about each other and this remarkable place. It was as though this family base generated new language energy. Many times in the years ahead Kurt would speak of this renewing community experience he found in Iowa City, something he had longed for in his writing life on Cape Cod, where he felt his neighbors either hadn't read his work and avoided him, or found it difficult to understand or appreciate. The nurturing support of that kind of community experience is sometimes difficult to sustain in the traditional academic setting of a university, and it was one of the extraordinary benefits of the Workshop. For Kurt, coming as it did after the frustrations of minimal recognition for his work, coupled with the family and financial stresses that must have had a draining effect on both him and Jane, it was a nourishing oasis of humaneness.

Thinking back on it as an adult, my daughter Leslie said,

In my young life [she was ten years old], I had never before met people who walked around clanging these invisible ropes of colorful richness, which was their art—their loving, passionate contribution to life. It was wonderfully curious and expanding for me as a youngster. I remember Kurt's house as this kind of delicious, go-with-the-flow chaos in his family's behavior. . . . Picnics with basic foods, sitting on old blankets on the lawn with all the kids running around, mostly Dubus kids with runny noses and dirty feet.

Years later, Kurt used the term "gang" to describe the community he later found in New York City. It was different, of course, but it was a culture of creative fellow humans among whom he felt stimulated and respected for the writer he was. It was a similar "we're in this thing together" kind of gang he needed and depended upon for the expression of his own art,

Back in Iowa City, however, with the reissue of Kurt's critically neglected early novels to increasingly positive recognition, along with signs of an emerging breakthrough in his twenty-year struggle to birth his "Dresden novel" (with its then working title, *Goodbye Blue Monday*), it seemed that a significant turning point was underway. A major part of that struggle would be completed within the next two years with *Slaughterhouse-Five*, and another would soon follow with *Breakfast of Champions*.

Even so, as the semester drew to a close, there came a growing sense that the camaraderie and intensity we had all enjoyed might be threatened. Within a few weeks, the acting head of the Workshop, Gene Garber, announced that Paul Engle would step down as the fabled director in the coming year. Soon another beloved and highly respected member of the poetry staff, Donald Justice, issued a harsh criticism in the *Daily Iowan* of the English Department's strengthened supervision over the Workshop. Distressing administrative and academic incursions threatened during the previous year were portending the possibility of change in the nature of the Workshop.

The end of the semester did arrive, and with it a grateful recognition that what the Workshop family had shared that year was an extraordinary experience of creative life at its most bountiful. For me, now it was time that I conclude my work and move on. My novel manuscript, substantially rewritten out of the ashes, had Kurt's assurance it would suffice at least for my thesis, if not for publication. The Vonneguts would be leaving for summer at their home on the Cape, and I would remain to finish my work in time for graduation in August.

Jane and I had had no real chance to talk privately, but I felt we both sensed the unspoken trust between us. I also felt she recognized by then the depth of my friendship with Kurt had not been a trivial teacher-student one. But I was grateful she knew it had expanded to include her and to honor their marriage. They would go home to Barnstable and return for another year or two at the Workshop in the fall. By then, after those months of job interviews and indecision, I'd be teaching at the State College in Cedar Falls, a hundred or so miles to the north, where I'd done public relations prior to the Workshop adventure. I definitely hoped I might see Kurt again, but I was less than sure that would be possible. I knew he wanted his marriage to continue, stressed or otherwise. But our love had been a new, if not profound experience for me. Being family friends was fine with me, so long as we had *some* kind of relationship, however it played out.

On a warm June morning I took my kids and the new Vonnegut novels I then owned over to their house to say goodbye and to get Kurt's signature. It was frantic with their moving preparations. Kurt went off and sat by a tree with my books. The kids and I helped haul stuff to the Vonnegut cars and shared lots of hugs. We all promised to meet again in the fall . . . have a great trip . . . goodbye . . . drive safely . . . be sure to write . . . goodbye . . . goodbye . . .

Later at my apartment, I looked at the books Kurt had signed. Inside one was a yellow lined tablet paper folded in quarters. It was the beginning of our epistolary friendship. He had written, "If we are not sad when we part, we must have done something lovely."

Loree Wilson (Rackstraw) and Kurt, workshop surprise party, 1966.

2

Fame at Last, 1966–1972

Welcome to the Monkey House, Slaughterhouse-Five, Happy Birthday, Wanda June

The summer in Barnstable was going great for Kurt: in July he wrote that producer Hilliard Elkins had taken an option to produce *Cat's Cradle* as a musical, which meant Kurt would devote the remainder of the summer to transforming it into a script on speculation for a percentage of the box office gross, although with virtually no advance money. As he said, "It's all a thrilling speculation."

Back in Iowa City, where I was finishing up my thesis and my job editing the alumni magazine, we had a little thrilling speculation of our own when my first Workshop mentor Verlin Cassill passed through town. In a call prior to his arrival, he had asked me to arrange for a duel between himself and Kurt Vonnegut, downtown in front of the Hamburg Inn No. 2! He was outraged at the changes proposed for the Workshop and may have thought Kurt had something to do with them, which was not the case. While Cassill was in town, he declined my invitation to read my thesis manuscript. I learned he had met with Paul Engle, newly arrived from Europe, in order to conclude his relationship with the Workshop, vowing never to return. Cassill would later take a teaching position at Brown University in

Rhode Island, where he had a fairly turbulent career and produced several substantial novels. He and his wife Kay lived in Providence until his death in 2002. As predicted, the Workshop was never quite the same without him.

My summer was a marathon daze of getting my completed thesis properly typed for submission to the Graduate College and concluding my studies. Kurt had arranged with his Workshop colleague, Vance Bourjaily, to do the final sign-off on my thesis, which he did. Then, with several Cedar Falls commutes to secure housing and re-enroll my kids in the College's Laboratory School, I finally got us ready for our August move and reorientation to a new life.

Kurt wrote from Barnstable when the Dubus family passed through on their way to New Hampshire where Andre, MFA degree intact, would begin teaching at a private women's college. Kurt had by then sent off several scenes for the *Cat's Cradle* musical to producer Elkins (now "Hilly" Elkins), and composers were working on the music. He had also connected with Allan Pakula, producer of *Up the Down Staircase*, who had come by to express his "abiding interest in all my work, which he had discovered only recently" (8/18/66). Kurt's love for the stage had sparked new energies, and he suggested he probably would teach only one more year at Iowa. His summer had been productive, though he never explicitly mentioned his war novel.

*   *   *

Kurt's optimism that late summer was not shared by author Richard Yates, with whom I'd studied my first year at the Workshop, and who had returned in early August to Iowa City from Hollywood, where he'd been working on a screenplay. Some years earlier he'd successfully adapted William Styron's *Lie Down in Darkness*, but this time he'd not done so well.

Iowa City was absent most of the Workshop students and faculty Yates had known from the previous school year, and his summer solitude was being drowned fairly regularly at his favorite bar, The Airliner. His first call to say hello suggested a state of mind reminiscent of Scott Fitzgerald's after his infamous Hollywood gig. We made a date to meet at the Airliner for lunch shortly before I was to make my permanent move to Cedar Falls. I wanted to say goodbye, but also to apprise him of the new staff members, both Vonnegut and Donoso, especially since his pals, the Cassills and the Dubuses, were no longer there to keep an eye on him.

Yates had initially been invited by Cassill to join the Workshop fiction staff in 1964, the year I first arrived there, on the merits of his highly successful first novel, *Revolutionary Road* (1961), plus an earlier collection of superb short stories. My first social experience with him had been at the Cassill home for dinner shortly after both he and I first moved to Iowa City. In the course of the evening we heard Yates's story of his health and psychiatric problems, as well as his praise for his famous New York psychiatrist "who didn't believe in that crap about talk therapy, but only in drugs." Iowa City was a far cry from New York City or from his former employment at the Rand Corporation, but it always amused me that Dick found Iowa City "over stimulating." My kids and I, as well as the Dubuses and Cassills, were among the Workshop families who had tried to see he had an occasional nutritious meal, and in return he had become a valued friend and mentor.

Yates was a writerly novelist who, understandably, seemed not to have quite recovered from being terrified he'd never write another book as good as his first one. *Revolutionary Road* had been runner up for the National Book Award. His short stories were beautiful, if full of the angst of Dick's own life. He was highly admired and appreciated by his students that 1964 school year, which perhaps made him feel less defensive about not having a college degree.

Now, nearly two years later, I tried to bring him up to date on what to expect. I believed he and Kurt would have some common ground, especially because both had seen European service in World War II. In fact, Kurt did become a caring friend of Yates that year, which continued when both were living in Manhattan.

As for Yates in Iowa City after I had left, Kurt wrote his early impression after returning, on September 22:

...tes and I get along fine—the way you wanted us to. He sure seems bloody and bowed, though. I guess he's had a hell of a life. He is an extra-good university citizen, repeating rules and policies and meeting times until he's got them straight. He'd like to stay on forever, and there's no reason why he can't. He is much loved as a writer by the kids, as was evident at registration. Shoals of people want to study under him.

The Workshop was still under the acting directorship of Gene Garber, although George Starbuck had been given a unanimous nomination by the Workshop staff to take over the post in the coming school year of 1967. Kurt wrote in November (14) that he'd had some interest in "becoming the boss of the joint . . . but we didn't stay on that razor edge very long. . . . A writer is the thing to be." He added that conversation with Bob Scholes had convinced him that Paul Engle was "switching to foreigners now . . . because he enjoys being the bull seal in a small herd of people who feel damn lucky to get small amounts of money for anything."

So when Kurt presented his resignation to John Gerber, the chair of the Department of English, and received "no counter-offers of more dough and less work," it confirmed his "impression that the Workshop is a device for getting good teachers cheap." Nonetheless, he felt Starbuck was in a great position to bargain for the directorship because he had had many offers from the outside. He wrote that

> it is slowly seeping through the thick skulls around here that anybody who works in the Workshop is actually doing the University a favor. Paul has always led them to believe the Workshop was a branch of the Salvation Army rehabilitating drunks, giving them soup and clean, second-hand clothing. (Spring 1967)

That spring, however, he wrote that Starbuck had given up on his hopes to head the Workshop because of frustrating lack of support from Engle. Kurt was outraged that Gene Garber, who was so conscientiously directing the program, hadn't been able to get his own novel published. But he was glad Donoso, who'd be leaving in June for Spain or Portugal, had "finished a perfectly brilliant book," even though "Knopf thinks it is only so-so. I'm crazy about it, so is Yates."

Kurt's big news by April was that he'd received a Guggenheim to revisit Dresden, along with a three-book contract arrangement with Seymour Lawrence and Delacorte Press. That would finally relieve the financial pressures that had dogged him for years and would provide the peace of mind he and Jane had never had.

By then, I was getting accustomed to my new role as an instructor of English, and had met an interesting fellow writer who'd joined the faculty the same time as I. Dick Rackstraw had been helpful in getting me past the first terrors of teaching and had gradually become a more frequent visitor in our home. In the process of divorce, he missed his own children and was dear with mine. Although he didn't know Kurt's work, he helped persuade my department head to sponsor a visit from Kurt for a speech on "Teaching Writers To Write."

*   *   *

I was excited about seeing Kurt and Jane again and invited them to spend the night at my newly rented home near the campus.

While Kurt wasn't exactly a household name by that time, enough faculty and students had read or heard of him that a modest but enthused audience soon was howling with laughter. He met with my writing students, kids who had little serious interest in novels or novelists, let alone World War II. But Kurt intrigued them with anecdotes about the difficulty of writing about his war experiences—and of how, when he tried to write about the Dresden fire bombing and its after effects, he kept coming up blank. Recently, he'd found and interviewed army friends in the same boat. Nobody had the same story or could remember details. At one time, he said he'd even toyed with the idea of printing techniques to gradually darken the pages as the narrative drew closer to the actual fire bombing—and then, during the event, to make the pages completely opaque. All this he described as an entertaining story, but of course he wasn't kidding.

Years later, the summer of 2005, I visited the Lilly Library at Indiana University in Bloomington, to examine for myself some of Kurt's documents archived there. In Box 10, beginning with file fifteen, were the hundreds of laborious pages of his early *Slaughterhouse-Five* drafts. When I opened the folder of pages written during the year I'd first met him, I found myself near tears with a sudden feeling of tenderness. How he had labored over those pages and pages! The manuscript versions were directed to Littauer & Wilkinson, Inc. in New York—agents who had managed some early sale of his work. Several versions of a chapter titled "Captured," were written in first person about a Private Arnold Moon who had been shot by a firing squad and whose mother the narrator had visited after the war. The typed pages were, of course, crossed out and overwritten, long before computer "word processing."

Another version began with a dedication "For Bernard V. O'Hare, Private First Class," edited to read "For Bernard V. O'Hare, A First Class Private." (This was his wartime buddy and fellow prisoner of war.) The dedication is followed by the author's statement: "I have lived this, dreamed this, changed all the names and faces, and dreamed this again. Nobody is real—not even I." With "not even I"—crossed out. The epigraph for this version was from Leviticus: "And fire came forth from before the Lord. . . ." In several other versions, "Private Moon" starves himself to death and "David McSwan" becomes the character shot by the firing squad. It was easy to sense Kurt's struggles as the narrative evolved toward the novel's true core and its resolution.

The finished *Slaughterhouse-Five* would, of course, eventually be dedicated to Bernard's wife, Mary O'Hare, and to Gerhard Muller, the taxi driver whom Kurt and Bernard met when they revisited Dresden in 1968 on Kurt's Guggenheim Grant. (This is the actual driver who, the novel states, sent a Christmas card to Kurt, saying he was glad to have met the author and would like to see him again, "if the accident will," a serendipitous statement that becomes a profound theme shaping the novel's final version.) By file twenty-four, apparently early in 1968, McSwan becomes Billy Pilgrim, and the manuscript takes on the tightness and flow of what would become the completed story that begins with the Preface, "All this happened more or less. . . ." Of particular profundity was the statement on manuscript page ten that "What made Billy [so happy] was his belief he was going to comfort so many people with the truth about time."

But in the spring of 1967 in Iowa, the author obviously was still struggling, both with work on the novel and with teaching at the Writers' Workshop. After his speech, I invited some faculty friends and a few students over to meet him and Jane at my home. I was glad to introduce them to my new friend Dick Rackstraw and hoped it defused any possible leftover tensions for Jane to know I was in a close relationship with him. Later, my ongoing conversation with Kurt and Jane went long into the night, shaped by our reminiscences about the great times of the previous year and celebrations of the Dubuses and all the Iowa City pals we missed. "The trouble is there's nobody there any more," Kurt had said.

So when the Vonneguts pulled out of Iowa City permanently that June of 1967, it was to drive back to the Cape with Kurt's Dresden novel nearing completion. Within two years, it would make him internationally acclaimed as America's most successful writer. (And it gave me considerable pleasure that the next time he returned to Cedar Falls to speak, with *Slaughterhouse-Five* still a best-seller, he would fill the school's largest auditorium with a standing-room-only crowd of wildly cheering fans.)

Later that summer of 1967, however, he sent me his whimsical article poking fun at summer writers' conferences from the front page of the *New York Times Book Review* (August 6). The front page! With the title "Teaching the Unteachable," the article focused on a summer conference sponsored by Western State University in Macomb, Illinois, where he and Yates had taught along with two other former Workshop staffers. His satirical style contrasted the brevity of the conference with the two-year Iowa graduate program, nonetheless asserting that

Nothing is known about helping real writers to write better. I have discovered almost nothing about it . . . I now make to my successor at Iowa a gift of the one rule that seemed to work for me: Leave real writers alone.

A scathing reaction appeared by poet John Ciardi the following month in the *Saturday Review* magazine (9/30/67). Writing in his weekly column, "Manner of Speaking," Ciardi—who was the famous director of the even more famous Bread Loaf writers' conference held each year at Middlebury, Vermont—bitterly denounced Kurt as a bumbling fool. Not only did Kurt lack "God's permission to write well," but he "writes like a slob and thinks like a blob," among other things.

In a letter to me soon after, Kurt wrote, "What a mean old poet [Ciardi] must be," noting that even though he didn't subscribe to *Saturday Review*, he'd sent a telegram canceling his subscription. He said Algren had written to Ciardi too, and that he'd "received several letters from people who went to Breadloaf [*sic*] and figure they were robbed."

As acerbic as Ciardi's piece was, it nonetheless was a foretaste of one kind of criticism that sometimes would be leveled at Kurt's style as his novels' popularity grew in the years ahead. Black humor, satire, and insistence on using the voice of "a man from Indiana" would rile some reviewers into bitter attacks. Although he never really grew used to that reaction, he did shrug it off more easily as time went on. It was not unlike the derision sometimes leveled at Mark Twain at the height of his writing career, among many similarities between Vonnegut and the nineteenth-century humorist, one of Kurt's favorite writers. And of course it was partly Kurt's style that made him popular to readers from all walks of life, and also helped make his Dresden novel so powerful. Humorless Mr. Ciardi doubtless winced when *Slaughterhouse-Five* sat for months on the the *New York Times* bestseller list.

Meanwhile, *Slaughterhouse* needed only final touches following Kurt's return from the Guggenheim trip in October. In a (10/29/67) letter he said, "Dresden, which was known as 'The Florence of the Elbe' before it was bombed flat, now looks like Cedar Rapids in 1936—the buildings, the clothes, the music. All of it." Traveling with his old war buddy, Bernard V. O'Hare, he said they'd been "thrown out of every iron curtain country within twenty-four hours. We didn't do anything wrong, but everybody was offended by two middle-aged Americans in business suits going here and there for pleasure. They knew damn well we were C.I.A." He was obviously pumped and ready to end work on his hard-wrought war book.

And so he did, during a period when the United States was moving into a turbulent election year, which was made all the more dramatic by political and social eruptions in civil rights, environmental concerns, and the feminist movement. To say nothing of the Vietnam War. By 1968, half a million U. S. troops were fighting there, with the body count growing daily. The Tet Offensive had been launched, requiring even more U.S. troops. This was the year of the My Lai Massacre and the second communist offensive, with B-52s bombing near the Cambodian border. In the height of the fray, President Lyndon Johnson announced he would not run for reelection.

The turbulent Democratic Convention in Chicago the summer of 1968 only made Kurt's popularity soar with college students. His new short story collection released in August, *Welcome to the Monkey House*, didn't hurt his popularity on American campuses, and he was using that role to insist on avoiding war and abuse of the planet.

By then, my friendship with Dick Rackstraw had transformed into marriage. I wrote to inform Kurt after the fact and didn't hear from him for some time. Dick and I may not have been quite ready to be married, but any hesitation was consumed by the waves of crisis and passion inflaming our campus and the country. We felt our commitment was empowering and could only strengthen our children and our work. We threw ourselves into peace marching and protesting, along with writing and teaching. Richard Nixon's election that November precipitated a horrendous escalation of the Vietnam War as well as campus agitation throughout the country. The presence of the FBI continued to grow at American universities, including ours at the

State College of Iowa. Dick and I joined protests against the draft but also embraced those grim-faced vets who returned to a country largely unsympathetic to their heroism and sacrifices. It was a time of escalating paradox and ambiguity both nationally and personally.

Along with the political turbulence, I couldn't deny a vague personal ambivalence involving my friendship with Kurt. Eventually, he acknowledged my wedding with kindness and only a hint of concern about what he had perceived as Dick's "nervousness." I'd acknowledged Dick's emotional crisis requiring hospitalization before we'd met, but because we both were seeing counselors, I felt assured we'd both benefit from our marriage. I felt no equivocation about my love for my husband, nor for my continuing loyalty and friendship with Kurt, but at the same time I was grateful when he acknowledged my marriage warmly.

It seemed certain to both Dick and me that our union strengthened his ability to end the psychiatric medication he'd been taking when we first met. And we shared the hope we'd soon be able to bring his three children into our family. Unfortunately, his previous "nervousness" would eventually spiral into a state neither of us could manage. But at the time, we were both exceedingly happy and deeply committed to our kids and our students. We cherished the welcome synchronicity of our mutual concerns and its enrichment of our relationship. We were high on the intellectual nurture we gave each other and energized in ways neither of us had experienced before.

In my marital delight, I was unprepared late that year (12/1/68), with Kurt's "Dresden book" at press, to hear from him that he was in what he called a postpartum slump. He wrote from Barnstable that he was "sort of hankering to teach again, or do some damn thing besides write. Sure is quiet here. There isn't just one hell of a lot I'm eager to get down on paper, now that the war book is done." He noted that only one of his students, John Irving, was "behaving in a big time manner these days." Random House would bring out Irving's first novel, *Setting Free the Bears*, in January. "All I did was admire it while he wrote it. Some teacher."

A couple months later, in February 1969, a copy of Kurt's *Slaughterhouse-Five* arrived in the mail, with no accompanying letter. His inscription read: "For Loree with thanks and love. Most of this was written during my first year at Iowa. Peace."

I was awed by how the book played with time and events to draw readers into questioning the logic of cause and effect. His insistent toss-off of multiple deaths with repetitive shrugs of "So it goes" became both cynical and amusing at the same time. Anti-war was the story's drum beat, but it mixed hilarity and cruelty together with heroism and pornography. *Slaughterhouse-Five* didn't just *imply* the contradictions of history and values, it showed their inevitability, given the flaws of human awareness.

I figured Irving's book was going to have a hard time keeping up.

By the following month, *Slaughterhouse* reached the top of the *Times'* best-seller list and was lighting fires under resistance to the Vietnam War. The reviews everywhere were raves and gave Kurt the status he held from then on, including with college students.

I wondered how his "postpartum slump" was faring when I finally sent my congratulations. His book *had* to be having some influence on the country's rising turbulence against the war. In November 1969, he wrote to say he and Jane were going to the big march in Washington:

> If the troops are going to fire into a crowd, and if the crowd is going to storm the Winter Palace, we want to be there. Do you know what the leaders of the crowd that actually stormed the Winter Palace shouted when they got inside? "Comrades! Don't harm anything! This belongs to the people now."

He said he'd been giving a lot of speeches and was

> very much into the generalized love thing just now, having spent four days in New York with acid heads, without being an acid head myself. Everybody is supposed to love everybody, and I'm finding it

a pleasant thing to do....Anyway—this hilarious rise in my spirits, originating from a deep purple depression, began with loving you.

Apparently ready for a change, he said he'd put aside novel writing and picked up an old play called *Penelope* he'd written years before, based on *The Odyssey*. Always in love with theater, he was re-working it and searching for a producer and director. It would eventually become *Happy Birthday, Wanda June*.

But before the play would become a reality, in January 1970, he agreed to undertake the grim task of traveling to Nigeria to report on the starving citizens of Biafra in their failing three-year struggle for independence. The success of *Slaughterhouse* by then assured that anything he said about the horror there would receive attention. He and his old buddy, Vance Bourjaily, made the risky trip, hoping to marshal rescue for the Biafran people. But as Kurt said later in his *New York Times Book Review* story, "Biafra: A People Betrayed," "It was like a free trip to Auschwitz when the ovens were still going full blast." His report celebrating the greatness of the Biafran people and testifying to one of many humanitarian failures he'd witnessed can be read in his collection of essays, *Wampeters, Foma & Granfalloons*.

He used his Biafra experience when he addressed the graduating class of Bennington College later that spring, to introduce a theme he'd repeat many times: the benefits of "skylarking." Or, as he would often say later, "We are here on earth to fart around. Don't let anybody tell you any different." He wanted them to realize efforts to "save the world" can and often have resulted in the opposite of the desired effect, so he urged a gentler alternative of equitable distribution of wealth. This theme from previous novels became considerably more explicit about then.

That spring of 1970, he met Lester Goldsmith, an independent producer of political films, who agreed to option his reworked play. Kurt spent the summer feverishly rewriting before moving with his daughter Edith into a borrowed Manhattan penthouse close by the Theatre de Lys to be near the rehearsals. As he says in the Delta Book introduction ("About This Play") to *Happy Birthday, Wanda June*, "I was writing new beginnings, middles, and ends. My nice manners and neat appearance decayed. I came to resemble a madman who was attempting to extract moonbeams from excrement" (p. xiv).

The play opened October 7 to mixed reviews. Kurt kept trying to make it work. (In fact, he was still writing new endings as late as 2001 when it was produced in Los Angeles.) In the Delta edition, he acknowledged the play's flaws and admitted he had always been "chicken-hearted about villainy" noting his true feelings that

> everybody is right, no matter what he says. I had, in fact, written a book about everybody's being right all the time, *The Sirens of Titan*. And I gave a name in that book to a mathematical point where all opinions, no matter how contradictory, harmonized. I called it a *chrono-synclastic infundibulum.* (ix)

This "absent villain flaw" might have been one of Kurt's himself that made him a person of considerable compassion and tolerance who avoided confrontation. The character of Billy Pilgrim as the anti-hero of *Slaughterhouse-Five* came close to his own desire to refrain from harsh judgment. He was likewise intrigued with unusual persons whom others fail to understand or respect. Although I never witnessed his temper, I was always impressed with how reluctant he was to see villainy in others, let alone *create* a fictional villain. One of his favorite quotes was that of his socialist hero, Eugene Victor Debs: "As long as there's a lower class, I'm in it. As long as there's a criminal element, I'm of it. As long as there is a soul in prison, I am not free."

Although Kurt Vonnegut was not alone when it came to the transforming experience of sudden fame on beneficiaries, it likely did contribute to his disequilibrium about that time. He was exhausted from writing, public speaking, and the intense pressure of work on *Wanda June* in 1970. Photographs during this period show him haggard with dark circles under his eyes. And it can't be ignored that the primary photographer for this play's published version, Jill Krementz, was contributing to substantive changes taking place in his life. Krementz, who had built her professional reputation partly upon author photographs for the *New York Times,* was then doing a photographic essay to document the play's rehearsals and production. Kurt was increasingly impressed with her and had told me with considerable awe about her earlier adventure of flying in the cockpit of a plane with Ariel Sharon so she could photograph and interview him.

Another influence was the fact that Kurt had been experiencing the empty nest syndrome in his home life in Barnstable. As he says in "About This Play," his

> six children were children no more. It was a time of change, of good-bye and good-bye and good-bye. My big house was becoming a museum of vanished childhoods—of my vanished young manhood as well. . . . I was drinking more and arguing a lot, and I had to get out of that house. (vi)

Empty museums and confrontation were not experiences Kurt found comfortable. In late October 1970, he wrote from Barnstable that:

> It's not such a good old house any more. It's the shell of a Utopia that lasted for a little while. Mark isn't here any more. He's on a farm he bought in British Columbia with his girl. He can reach his property only by water, which is beautiful from his point of view. When he left, I played "Hey Jude" over and over again. . . . Edith is in Jamaica with her lover. . . . She's living on the mountainside farm of Jim Adams, my oldest boy, the former Peace Corps boy—and painting passionately. . . .

Although his family life might have lacked tranquility, it had certainly been central to his life and at least one major reason for slugging away at his typewriter for all those lean years. He wrote that before Edith left for Jamaica, she told him he had spent his life taking care of his family, and that now "I should go be happy any way I could be happy, which I am now trying to do." He said he was working on another play. "Write a play, lamb. . . . You don't have to describe characters in depth. Simply put words in their mouths. Then your producer hires graceful, enchanting people to speak and move. How long is a play? About 100 pages and a lot of every page is white space" (10/27/70).

It's worth noting, again from his candid discussion in the introduction to *Happy Birthday, Wanda June*, that his main advisors in the rewriting orgy were the *actors*, whom he called his "new family." When the play closed on March 14, 1971, after 142 performances, he credited that family with saving the play, but sadly added, "Things die. All things die. My new family dissolved into the late afternoon. . . . (xiv)"

The new family member who did not dissolve, however, was Jill Krementz, whose photographic essay illustrated the *Wanda June* book.

Part of his old Vonnegut family concerns, however, had involved his son Mark, who'd been among the many youthful dropouts disgusted with Nixon war policies and corporate power structures that betrayed their ideals about America. Having graduated with a religion degree from Swarthmore, Mark had "beat the draft with an uncanny schizophrenic act (*The Eden Express*, p. 7)" and spent the better part of 1970 at a "do-gooder" job and in recruiting other friends to start a commune in British Columbia. The extraordinary story of this adventure, and in particular of Mark's breakdown, can be read in his book, *The Eden Express: a personal account of schizophrenia.*

After packing basic necessities into his Volkswagen Bug, Mark and his girlfriend drove cross-country and met up with friends in Vancouver. They located a ramshackle old house in a wilderness area, finagled a boat and motor, and began to establish a new life free from the pressures of political and economic corruption. Despite his saxophone and a supply of basic necessities and recreational drugs, all did not go well. He eventually succumbed to increasing delusions and erratic behavior despite his friends' best efforts to help.

Shortly before *Happy Birthday, Wanda June* closed, Kurt had flown out to Vancouver where Mark was hospitalized for a time. Later, after a second hospitalization, Jane took temporary lodging near Vancouver to help monitor Mark's recovering condition and provide sustenance.

In a phone conversation with me, Kurt expressed awe at his son's extraordinary powers of strength and agility during his psychotic episode (e.g., leaping to impossible heights in a locked, padded room to break a ceiling lamp), and supported the psychiatrist's diagnosis that his case resulted from chemical imbalance. Apparently this was treated successfully over time, primarily with mega-vitamin doses. Mark returned to the Cape where he continued to benefit from a more structured life, with adequate sleep and careful diet. It was his intrigue with his own "chemistry" that led him eventually, to enter medical school. He is now a successful pediatrician with a practice in Massachusetts.

I think it's fair to suggest that the explicit nostalgia in Kurt's introductory remarks in *Happy Birthday, Wanda June* were partially intended as a kind of public apology to the many friends who knew and admired him and his personal family, perhaps even to his wife Jane. He had been seeing Jill Krementz regularly, and although he'd only mentioned her to me a couple times, I sensed this was a serious relationship.

He called again about that time. It was clear he did not like living alone, but he would do his best to avoid hurting the feelings of others in actual face-to-face confrontations. When I congratulated him on his play and asked how it was going with Jill, he replied quietly, "You changed your name."

I wasn't very good at confrontation either, and that caught me speechless. Was this his way of expressing the significance of his new relationship? I knew I would have found living with Kurt's mood swings daunting. Beyond that, there was no way I could have lived in New York, where the city's constant stimulation was welcome adrenalin that kept him going. I was a country girl. Nonetheless, in hindsight it seems likely we both had been somewhat knocked akimbo by the turbulence of all that was happening around us, as well as by the power of our impossible relationship in Iowa City.

Kurt and Jane did not divorce at that time, but they permanently ceased living together, and he never really did live in West Barnstable again. Instead, he took up permanent residence in Manhattan within the year with Jill Krementz.

Howdy Stranger, one of Kurt's "Enchanted I.O.U.s"

3

Monkey Gland Transplant, 1972–1978

Breakfast of Champions, Wampeters, Foma
& Granfalloons, Slapstick

Halfway across the country from Manhattan, the permanent residence for the Rackstraw family in Iowa gradually mellowed into
a fully furnished domicile, brimming with the substantial energy of
five youngsters. By 1972 they ranged from darling seven-year-old
Didi, Dick's daughter who was skilled at charming her elders, to an
adept pair of adventurous Wilson adolescents, Leslie and Robbie, at
the other end of the spectrum. In between were the two fully charged
Rackstraw sons—Kevin, nearly fifteen, and Geoffrey, eleven—who
were quite ready to defend territories but were gradually making inroads toward new sibling bonding.

In fact, all five were pretty good at holding their own, but Dick
was a skillful nurturer of domesticity. Together we worked toward
mellowness and a calendar of household chores that eased us toward a
semblance of order. Sacred territorial lines were established, equipped
with everything from blessedly quiet Tinkertoys and dolls to electric
guitars and stereo systems. Television in the sunroom, plus books, and
Monopoly helped with indoor entertainment. Best of all, a large yard
afforded plenty of space for testosterone-releasing football. We even

picked up a canoe for exploring Iowa rivers and a jerry-built camper for special outings.

Our major coup as parents was the hire of a reasonably mature college student who could cook. She was on the premises by 3 p.m. five days a week to monitor the troops and prepare the evening meal so Dick and I could enjoy a brief, semi-quiet moment after a day of teaching. The gift of an automatic dishwasher from my mom was a blessing.

Meanwhile, in Gotham City, Kurt did *not* come forth with another play as he'd intended. Rather, he and Jill collaborated on the National Education Television Playhouse production of *Between Time and Timbuktu: A Space Fantasy* based on his writings. The slaphappy amalgamation aired in March 1972, incorporating characters, scenes, and themes from his previous novels with a cast of his favorite radio comedians, Ray Goulding and Bob Elliot, and some players from *Happy Birthday, Wanda June*. Drafted into a script by the NET Players and tinkered with by Kurt, it was later published in book form by Delacorte, with photographs by Jill, a creative, if wacky collaboration of the new couple.

Kurt's acclaim continued unabated. He sent a copy of his first commencement speech, presented in May 1972, at the State University of New York at Albany, where his beloved older brother Bernard taught. His only living sibling, Bernard, was famous by then for discovering that silver iodide could be used to "salt" clouds to produce rain. Aside from standup hilarity, Kurt's speech stressed the urgent importance of Americans forming a national family unafraid to touch and care for one another as therapy for the persistent Vietnam War.

Kurt also resumed teaching creative writing, first at Harvard and later at City College in New York, while continuing work on his seventh novel, *Breakfast of Champions*. But he also made public appearances, gave interviews, and enjoyed growing fame and fortune in the New York scene, with Jill Krementz at his side.

In the summer of 1972, he covered the Republican Convention in Miami Beach, which eventuated in Richard Nixon's reelection, but not before Kurt wrote a damning satirical report for *Harper's Magazine* (11/72) prior to the election. With photos by Jill, and titled "In a

Manner that Must Shame God Himself," it concluded that: "The GOP Council at Miami Beach began with a sermon on the Divine Right of Presidents and ended with a cool certainty—the meek shall not inherit the earth" (p. 68). With his powerful satirical style, he justifiably became a contributing editor at *Harper's*. He was teaching a sophisticated public how to read him in language that even lowbrows could appreciate.

I hadn't been in direct communication with him since *Wanda June* closed, but since I never missed congratulating him on his November 11 birthday, I sent my appreciation of his *Harper's* article and included an account of my new domestic life. He replied with an energized greeting:

> You're full of white magic, as always. I eat it with a spoon. There is plenty for everybody.
>
> I'm fine at fifty. New York jazzes me up. It's my monkey gland transplant. People speak to me on the street. I glow. I feel like a useful citizen. I like famous people. I had supper with Dan Ellsberg last night. He is high as a kite on virtue and notoriety. I asked him if he thought the F.B.I. was clever. He thought it was dull but dogged. I asked him what he would be doing now, if he hadn't given away the Pentagon Papers. He guessed he'd still be working for RAND. He at first intended to commit civil disobedience and pay the price.... Now it turns out that he has probably broken no law. He has a 50–50 chance of going free, his lawyer says. The cost? Oh—$100,000 or so.
>
> I've finished another book [*Breakfast of Champions*], which will be out in April. I never thought I'd finish another book. I thought I was all through. The natural mourning period for my marriage seems to be over—and for Jane, too. I felt as though I had committed the crime of the century. So did Jane. She has a better life now, though—out of the kitchen and into the world.... When she had nothing going for her but my ups and downs, we were like Siamese twins.

The woman I live with, Jill Krementz, gave a smashing birthday party for me last Sunday. There was live music. Dancers you would have recognized were Edith, Mark, and Nanny, Bob Scholes and his new wife, and Barry Kaplan. Edie, as you probably know, married a sensational Puerto Rican named Geraldo Rivera, who is the hottest thing on local television news. I am crazy about him. He gets sore or cries on camera frequently. Nanny is an art student in Oakland, California, homesick for the East. Mark is writing on Cape Cod. . . . He is miraculously recovered now, and much calmer and wiser and capable than before. He has become a first-rate musician and painter since coming apart and putting himself together again.

He concluded with a sweet reference to my kids: "I look at the picture of Rob and Leslie, and I realize that I still love them a lot. Please tell them so" (11/15/72).

* * *

Kurt really *was* impressed with celebrities, at least until he grew used to being one himself, although his delight with Rivera waned as the short-lived marriage with Edie turned sour. (By which time he called Rivera "Jerry River.")

His enchantment with celebrity might have reflected his sometimes nonjudgmental openness, almost to the point of naïveté. It was a trait that sometimes made friends feel protective out of concern he'd be exploited. But he could make fun of his own naïveté with an endearing narration of his daily trip to the convenience store to buy an envelope, to the post office for a stamp and silly conversation with strangers, and finally to the mailbox. All for asserting he "has had a perfectly wonderful time," concluding with his now famous moral that "We are here to fart around. . . ."

Kurt's whimsy seemed a charming antidote to the competitive nature of enterprise he observed as wreaking havoc on the life of the planet and on growing numbers of homeless humans. A freethinker socialist by heritage, he was increasingly outraged by corporate greed, even as he ironically moved toward increasing prestige and wealth.

Surely a major part of his genius as a writer was his ability to consciously sublimate his political outrage into disarming humor or satire. Consider, in *God Bless You, Mr. Rosewater*, his tippler character of Elliot Rosewater who acted like a sentimental buffoon by giving useless people small handouts to keep them from committing suicide. Elliot's self-deprecating generosity was fundamentally characteristic of Kurt himself, and of course it remained one reason why he was so beloved by readers.

When *Breakfast of Champions* came out in April 1973, he was at a popularity peak where he stayed longer than many. He wrote

> My new book is selling spectacularly. Money is becoming a sort of Parker Brothers game. I manage it in order to manage it. I keep trying to think of things to do with it. The latest scheme is to buy a studio ... and be a painter during the summer months of each year. (5/7/73)

That he could even fantasize the luxury of painting must have seemed a miracle. I was delighted he was finding more balance in his life and family relationships.

Not only was he adjusted to the rock star adulation following *Slaughterhouse*, he was taking his new role as a significant literary figure seriously. He'd accepted a teaching job at City College, and both he and Donald Barthelme had been American P.E.N. representatives at the International Conference in Stockholm that spring. It was there he heard Heinrich Boll deliver his Nobel Prize lecture "in folksy German. . . . He is a darling, sad, whimsical man, and, as President of International P.E.N., is the loving Dutch uncle of writers everywhere," Kurt wrote. "He loves you, me, everybody. We told each other war stories in English" (5/7/73).

I shared with Kurt that spring, however, my less cheerful concerns having to do with my husband's increasingly fragile psychological state. Dick had begun working regularly with a psychiatrist in a neighboring city following a period of intense writing that resulted in severe insomnia and hallucination. I was concerned about a possible recurrence of the mental crisis he'd suffered before we met. His condition had recently grown more turbulent, particularly during an intense period when he'd written some of his most powerful poems.

Kurt phoned to remind me of what his son Mark had learned about chemical imbalance and the similarity of his symptoms to Dick's. In fact, I did talk with Mark about his mega-vitamin treatment, but it was never implemented.

In July, despite his horror of psychiatric hospitals, Dick insisted I get him admitted to one, with what appeared to be a serious breakdown. Unfortunately, the therapy he received over a three-month period with yet another new psychiatrist, despite my efforts to the contrary, included both drugs and repeated shock treatments—a therapy that fully erased the abundant poetry that had sustained him and his teaching, leaving him increasingly fragile when he returned home to recover on a disability leave.

The opposite of fragility was true for Kurt. That fall (1973) he wrote that he and Jane would be divorced by the end of the year and that he'd just purchased a four-story brownstone on Manhattan's east side where he and Jill would have work space, and she could run her photographic business from an attached basement apartment. "There'll be rooms and rooms in the house—a ping-pong table and all that. I do wildly materialistic things from time to time" (11/19/73).

His childlike joy in managing this feat was an upper. His persistence through the decade since those struggling Iowa City days and his family's turmoil had brought him success that few could have imagined back then. Although I don't think he ever doubted his ability as a writer, to imagine that his kind of dark humor and playful satire could surpass his small cult following to the wild enthusiasm spreading across the country—well, it could only have been in his dreams. I knew of only two persons who'd believed early on he was a creative genius whose work was deeply significant—Jane Vonnegut and myself.

* * *

Alas, there is a price genius writers sometimes pay for their gifts, not excluding Kurt, but certainly not excluding my dear husband who died of carbon monoxide suicide in January 1974.

Of the many writers I heard from that dreadful month, every one of them shared empathy for Dick they'd *earned*, as poet Ted Roethke put it, by going where they *had* to go as writers. That works for many, but not all. I came to believe there is a level of raw sensitivity and imagination in some artists that can take them to an exquisitely intolerable awareness—a state of mind that can be dangerously close to the abyss. The survivors are those who are successful in finding some way to balance their work so they can step back soon enough from the precipice. But it can become deliriously compelling to take the plunge.

One of Kurt's first questions when he learned of Dick's death was whether he had a body of work that could be published. He did. My friend and colleague, Robley Wilson, editor of *The North American Review* journal, helped collect and then edit Dick's work. It was published in 1977 as a gathering of poems called *Learning to Speak* by *The North American Review* Press. It is perhaps fitting to illustrate what I mean by the "abyss" by quoting from the gorgeous verse Dick was writing when he first approached the chasm, a poem called "The Peaceable Kingdom."

> *We are not trembling now and we think*
> *in circuitries the mind we know*
> *cannot. It is alternating current*
> *B-flat easy on us and he*
> *does not dream I am sleeping in his*
> *belly, softer than orange flame*
> *licking the tongue and face of the*
> *One God. I am Aaron and lion at once.*
> *The fish blinks away in the mystery*
> *of the shallow river I have crossed.*

Some writers, perhaps artists in general, *do* "think [at times] in circuitries the mind we know cannot." But to cross that river and become Aaron speaking, as if for the Biblical Moses, may be dangerously alluring. Especially without any distancing protection, like humor, which Kurt used intuitively. Nor did Dick pace himself, limiting work to a few hours at a time. And perhaps if the writer can temper a profound vision with irony or making a joke of it, both author and reader can more easily wade back to a sunny rock to meditate peacefully on the dream—or to simply enjoy a laugh. Simply put, Dick was not that writer, that person, for whom humor was an antidote. He did not know how to wade back at that time.

His untimely death that miserably cold January in 1974 left me as close to exhaustion as I've ever been. Had it not been for family and friends, I cannot imagine how we could have survived. Dick's parents and his brother and family came to help, even as friends provided ongoing food and cheer.

Kurt wrote of his concern, after a visit with some of his former students:

> I told them the sad news about Dick. People spread the news. Andre Dubus called Dick Yates on Staten Island, where Yates is writing brilliantly, they say. Yates called me to tell me, in case I didn't know. You're the wampeter of the lives of a lot of good, warm people....I remember telling you one time that I worried about women, that I thought their lives were so much more dangerous than men's. And you replied with the little kid bravery which makes a lot of people think you're tough: "Don't worry about women. They're fine." I dunno. I think you're going to be in a pisspotful of trouble....This is a mean son of a bitch of an economy....
>
> One time I told a woman I was inexplicably happy. She said, with complete friendliness, "That's because you aren't thinking about anybody but yourself for a change." She was right. I wish you the same refreshment.

I will always write you letters which are clunky and incomplete. I'm sure you understand why.

It's because I love you so much. (1/20/74)

In March, old family friends of Dick's from Michigan insisted I join them on a trip to the Virgin Islands—where I *did* mostly think only of myself, and even learned to scuba dive with lessons bought with Kurt's gift money, insisting I must "use every bit of it on yourself." Almost miraculously, the images of stunningly beautiful underwater sea life began to replace the flashbacks of my husband lying dead on the garage floor.

Beloved faculty friends back in wintry Iowa fed, sheltered, and entertained our five dear children and helped them recover. Dick's youngest son, Geoffrey, got a starring role in a Dickens play at the university. Our eldest three somehow survived various adolescent crises and triumphs. Didi's tender age may have shielded her somewhat from her father's loss, but I was grateful for the tenderness of her teachers at the Laboratory School. It would be hard to document the immeasurable kindness of friends to all of us. When I returned from the Caribbean, I bought an old upright piano—the only positive thing I could think of doing was to make music or listen to it.

That following summer, Dick's parents took the Rackstraw kids to their home in Michigan to enjoy their backyard pool and soak up love from adoring relatives. My daughter, Leslie, traveled to Maine for an extended visit, and son Rob provided abundant healing energy before embarking on his long-anticipated motorcycle quest to the Pacific. The only productive thing I did that summer was teach a literature class and dig crabgrass in the yard. It worked. The sanity of order was gradually restored, and we all survived.

University of Iowa psychiatrist Dr. Nancy Andreasen, who also holds a doctorate in literature, undertook a study of creative writers later that year and interviewed some of the Workshop writers, including Kurt, in the course of her study. Her general conclusions were that poets tended to experience schizophrenic episodes in higher frequency than the norm, and that fiction writers tended more toward the malady of depression or bi-polar disorder. She told me that Richard Rackstraw would have been the second Iowa City poet she knew of who'd died of suicide by then.

The irrational forces that plague some of our great artists may be the underside of powerful creativity that also brings beauty and transformation to human experience. I continue to be awed by the paradox and was occasionally even concerned about Kurt's imbalance of highs and lows.

It's never been a secret that he struggled with depression, nor that he was one of the less-traditional American fiction writers. An editor asked me a few years back what Kurt Vonnegut was "really like." What made him so unique, I think, was his incredibly imaginative mind, crammed to bursting with history, hilarity, pain, paradox, compassion, patriotism, irony, the creative arts, and even outrage at public injustice. He had a huge sense of curiosity, read incessantly, and truly loved conversation—asking questions and conversing often with total strangers. It appeared to me he couldn't get enough of the wonder of human inventiveness, and was easily bored with the mundane. He hardly ever took himself too seriously.

A new collection of some of his best previously published essays and interviews strung together with new material was released by Dell in 1974, under the title of *Wampeters, Foma & Granfalloons*, again to positive reviews. Some of the material in *Wampeters* comes as close to revealing what Kurt was like as anything I've read. It's a remarkably frank and open expression of his opinions and values, beginning when he was forty-three and lived in Iowa City, through the age of fifty-two when he'd made his mark as a major American writer living in Manhattan. It reveals his humility, rage, and generosity, his pessimism and joys, his feelings about religion and death, about cultural relativity and politics, and about the ideals of American democracy and their betrayal by greed and ignorance. In language anyone can understand, he celebrates the beauty of creative potential in humanity, even as he mourns the mistakes and betrayals that block it. I was among those in awe of his often-expressed wish to "stay as close to the edge as I can without going over. . . ." Dick Rackstraw was not that lucky.

By the time *Wampeters* was in print, Kurt was nearly finished with his eighth novel, *Slapstick*, which would see print by October of 1976. But his big news in October of 1974 was that he was going to Moscow to see his seventy-seven-year-old translator, Rita Rait, whom he had tried unsuccessfully to bring to the United States for a visit. She'd been introduced to Vonnegut's writing by Don Fiene, a Slavic professor from the University of Tennessee and a Vonnegut fan who'd become a good friend. Rait had also translated William Faulkner, John Updike, and J. D. Salinger. Kurt had only met her the year before in Paris when she'd been "let out" for a brief visit. He wrote that she was now a virtual prisoner in her own country because, "She has infallibly made friends with all the wrong artists in the U.S.S.R., so her life is a cramped one." He was impressed that

> She is one of those who want to stay there, but who is heart-broken over the regime's cruelty to its artists and intellectuals. I am supposed to bring a lot of razor blades, so her friends can be clean-shaven in jail. Some lark. . . . I'm supposed to have some rubles over there, since they have pirated five of my books so far. (10/6/74)

They were rubles he couldn't use because of Soviet restrictions about purchases. He added whimsically, "It's fun to be rich in rubles."

When I spoke with him after his return, he was utterly delighted to have seen how Rita lived and how she and other Soviet artists celebrated the creative and intellectual spirit. "They even call their scientists 'poets'." Later a visiting Russian scholar gave me photographs taken in Rita Rait's home, one of which shows her in her kitchen with a box of Wheaties (the "Breakfast of Champions") hung on the wall. A petite, gray-haired lady looking twenty years younger than her age, with a sparkle in her eyes, she appeared to be as much in love with Kurt as he was with her.

*   *   *

If anything gave him hope it was being in touch with creative energies like hers and her friends', despite draconian strictures the Soviets imposed. Kurt was in love with the arts, period, no matter whether they flourished in theater or visual media or music or the written word. And he put his own creative energies into all of them whenever and however he could. Without them, and without the community that produced and supported them, I doubt he would have opted to live.

Since I understood the struggle to stay alive, especially during my poet husband's despair, madness, and eventual suicide, I was especially appreciative of Kurt's healthy enjoyment of success within his own creative enterprise. I still had family problems to resolve, but my vegetative summer of rest had been restorative, my kids were healing, and my teaching was going well as the school year progressed. I was pleased to learn from Kurt that Jane had been traveling and writing and was involved in a new relationship. Their son Mark would enter Harvard Medical School in 1975, with his finished book about his mental breakdown, *The Eden Express*, due to be released toward the end of that year.

So that springtime of 1975, when Kurt phoned with a totally unexpected and rare proposal for an extended weekend with him in Key West, I hesitated only briefly.

I stepped off the plane in Key West into a reunion filled with delight. I want to say "pure" delight because it felt that way. Only, here we were—two middle-aged people with all kinds of responsibilities and obligations freely enjoying an extravaganza of childlike joy. It was a gift, truly and simply magical, with no expectations of anything more.

Certain things stand out. A phone call from author Jose Farmer hoping to verify Kurt would allow his use of the name Kilgore Trout as "author" of Farmer's forthcoming *Venus on the Half Shell*—the only time tension came into Kurt's voice that week. (He later was outraged by what he felt was Farmer's betrayal of agreements they'd made.) We dined on exquisite dinners of fresh seafood. We spoke at length about my late husband, with Kurt wanting to know the diagnosis and details of my later conversation with Dick's first psychiatrist, who'd been unavailable when Dick went into crisis. He wanted to be sure I had adequate funds and support for the children, which I felt I did, or would eventually have. By then, Dick's two youngest, Didi and Geoffrey were living with their mother. His eldest son, Kevin, lived with me and would finish high school and begin college in the fall. My two were already fairly well set in college. President Ronald Reagan had not been elected yet so had not yet pushed for limiting Social Security college aid benefits, which were a great help to my kids' higher education goals.

*   *   *

Kurt and I toured the town of Key West, hand in hand like kids, and took photographs of each other beside somebody else's catch of a huge fish. We enjoyed coconut daiquiris at Sloppy Joe's, Hemingway's favorite bar, and visited, largely unrecognized, at Hemingway's historic house, still occupied by the abundant descendants of his cats. We rented a little sailboat at a resort, where the wind made the halyards of beached sailboats chatter, and swamped the little craft far from shore, half-drowning with laughter in the waves until we righted it again. (Both of us had sailed as kids, but righting the craft in fairly high surf and getting underway and safely back to shore may have been the triumph of the whole week.) Later, we danced barefoot under moonlight on that beach, to ragtime music from the piano bar.

One day Kurt chartered a fishing boat that guaranteed a catch. We carried onboard our box lunches and beer and prepared for a major adventure. Instead, we happened to have one of Kurt's many chance meetings of Dresden survivors: We heard stories from the German captain about how he had been sent as a child to the countryside and thus missed the firebombing. Eventually, rather than catching reluctant fish, we snorkeled and swam off the boat with graceful stingrays.

Once onshore, still in damp bathing suits, we drove to the hotel where Kurt thought Truman Capote was staying. I was thrilled to be meeting the man, even if not dressed quite this informally. There he was sitting in the garden lounge with his companion, staring at the *New York Times* opened to a stunning photograph of himself in his fedora, taken by Jill Krementz! He looked up as we approached, and gesturing toward the *Times*, said to Kurt, "A nice likeness, don't you think?"

I gulped, thinking he might wonder about me, but not so. As Kurt introduced us, he extended fingers in a delicate greeting and immediately began talking enthusiastically with Kurt as though just resuming conversation after a brief interruption. When Truman signaled a waiter to order drinks, Kurt told him how much he admired his new short story collection, *Music for Chameleons*. Truman was obviously delighted, "You really loved it?" The collection had received decent critical response at that time, prior to his scandalous "La Côte Basque, 1965" publication in *Esquire* later that year, which did not.

Meanwhile, Truman's friend Jack sighed and stared into space, dramatically uninterested. I attempted unsuccessfully to engage him in conversation, but since I knew nothing about him, I hardly knew how to start. I figured he was surely Jack Dunphy, Truman's lifelong companion, but he clearly found me quite tedious and would have much preferred a nice nap.

As we said goodbye, Truman demanded enthusiastically, "But have you seen *the sunset*?" Admitting we had not, we were dispatched to the proper beach for observing the possible phenomenon of the "green flash" event that sometimes can be observed at the precise moment the sun dips below the sea's horizon. We saw flame swallowers and jugglers and performing iguanas and returning shrimp boats— and a very nice sunset that just *maybe* provided a split-second flash across the horizon before the sun disappeared. That question remains unresolved. Whatever it was, it was enough.

Experiences like sitting poolside with Kurt to read the morning papers gave me an insight I hadn't been aware of before. This was his usual time to be writing. Instead, as he scanned the newspaper, he kept up an almost continuous monologue of extemporaneous whimsy, editorializing, and historical backgrounding that I found quite astonishing. ("Did you know Gerald Ford won a Heisman Tro-phy in college? Some Boy Scout! He even tried to impeach William Douglas from the Supreme Court!")

I'd always admired his knowledge of history, but his ability—more of a compulsion, actually—to historically contextualize almost any-thing he read was quite uncanny. ("Henry Kissinger thought Laos and Cambodia wanted to hook up with Vietnam. Those poor Vietnamese hiding in Cambodia will have about as much chance of surviving the Khmer Rouge as the Lakotas did the American militia at Big Horn.") One of his concerns had always been the average citizen's lack of such knowledge, thus unable to adequately evaluate political or economic decisions, and more recently, those that affect environmental or social issues.

It was his ability to almost instantly perceive contrasting ideas that don't initially seem related or to suggest historical parallels that most of us would miss—that marked his unusual creative dexterity and richly complex wisdom. He once told me he thought Gore Vidal was the most brilliant writer alive, but I think Kurt could hold his own quite nicely.

He distilled this gift into the imaginative crafting and playful cari-caturing of his characters that sometimes seemed to have fooled his harsher critics into thinking his novels are fluff. Take his novel *Jail-bird*, for example, in which its New York City setting reflects the three levels of Dante's *Divine Comedy*. In fact, it's that rich reserve of facts and insights hidden in whimsical disguises that suggest to me a writer of genius, albeit one who never expected he'd continue to be read long into cultural history, let alone provide a remarkable store of material for Ph.D. dissertations. Being witness to his unusual mind playing ex-travagantly with unremarkable journalism was a surprise and delight in an unexpected holiday venture.

When our rare holiday came to an end, Kurt drove me to the air-port in silence. We sat outside in a little park to wait for my plane. Who would have guessed this tourist carving our initials on a wooden picnic table near the tiny Key West airport was a creative genius care-fully defacing public property?

"I think it's possible to love two people at the same time, don't you?" he asked, looking up from his work with a grin. I agreed it was possible, and OK, too.

Nonetheless, it was heartbreaking to get on that plane, with Kurt waving goodbye as I flew away from the paradise of experiences we'd shared. For a moment there, it was difficult to imagine how the attractions of New York City could better fill his creative needs than the simple bliss we'd experienced, yet I knew that was true. His actors in *Wanda June* had been a new family for a time, rather like the Iowa Workshop had been. And there could be more plays. In the city, he also had a partner much more at ease than I with its inspiration and challenge.

I returned to Iowa revitalized, grateful that Kurt and I would continue to be loving friends. He wrote soon after:

> I assume that we are in touch telepathically, and that you know I am O.K., and even, probably that I am happily smoking again and writing again, and that I will love you always. . . . I am thunderstruck. It was surely the most intelligent adventure of my life, impossible without you and salt water. I will try to write you a long letter about it, and put it in a book. (3/31/75)

Later, in May, he did write a longer letter (which included a flyer from our Key West hotel), comforting me about some legal decisions regarding Didi and Geoffrey's custody:

> No matter what lawyers . . . do to them, they tend to be generally O.K. We are as much sustained by our ideas of people as we are by the people themselves. (If we don't know that, who does?) And the Rackstraw children's ideas of you as sane and wise and loving will accompany them wherever they go.

However, his letter also described a difficult prospect he was facing—a trip back to his old home in West Barnstable was giving him "two and three headaches a day—all psychosomatic." What he dreaded was the prospect of mingling with his old Cape associates: "I'd no idea I'd been that badly bent while living up there," where, he believed, "my neighbors had no respect whatsoever for what I did." In New York City, at least "there are enough artists to constitute a sort of extended family." He continued

> You, at any rate, are engaged in one of the major enterprises in Cedar Falls, which causes your neighbors to support and admire you almost absent-mindedly. This ambience may seem common and tiresome to you. It is in fact valuable and rare. I have been able to cobble together something like that only by coming to New York City, where there are enough artists to constitute a sort of extended family. It isn't all that great, but it's something. (5/22/75)

Anecdotes of his painful Cape visit were later shared by others—confirmation of how tough it had been for Kurt to handle perceived contradictions of love and contempt, and perhaps even his own personal dismay about unintentionally hurting his extraordinary Barnstable family.

It was not until nearly a year later that I heard from him again "because," as he said, "it's so cumbersome to be any kind of lover from so far away. So I feel wooden." In response to my query about whether he'd completed his book in progress, he said he'd be sending me page proofs of the manuscript he'd turned in on March 8, for his so-called autobiographical novel, *Slapstick*. "It was a mess," Kurt wrote, "but I thought I had better publish even a complete disaster." It was the first time he'd expressed this kind of anxiety to me:

> One thing that troubles me is that anything I write now sells like crazy and my publishers won't tell me honestly what they think of my work, since their opinion doesn't mean a damn thing commercially. Nobody's opinion matters commercially. We just publish, and off we go. (4/25/76)

He was cheered, however by the news that his daughter Edith would present a one-woman sculpture show in "a fancy store on Fifth Avenue." Plus, his son Mark had just received a big check for his newly published book.

I had sent Kurt my essay on "The Future of Energy and Imagination" I'd presented at an academic interdisciplinary conference, to which he generously responded, "I am amazed . . . by your poetic understanding of thermodynamics and all that. . . . I'll bet it is over the heads of most of the scientists out there." And it was here that my former teacher became one again, suggesting, "Since you are capable of such direct thinking and expression . . . I wonder if fiction might not now be a waste of time . . . you have read so much and thought so well, that I see no reason for you to tangle yourself in all the froufrou of fiction" (5/8/76). It was probably the best advice he'd ever given me.

By late May, he seemed more relaxed and introspective when he wrote from "the final and modest home of the Gerald Murphys" where "there are French farm tools hung on the wall, all carved from wood." He had rented this Long Island beach cottage from the Murphys' only surviving heir, and it must have thrilled him to be living in space once occupied by the famous East Hampton expatriate couple who had hosted writers like Hemingway and F. Scott Fitzgerald while they lived in France. He continued,

> I am here alone on a Monday morning. There are lots of rabbits and birds. Fishing boats are busy about a mile offshore. . . . I suppose I'll always be a tenant, without a place anywhere I truly feel is my own. That's an easily bearable curse, no worse than athlete's foot, but a curse all the same. (5/24/76)

It was this mood of loneliness and rootlessness that somewhat informed the page proofs of *Slapstick* he'd recently sent me. It was a story dedicated to the memory of his beloved deceased sister, Alice, whom he'd identified as the primary reader for whom he wrote. He'd often described slapstick as the form of humor that had cheered him up when he was lonely as a child.

I had thought the manuscript a bit uneven compared to his previous books, but nonetheless extraordinary as a wacky allegory of Western history, the achievement of which I conveyed to Kurt. This is the story in which the twin brother and sister protagonists are confined as lonely orphans in an Edenlike forest and as adults, discover that if they put their heads together, their orgiastic transformation yields universal secrets. I smiled when I read that passage, remembering the whippoorwill's cry and the Stone City epiphany Kurt and I had shared. In the decade since then, he had certainly managed to transform some fairly profound "secrets" into hilarious satirical fiction to chill readers with concern even as they laugh. And he was no longer wondering where the next dollar was coming from.

On this day, however, Kurt was reading proofs of his friend Vance Bourjaily's new novel and could also convey the cheerful news that our mutual friend Dick Yates had "received a medal from the National Institute of Arts and Letters for the best book of the past year . . . an artistic, but not a financial sensation." He said he and Yates, both under contract to Delacorte, had gone to lunch at the Club Twenty-One with their editor, Sam Lawrence, to celebrate. "Yates has always wanted to jump into the Plaza Fountain, like his hero, Fitzgerald. Sam and I told him he was entitled to do that now— wearing his medal, and clamping his Book of the Month Club contract in his mouth."

Dick's award-winning 1976 novel, *The Easter Parade*, had been well received by critics and an as yet small following of avid readers. It was such a wrenchingly moving book that it left me as awed as I was saddened by it. Awed because it used such believably convincing dialogue and scenic narration, but saddened because it was so transparently autobiographical. The "two sisters," whose painfully sad lives growing up in New York City are central to the story, were actually the lives of Dick's own sister and himself.

Unfortunately, a month or so later, Kurt wrote he had just visited Dick in Bellevue Hospital where he was recovering from accidental burns from a cigarette-started fire. Kurt said the good news was that despite losing his entire wardrobe to the fire, Dick's unfinished novel manuscript was intact:

> He was in bed last Sunday morning—alone, as usual, but cold sober and no doubt thinking about all the people who had told him truthfully that his latest book, *The Easter Parade*, was better than *The Great Gatsby* and on a level with *Madame Bovary*. . . . He was found unconscious, burned on his hands and chest and face . . . he is going to live. . . . He can't open his swollen eyes yet, but doctors pried them open for a moment, and found out he can still see OK. . . .
>
> And he is ruefully cheerful, as always . . . the same old Dick, but with his eyes shut, and with his hands in plastic bags. There doesn't seem to be much pain, thank God, and even less surprise. He has seen it all so many times.
>
> Curiously: We are both publishing books about our sisters this fall. It was time for both of us to talk about that.
>
> He asked for a drag from my cigarette, which I had to hold to his French-fried lips. He coughed his head off, thanked me, and asked for another drag.
>
> We talked a lot about you. (7/1/76)

It was such a sweet account from Kurt that it brought tears to my eyes. And how curious they both would have written of their sisters at this time. Unfortunately, I had another letter from Kurt about Dick a month later:

> The Yates saga goes on and on. The poor man, who has tons of money now, and reputation, has had another mental crackup, even as his burns were healing. . . . He went crazy last weekend, during a peaceful visit to friends on Long Island, and had to be put into a VA hospital. He likes his room-mates, I hear, and has begun to write already.

Kurt's compassionate account would be repeated over the years, as he continued to stand by his old colleague and fellow writer through the harrowing persistence of Dick's continuing crises.

Before closing this letter, Kurt also described a poker game he'd been in recently with Irwin Shaw and some friends at the home of James Jones. Although Shaw and Jones had been portrayed in an unfriendly remark as "a couple of moth-eaten old lions," he said

> it made me feel very tender about them. They are so brave and gentle—and so damaged by cigars and booze and war and manliness. Shaw would enter the hospital the next day with an ulcer. Jones was upstairs in bed with heart trouble. There wasn't any booze-drinking or any cigar-smoking at that poker game that night. Think of that. Somebody had a Tab.

He concluded by referring to his own work: "The new book is going to sell a gazoolian copies, they say. We'll see. It's a game" (8/4/76).

Despite Kurt's relative isolation that summer, the reality that he was mingling with the shades of Gerald and Sara Murphy, and the likes of Irwin Shaw and James Jones in the Hamptons must have seemed like a dream to a man who only a decade earlier was virtually unknown, nearly broke, and closing in on a twenty-year struggle to complete a novel about his war experience.

After the acclaim and notoriety that decade had earned him, Kurt was correct about the rush to get *Slapstick* into print. Review copies were out that fall, with publication set for October 1, when eighty-five thousand copies of the first edition were issued. His (and my) uneasiness about the book may have been confirmed when a number of reviews were less than enthusiastic. However, John Updike in the October 25 *New Yorker* magazine took more than six pages to write not only a positive review but also to use Shakespeare's *The Tempest* as a comparative master narrative and to seriously extol most of Kurt's novels to date, beginning with *The Sirens of Titan.*

Slapstick was the first of Kurt's books that I reviewed for my university's literary journal, the *North American Review,* published in

November 1976. Although the novel wasn't his best, it was nonetheless brilliant when seen as a zany parody of Nietzsche's *The Birth of Tragedy*. I wrote that it was a reflection of Kurt's relationship with his own sister as the Apollonian-Dionysian synthesis from which, as Nietzsche had argued, the Classical Greeks had created their magnificent tragedies (the opposite of slapstick, but nonetheless renewing). In this review, I began to examine seriously that rich intellect and historical context I believe informed Kurt's work, something that has never since ceased to amaze me. I sent him a copy just prior to his November 11 birthday and received the following telegram in reply:

> You have given me the perfect birthday present. How could you have known that what I wanted more than anything was a rave review. (11/10/76)

Kurt said many times that life is a joke, implying it's a cruel one at that. In fact, *his* life was shaped by an unusual amount of violence, accidents, and painful ironies, including his mother's suicide on Mother's Day shortly before he was shipped overseas during World War II. Thus, I think he was quite serious about creating fiction that reveals strategies capable of transforming life's tragedy into something entertaining for a reader, but at the same time, actually *useful*—as slapstick had personally been for him.

In the first page of the prologue to the novel, he says, "This is the closest I will ever come to writing an autobiography. I have called it *Slapstick* because it is grotesque, situational poetry—like the slapstick film comedies, especially those of Laurel and Hardy, of long ago. It is about what life *feels* like to me."

Kurt's effort to transform his own personal experience was—ironically—something he took quite seriously. While he shunned the notion of being an intellectual and denied he'd been a serious scholar of philosophers like Nietzsche or Goethe, he *had* read these writers, and their philosophies did lurk beneath the surface of his own life and work. Even so, he wrote largely from his own experience and intuition, rather than from literary or philosophical scholarship.

That *Slapstick* was not a rave, critical success was a disappoint-ment—and also one that Kurt himself severely awarded only a grade of "D." However, it certainly did not diminish the affection of his fans wherever he went. I think it was the book's simple comfort of "human decency" that readers found so appealing.

Kurt was making an increasing number of public appearances and had hired a professional agency to manage speaking tours into inten-sive two-week marathons twice a year, to balance his writing time more efficiently. In the spring of 1977, he made another trip to Iowa to speak at both the university in Iowa City, as well as my University of Northern Iowa in Cedar Falls.

His initial intention had been to introduce his eighty-eight-year-old Russian translator, Rita Rait, to America. In January, he wrote that he had

> taken all the proper bureaucratic steps . . . but have yet to hear whether or not they [the Soviet government] will let her out. She has consistently made friends with people who later became jailbirds. I am putting up the money for her trip. She is that important to world literature and that important to me. (1/19/77)

However, he later wrote in disappointment that the Writers Union of the USSR would not allow the visit, "Probably because she is too funny and talkative and beloved in the outside world" (3/12/77).

Despite Rita's absence, Kurt's two-day presence on the University of Northern Iowa campus in Cedar Falls on March 31 and April 1, 1977, was a spectacular success. I'd gone to Iowa City to hear his speech there and to drive him to Cedar Falls. In the meantime, I'd sent a bouquet of daffodils to be placed in his motel room to reflect the "new middle name" ("Daffodil-11") of the protagonist in *Slapstick*.

Arriving in Cedar Falls after a pleasant drive through the spring-time countryside, he wore one in his lapel at lunch when we joined Jerry Klinkowitz, a UNI colleague and one of Kurt's strongest aca-demic celebrants. Kurt's friend Don Fiene from the University of Tennessee joined us for the weekend festivities. He was particularly sorry about Rita Rait and had to be satisfied only that his written celebration of her and Kurt, "Vonnegut—Big in Russia," appeared in that Sunday's *New York Times Book Review* (4/3/77, p. 3).

Following media interviews that afternoon, Kurt spoke that night to a wildly enthusiastic, standing-room-only audience and then a party at my home with faculty and writing students.

His speech took place on an auditorium stage that happened to be cluttered by a set-in-progress for a university production of *A Midsummer Night's Dream*, an appropriately whimsical setting for a Vonnegut presentation. His comments made up a largely humorous montage that included praise for Iowa's support of writers and readings from three current works. These latter included a "Self-Interview" about his war experience to appear later in the *Paris Review* (No. 69), one of several he did with its editor, his friend George Plimpton. He also read from his introduction to a new collected works of Mark Twain; and an excerpt from a novel in progress called *Mary Kathleen O'Looney* or *Unacceptable Air*. The latter would eventually evolve into his next published book, *Jailbird*.

The following morning, April Fool's Day, he fielded questions for two hours at a well-attended forum at the student union and in the afternoon signed books at a beer and pretzels reception. He seemed genuinely pleased to sit at a table and speak individually with the many fans who lined up with books to sign, something he'd never done before.

That evening it was time to relax. At Kurt's suggestion, we ordered take-out chicken and picnicked at my home with my kids and close friends. We all regretted Rita Rait hadn't been there to share in the celebration so she and Kurt could be "Big in Cedar Falls," too.

I drove Kurt to the airport Saturday morning for his next gig—the opening of a theatrical production based on *The Sirens of Titan* that night in Chicago, and then making rounds on Monday with doctors at Cook County Hospital before giving a speech there.

I'd been concerned that we'd exhausted him with the overwhelming crowds but later had a sweet letter from him:

Dearest Loree—

You utterly elate me. What good times we have together—
and how obvious it must be to one and all that we love each
other so....

The play in Chicago has a certain clumsy charm. No one ever
succeeded in jamming a whole book into two hours of theatre. It's
a local hit, and the profits are going to P.E.N. (4/15/77)

He assured me he'd felt so energized by the crowd at his UNI reading that he'd decided not to scrap the novel that would become *Jailbird*, and which would suggest that people take on ideological beliefs in
order to make friends. I was delighted to find he'd included the *Mary
Kathleen O'Looney* manuscript from which he had read in Cedar Falls.

That summer of 1977, he and Jill again rented the Gerald Murphy
summer home in East Hampton. In July he wrote he was planning an
October business trip in Europe to visit his publishers in Scandinavia,
Germany, and Holland. This would include a side trip to Leningrad
to see Rita Rait, since she'd finally given up on permission to visit the
United States. He planned to schedule a visit to the Frankfurt Book
Fair as well. I, too, would be in Europe that fall for three months on a
sabbatical leave to prepare for teaching two new interdisciplinary
courses. It would be my first trip abroad and would include study in
Egypt, Greece, Italy, Switzerland, and England.

My intent was to track the roots and early development of Western
civilization as preparation for an introductory course in mythology
and another in the history of Western culture. I was mostly interested
in soaking up the general culture—how geography may have helped
to shape ancient myths and arts as well as values, and what artifacts
reflected those cultural visions. I had the great advantage of touring
Athens, Santorini, and Egypt with my old friend Solveiga Rush, an
art historian—and got some good slides for my courses. We abandoned plans for a bus trip into Turkey when Greek travel agents dis-
couraged us with horror stories about the current conflict over

Cyprus. It was mid-September when my friend bade me farewell at the bus departing for my Peloponnesus tour, and I finished my explorations of Greek culture alone in Crete and Corfu before boarding a ferry to Italy, luxuriating in golden memories of mountains, sun, and sea, and the glorious art of the Greeks.

I was still trying to digest how Greek art and architecture contrasted with Italian in mid-October when I reached my hotel in Florence, to find a cheerful letter from Kurt waiting for me. Writing from Stockholm, he said he'd found people "on the rim of the Arctic Circle to be the most honorable and intelligent inhabitants of the planet. . . . Amsterdam and Oslo received me as though I were a blood relative. Munich, Copenhagen, and now Stockholm have been stiff and correct with this stranger."

Then he noted tersely the irony that in two days he would "ride a sleeping train from Helsinki to Leningrad, a city younger than New York and built by a man who tortured his own son to death," wryly adding that Peter the Great "might be thought of as the inventor of Fathers' Day." While his distress about the Communist government's treatment of Rita Rait recognized deeper historical roots in Russian culture, his expectations about reuniting with her were framed by his affection and concern. He wrote that he would be bringing her

> an enormous magnifying glass and a dictating machine, since she is now going blind. She was born an aristocrat, and learned all languages as did Nabokov. When she and a few others like her at last die off, Russia will again have sealed itself off perfectly, without a single leak into the outside world. (10/5/77)

On a less serious note, he was disappointed in not seeing beautiful girls on this business trip: "We saw one in Holland, and that was the end of it. I blame this on the Hite Report, which has now been published everywhere." One of the major events of his trip would be the visit to the Frankfurt Book Fair, where he'd connect with Jill and then proceed to tour Italy, arriving here a few days after I left.

What I wouldn't have given about then to stroll across the Ponte Vecchio with Kurt that evening. The balcony of my *pensione* in Florence overlooked that famous bridge, from which I could hear the laughing voices of young Italians long into the night.

I never heard Kurt's impressions of Italy, but mine were nearly overwhelming at times—negative in terms of traveling solo, but being delightfully stunned by the wonder of its Renaissance art and architecture. Along with occasional help from another English-speaking traveler or guide, I appreciated the quiet time to digest it all over my increasingly tattered green Michelin guide book in the evenings.

Approaching the end of my tour by late October, I took a train from Venice to Zurich to participate in a panel at the Jung Institute and attend a conference on creativity and Jung's theory of individuation. Growing increasingly restless and lonely, I was ready to return home and almost prepared to deal with my son Rob's surprise marriage plans and a visit to my two youngest step children, Didi and Geoffrey, now living with their mother in Texas.

Such were those events that again, I was out of touch with Kurt for nearly a year during which time he was working hard to finish *Jailbird*, his book reflecting the Nixon years and the Watergate scandal. Doubtless, he was also enjoying the fruits of more public speaking and his "failed" novel, *Slapstick*, which was by then being published in England, Brazil, Holland, Switzerland, Argentina, Norway, Bulgaria, Japan, Germany, and Hungary. All his books were still in print, due, he claimed, only to the shrewdness of his publisher, Sam Lawrence.

Kurt and Loree, Loree's backyard, Cedar Falls, Iowa, 1977.

4

A New Lightness of Being, 1978–1982

Jailbird, Palm Sunday, Deadeye Dick

By October 1978, Kurt wrote he was still "hacking away" at his new book: "The trouble is that it gets better as I rework it. I wish to hell it wouldn't improve so with work, so I could just hand the mother in. Looks now like it might be done in January."

I was to be in New York for a conference and was delighted when he suggested we meet for lunch. It was a lovely fall day, just after the horrific news about the "Jonestown suicide" tragedy in Guyana. Somehow the craziness of that event, in contrast to the "Conference on Consciousness and Culture" I'd been attending, had begun to suggest opposite poles of unearthly fantasy: Mass suicide commanded by a charismatic "priest" in an unheard of tropical jungle seemed about as real as the slide lecture that morning by Fritzjof Capra. It concluded with an image of the creative dance of the Hindu god Shiva superimposed over one of scattering anti-matter particles in a nuclear accelerator. So it seemed perfectly in keeping that I would have lunch with Kurt Vonnegut.

Afterward we strolled in Kurt's Turtle Bay neighborhood. His fondness for the area and its splendid architecture was obvious. We ambled into one of his favorite haunts: a hobby shop specializing in HO gauge toy trains. Exquisite brass models of famous railroad lines

71

gleamed from glass cases. His enthusiasm in identifying them all was charmingly reflective of the child in him, which had always delighted me, and I hoped his partner Jill found this boyish innocence as endearing as I did. I was reminded of the toy train we Workshop students had given him over a decade ago in Iowa City to celebrate his triumph of *Rosewater* and *Mother Night*.

He insisted we visit the Empire State Building. On the way he delighted in pointing out historic origins of various buildings, acknowledging the Chrysler Building as his favorite. In fact, that building's splendid crown tower would become the "harp sales room" in *Jailbird* next year.

We paused to observe one of those colorful shell games being performed on a corner, with Kurt whispering, "You could never outsmart this guy."

As we walked, he kept a going narrative about these streets, clearly an environment that both amused and stimulated him. Before leaving town a couple days later, my friend Bonnie Koloc and I met Kurt for breakfast. Bonnie, a singer-songwriter originally from Iowa, was performing that weekend at a club with David Amram and had never met Kurt. We connected at one of his favorite coffee spots, a warm and busy restaurant where the waitress called everybody "sweetie" or "honey." A few months later, when I read the page proofs of *Jailbird*, its street scenes and affectionate Manhattan waitresses were a flashback of that day.

New York was perfect for him. He was as jubilant as he'd been in Iowa City, but here, abundant diversity was endless. He seemed infused with a new creative vitality: thrilled by the great museums and performance halls, but moved to tenderness by waitresses in coffee shops and homeless street vendors, a bountiful tableau.

After I returned home, his letter announced a little Christmas package would be arriving. It was one of the exquisite HO gauge model trains—the bronze Long Island Express engine we'd seen in the Manhattan hobby shop. I was stunned by the extravagant sentiment . . . so like him . . . so dear to commemorate our tour that happy afternoon.

It was February when Kurt wrote to say he'd finally turned in his new novel, but "now I have the manuscript back with flags all over it . . . a tire in need of about a hundred blowout patches." But he was jubilant about an anticipated getaway: After not communicating for twenty years, he'd phoned his boyhood friend, Ben Hitz, to announce his dedication of *Jailbird* to him. A Los Angeles banker, Ben had invited him to the Baja Peninsula for a camping trip. "He knows a guide who takes people by muleback up into the mountains to see huge cave paintings there. So we will meet in San Diego next Saturday, and off we will go, sleeping under the stars, until March 17. I'm so excited." Kurt, the anthropologist, was thrilled about seeing paintings by unknown indigenous peoples, pictures thought to have pre-dated Spanish invaders by some two hundred years.

In the meantime, he had Delacorte send me a photocopy of his *Jailbird* manuscript. The more I read, the more I felt the book would be a hit. I loved the way its long "Prologue" incorporated Kurt's youthful memory of meeting socialist labor leader Powers Hapgood. It contrasted his father's and Hapgood's values about the 1920s' Sacco-Vanzetti trial and execution, and simultaneously echoed current concerns about the Watergate scandal, reflecting how Kurt's fiction rested on historical events still influencing ethical and political decisions.

I wrote a celebratory letter and promised a smashing review. But I also asked his reaction to my revised essay about space and time in world myths. I'd been encouraged by his earlier responses, despite new time constraints from parenting Geoffrey, my seventeen-year-old stepson who had recently returned to live with me.

In reply, he wrote

> Klinkowitz told me a few weeks back that you were at last being honored as a thinker by your employers. I was reminded of Louise Nevelson, who wasn't taken seriously as a sculptor until she was in her seventies. A fellow artist explained to me: "Everybody finally decided that she really meant it."

Then he reminded me of his article in the *Nation* magazine that week

> about Mark Twain as the creator of the fundamental American myths, without which we would never feel like a people. Does this fit into your thesis anywhere? . . . I think now of how inconvenient it must be for you to be reliable and resourceful as well. Geoffrey is a lucky boy. He had better be nice to women when he grows up. (7/12/79)

Kurt was then awaiting "reviews of *Jailbird*, anxious to know if my self-respect is to be returned to me. I am paired with Roth by The Book of the Month Club in September."

I knew he smarted if reviewers put down his work. In fact it puzzled me when they ignored his innovative crafting to focus instead on perceived thematic recurrences. But to be linked with Roth had to be an upper.

While awaiting reviewer response, however, he explained he was involved in his own new venture—a musical adaptation of his novel, *God Bless You, Mr. Rosewater*. His love affair with theater had never stopped, but this was imminent: that June, a successful off-Broadway adaptation of *Rosewater* had opened in the WPA Theater. It had been adapted and directed by Howard Ashman with music by Alan Menken, a pair who later went on to Disney animated film fame with their scoring of *Aladdin* and *Beauty and the Beast*. By midsummer the *Rosewater* production blossomed into a family affair: he had made his daughter Edith the producer! She was then readying it for the next phase: an opening production at the Entermedia Theatre, where many successful plays had been launched into Broadway fame. Kurt proudly reported that

> She has responded brilliantly to the responsibility—raising $400,000, hiring a big, beautiful, cheap off-Broadway theater, holding the cast together, getting Warner Brothers in as a partner, and on and on. She is wowed by her own bravery and intelligence,

and could make a fortune. I sure hope so. That would be hilarious and deserved.

He said the play would open officially in October. "It's such an innocent show. In the finale, every member of the fourteen member cast is onstage with a baby. I cry every time I see it" (7/12/79).

Excitement about the play likely softened an edge of anxiety while he awaited those *Jailbird* reviews, and perhaps took his mind off the angina attacks Edie had told me he'd been experiencing, something he, of course, hadn't mentioned. He was thrilled with her management of the enterprise, and so was she.

A couple months later, the reviews of *Jailbird* began. I smiled as I collected them, imagining how ecstatic Kurt must be. I opened his letter of September 21, anticipating his jubilance. He began

> I will be marrying Jill late in November—the first marriage for her and the second one for me. It's time. We've been together nine years and we get along better than ever. We're all calmed down, and my kids approve. Jane has been with Adam Yarmolinsky for six or seven years now, so she's O.K., too. Things have reached such a state that Adam and Jill now like each other a lot. Anybody sophisticated in thermodynamics will have no trouble understanding all this. You, of course, are part of the whole *gemutlich* system. Love, love, love . . .

Well, OK—that wasn't quite the jubilance I'd expected. But of course it was time. He knew Jill well, and they had even worked together professionally. He'd never discussed their relationship in any detail, although I knew he admired her gutsy independence. Jill appeared quite glamorous in photographs I'd seen, and I knew that was a quality Kurt always appreciated. And she had a considerable reputation with artists because of her photographic talent and specialty in writers' portraits. Her photo credits appeared quite regularly in the *New York Times*.

I could only hope the marriage would be right for him. Surely having lived with her for this long had given him time for certainty. From my comfortable distance, I was pleased to continue to be his friend.

His letter went on to report that, although looking "like a thirteen-year-old dumb toot despite her twenty-nine years" his daughter Edith was:

> now known as "The Dragon Lady." . . . She was up all last night, negotiating with lawyers representing Atlantic Records, Warner Communications, the composer, the lyricist, the theater owner—and me. At dawn, a single contract dooming all of us to eternal servitude was born. . . . The official opening . . . will be October 14. There are signs all over New York, saying, "Don't kill yourself. Call the Rosewater Foundation." . . . Any nuts calling the number (although the poster is clearly a theater hype) will be switched to an actual suicide hotline. (9/21/79)

Kurt had even bought gifts for the cast, staff, and backers: "Rosewater Fire Department" badges with the play's opening date functioning as the badge number. But it was Edie who was featured in the October 15 *People* magazine as the top dog of the show, along with praise for her professional life as a painter. (Kurt's delight with the play unfortunately was short-lived; it ran only a little more than a month.)

His letter closed with gratitude that "John Irving wrote such a detailed and heartfelt appreciation of my work for the *New Republic* that I nearly cried. Bread on the waters." It was fitting that Irving, one of his best Workshop students (1966–1967), used his now ample credibility to pronounce the virtues of his former teacher's work. Irving's fourth novel, *The World According to Garp*, published the previous year, was still topping best-seller lists. His praise of Kurt's *Jailbird* was just the beginning of substantial acclaim for the book that suggested a fictional recovery from the Watergate scandal. About half of his nearly eight-page *TNR* article (9/22/79) took to task critics who had recently seemed to compete for acrimony in their disregard for *Slapstick*. In fact, Jerry Klinkowitz and I had both puzzled over their particularly rancorous tone. Klinkowitz had already published two enthusiastic scholarly books on Kurt by then, believing him to be the most accessible American writer of the difficult fiction now being heralded as "postmodern."

Irving's article drew attention to criticism that took Vonnegut to task for being too accessible, for being an "easy writer"—or worse, for writing lowbrow *science fiction*. In contrast he agreed with another former Workshop student, John Casey, who'd praised Kurt's insistence that writers recognize the difficulty of a reader's job. Irving added, "Making a reader's job easy is difficult work, although there's always been a great misunderstanding of Vonnegut on this point" (p. 41). He noted a 1973 *Playboy* interview in which Kurt argued writers should be agents of change, something he could best do with a little sugar coating to make his writing entertaining, so: "You get him [the reader] without him knowing it by making his job easy for him." Irving adds, "Like the pharmacist who really knows what's good for you, he understands the need for sugar coating on some very bitter pills. So many of Vonnegut's critics have noticed only the coating."

He cites *Jailbird* as an encouragement of humanity's highest ethical calling without condescension, a calling Vonnegut dares to compare to the "Sermon on the Mount." Recognizing how such a comparison risks cliché, Irving says "Vonnegut's ability to freshen the clichés in our language by using them when we're most vulnerable to the truth in them has never been sharper." He concludes that *Jailbird* is his "best book since *Slaughterhouse-Five*. . . . It is vintage Vonnegut. . . . It is not an aesthetic of condescension, or of writing down to one's reader. It is an aesthetic of the most demanding order" (48, 49).

Bread on the waters, indeed. Irving's article almost made me cry, too. The review preceding his was Stanley Kauffmann's celebration of the Monty Python film, *The Life of Brian*. That film and *Jailbird* were a stunning contrast to the cultural changes that would evolve. What Irving characterized as "the demanding aesthetic" of 1979 came to have no status whatever in the years ahead. Vonnegut's humanizing message of compassion and humility seemed lost in the shuffle of the last quarter century, along with the nation's sense of humor and its critical perception.

John Irving's eloquent appraisal of Vonnegut's opus and *Jailbird* was not entirely reflected in reviews that followed, but there was enough to assure Kurt his reputation as a writer had been "restored." Hardly any failed to recognize his humaneness and compassion. In a January 1980 letter, Kurt's modest response to my congratulations was typically edged with sarcasm: "Almost everything I'm praised for was a lucky accident. I think scarcely at all."

My review for the *North American Review* magazine said quite the opposite about Kurt's thinking. In fact it speculated his novel could be read as a comedic parody of Dante's *Divine Comedy*, set as it was in the three-story Manhattan universe from which bag lady Mary Kathleen O'Looney (Beatrice) administered her RAMJAC Corporation to redistribute the wealth of America. Imagine Dante's *Commedia* set in *Jailbird*'s Manhattan, where the Grand Central Station underground garage is Inferno; the area around Forty-Second Street and Fifth Avenue where protagonist Walter first meets his Beatrice is Purgatory; and her penthouse garden showroom for the American Harp Company is Paradise, in the crystal crown of the Chrysler Building. And I echoed what most reviewers had thought by then—that *Jailbird* was his best book since *Slaughterhouse*.

One might say the year 1980 marked a high in the plateau of appreciation for the Vonnegut opus and his worldview. Unfortunately, at the same time it marked the beginning of a new politico-moral force that would turn United States policies toward polar opposition to the compassion and humaneness most readers found in Vonnegut's novels. By April 1980, President Jimmy Carter had to accept the failure of a rescue mission to release U.S. hostages in Iran. In November, a prediction about the American presidency that Kurt had made in *God Bless You, Mr. Rosewater*, came true: Ronald Reagan, movie star and former governor of California, would defeat Carter and begin implementation of a platform endorsing a 30 percent cut in income taxes plus a massive increase in military spending. What the balanced budget politicos dreamed of in 1980, led to cuts in social programs *and* a record-breaking deficit, all of which only spurred support for Reagan and his second-term election.

Those very problems became Kurt's context when he stood as the Palm Sunday guest speaker on the stage of St. Clements Episcopal Church in New York City, March 30, 1980. Text for his brief sermon was John 12, the Palm Sunday eve account of Mary's anointment of Jesus' feet with costly oil, to which Judas reacts that Mary should have sold the oil and given the money to the poor.

Kurt's "sermon" focused on Jesus' enigmatic reply: "Let her alone, let her keep it for the day of my burial. The poor you always have with you, but you do not always have me."

Acknowledging himself as a "Christ-worshipping agnostic," Kurt said he chose this text because he was troubled by how "much un-Christian impatience with the poor [has been] encouraged by the quotation." He suggested that an exhausted Jesus "was only joking, and . . . not even thinking much about the poor." Instead, it was "a divine black joke" that "allows Jesus to remain civil to Judas, but to chide him about his hypocrisy all the same: 'Judas, don't worry about it. There will still be plenty of poor left long after I'm gone.'" He concluded that this interpretation helped the story "harmonize" with the Sermon on the Mount, suggesting "a mercifulness that can never waver or fade." Kurt continued over the years to use his own celebrity as a bully pulpit from which to argue that "muscular Christianity" had increasingly neglected the core teachings from Jesus' "Sermon on the Mount." (See "Hypocrites You Always Have with You," *The Nation*, April 19, 1980.)

Happily, by the decade of the eighties, Kurt's comfortable financial success may have allowed him to begin taking time out for his own personal pleasure in creating visual art and amateur play reading and acting with friends in the City. He even devised a delightful children's story for Ivan Chermayeff's colorful abstract paintings, published as an oversized book called *Sun Moon Star* by Harper & Row. That summer of 1980, he sent me three small black-and-white lithograph prints he'd created—iconic images I took to be whimsical self portraits. One was a profile of a bushy-haired man's face with a flower mouth, who gazed at a similar flower in a vase; the other two both suggested twin images reminiscent of the *doppelganger* theme in his fiction. It was obvious he was having fun with visual art.

He also was growing increasingly angry about what he called "the jazzy new mania for the eighties with its fashion and increasingly dull scholarship in writing." In January I had sent Kurt an essay I'd written on gender differences in human perceptions as they affect environmental concerns, prepared for an Earth Day conference. Unasked, he sent my essay to Gloria Steinem at *Ms.* magazine.

I had argued that the feminist celebration of male/female "equality" wrongly implied both sexes had identical perceptions of life. Rather, new scientific research suggested that female biology actually shapes the brain's capacity to perceive conditions imperceptible to the male, for example, the life-enabling phenomenon of interdependency, as in pregnancy.

Kurt sent me Ms. Steinem's reply, which essentially disagreed with my essay as an outdated view "very popular in the First Wave" of feminism. Kurt called her lengthy letter "a well-intentioned but obtuse response . . . by a person who shops for conclusions which suit her. . . . I might as well have submitted your essay to Barry Goldwater. . . . I trust that her comments will do no more than annoy you. . . . I'm damned if we're all alike" 2/8/80.

I had a lot of fun writing a parodied refutation of her letter back to Kurt, including new research citations supporting my point. He replied that he did not pass along my

first-rate rebuttal . . . nobody pays any attention to rebuttals around here. This is a city of statues. Nobody softens or abandons a position—for fear of vanishing entirely. . . .

William Buckley dares to praise liberals eloquently, as he did yesterday at the funeral of poor Allard Lowenstein [the murdered liberal activist], only when they are safely dead. . . . What the hell. 3/18/80

He added he'd recently had a phone conversation with a Swedish woman who would be interviewing him: "she had just come back from the Illinois primary, and she was literally in tears about the stupidity and barbarism in the speeches of Ronald Reagan. We scare the shit out of her."

By October, he sent a poster from his one-man show of "60 drawings in colored inks!—at the Margo Feiden Galleries in New York!"— and was delighted when former Workshop students showed up for the opening. The show was comprised mostly of quirky and colorful icons, not unlike enlargements of the doodles that sometimes adorned his letters and scrap worksheets. It would be the first of a number of shows he continued to produce—with colorful magic markers at first, and eventually, in partnership with Joe Petro III, silkscreen print artist in Kentucky.

He also mentioned seeing our friend Andre Dubus with his new wife ("who appears to be about thirteen")—on a speaking visit to Boston the previous week: "He looked happy and his reputation as a writer has a nice heft to it these days." But about our other Boston friend, Dick Yates, he had less good news: "He is in an intolerably lonely condition, and is having bad luck in the marketplace, too."

He included an amusing story about Nelson Algren who he said had moved to Sag Harbor on Long Island, not far from where Kurt had recently bought a summer home in Sagaponack:

> I took Nelson out to supper in August and brought John Irving and Shyla along. It turned out that Nelson had never heard of John. He spoke very strangely to him, and we only realized a couple of days later that Nelson thought John was Clifford Irving, the crook [author of the fake autobiography of Howard Hughes].

Unfortunately, a few months later (2/25/81) he wrote that John and Shyla had separated, "although they might get back together again. All the money and fame is turning their life to garbage, as far as she is concerned. She could be right."

In this newsy letter he also managed to mention "I'll have a new non-book out in early April. I'll send you a copy in a week or so. I'm not very proud of it. What matters is a novel-in-progress called *Dead-eye Dick*." The "non-book" was *Palm Sunday*, his "autobiographical collage." A rich sampling of speeches, tributes, letters, and essays tied together with an autobiographical narrative, *Palm Sunday* lacked the coherence and punch of his previous collage, *Wampeters, Foma & Granfalloons*, which his critics didn't fail to notice.

By the spring of 1981, I was writing grant proposals to support research on how myths and literature connect with cultural and scientific views, with all shaped by our belief in linear time (inspired partly by Kurt's manipulation of narrative time lines that influence differing views of "reality"). Kurt wrote a recommendation for me, as did our mutual friend, Bob Scholes, another of my Iowa mentors who was now heading the semiotics program at Brown University.

When Bob invited me to join him and his new wife for a sailing venture to christen their new boat in August—they'd be sailing up the coast to their home in Providence, Rhode Island—I was quick to comply. I'd already made tentative plans to vacation in Cape Cod with my art historian friend, Solveiga, that summer, but when I mentioned the Scholes's sailing trip to Kurt, he immediately suggested a side-visit to Sagaponack. I had reservations, but he insisted he wanted Jill and me to know each other.

He'd said virtually nothing about Jill since their marriage nearly two years ago, and I was considerably uneasy about bouncing into their conjugal retreat in the Hamptons. Especially, since I had no idea how she would feel about me. Eventually, we put it all together that I would fly out to New York, connect with a limo he'd provide for the drive to Sagaponack, spend a few days there, and then hook up with the Scholeses, who could moor their boat overnight at Three Mile Island Harbor near Sagaponack. Kurt would pick them up for a quick visit before we sailed off for Providence.

That summer was an exciting one for me. I'd rented a cottage for the month of June at a nearby Iowa lake in order to concentrate on my writing and returned home to host my gala fiftieth birthday picnic before taking off for New York.

I was numb with anticipation on the two-hour limo ride to Sagaponack, wondering how I'd be received by Jill and whether I'd been a fool to come. The driver enjoyed providing a somewhat tedious geographical and economic history of the Island as we drove. When he pulled up in front of the Vonnegut residence, I heard loud country music coming from the open windows and door. It was a spacious two-story home with Shake shingle siding and roof, surrounded by large, old trees, and even boasting one of the old potato barns common to early Long Island farms. Quite suddenly a tanned and sleek woman in a white bikini pushed open the screen door and shouted lyrically, "Darling, Loree is here." Obviously, this was Jill.

Kurt came out grinning in a T-shirt and shorts, made introductions, and invited me to take a swim after I unpacked. My upstairs guest room overlooked a patio and the in-ground swimming pool on the back lawn. Kurt sat in a lawn chair by the pool while I swam and cleared my head. I wondered what he'd told Jill about me, and I wasn't quite sure how I should approach her. "So, is this really going to be all right?" I asked, toweling off and feeling a bit more relaxed.

"It's going to be fine," he promised. We sat on the patio and sipped a gin and tonic. "Jill's gone to the airport to pick up Edie. When she comes back, we'll visit a couple galleries where she has some pictures." He explained that this weekend marked the fiftieth anniversary of the East Hampton Art Association with gala shows in all the galleries. "Later tonight we'll go to a smashing party with lots of writers at the cottage where Arthur Miller and Marilyn Monroe spent their honeymoon." He was like a kid in his delight of showing off the Hamptons.

We talked for an hour. He was still working—slowly—on *Deadeye Dick*. I was eager to hear about Edie—it had been a long time since the Iowa City days where we'd played hide and seek with the FBI guys. He wanted to hear about my kids and my writing. I told him my plans for traveling in France and England next summer and my chance of an actual visit to the Lascaux cave because of connecting with the anthropologist John Pfeiffer. I complimented him about Jill's beauty and this splendid summer home. He explained they were in the process of restoring the house, a long-term job. It was great to see him again.

After showering, I was sitting on the patio alone when Jill joined me. She quite abruptly opened a kind of intimate "woman-to-woman" conversation that rather took me by surprise. She assumed I knew about Kurt's mood swings and how much time he spent at the typewriter. She was concerned about his health—apparently he still suffered from angina attacks and had to carry pills. She asked about Iowa City, and it was apparent Kurt had told her about our friendship. She was charming and seemed grateful I'd come to visit, which helped considerably to put me at ease, although I still wasn't sure whether she knew the extent of our Iowa City relationship.

Within an hour, Edie arrived looking tanned, healthy, and perky. She loved having a studio in New York, and her paintings and ceramics were doing extremely well. She was thriving and comfortable with the celebrities who mingled with her father and Jill. When she learned I was going to the Cape after the sailing trip, she insisted I pay a visit to her mom in West Barnstable. I was unsure about this, but she was adamant that Jane would be unhappy if I didn't come. We'd not been in touch since she and Kurt had parted ways and he'd moved to Manhattan for good. My affection for her had never changed, but I'd always felt it would be presumptuous for me to reach out to her after she and Kurt split. Edie later called Jane to explain my presence—and I was persuaded she really did want to reconnect, so we made arrangements for meeting. Her invitation was an unexpected and generous gift.

We left Kurt's house for the party about nine, navigating a balloon-bannered drive to a house ablaze with colored lights and an outdoor dance floor, with parking on the lawn behind the house. The party was already in full swing. Kurt started introducing me to people, most of whom expressed their concerns about his neighbor, Truman Capote, who had suffered a seizure the previous day. He especially wanted me to meet the widow of author James Jones, Gloria, who'd been a companion to Nelson Algren. She was a warm and amusing woman who loved telling me the story of how he was buried in a Catholic Cemetery here, something Nelson would have found bizarre. We made a date to visit his grave before I left. Throughout the evening I was astonished at the warmth and friendliness of the guests, not at all what I had expected. When Kurt finally gave me the sign we were leaving, it was very late, and I was inexplicably involved in an intense conversation about the Heisenberg Uncertainty Principle with an elderly man who was asking me questions I couldn't answer.

"Thanks for the rescue," I exaggerated as we headed for the door.

"That guy is a multimillionaire broker," he said.

"Of course," I said. "Couldn't you tell I was in my element?"

"So now you know what celebrity society is all about," he grinned. "Jill's waiting outside."

I was wound up like a clock and appreciated the books left at my bedside table. Early in the morning, I could hear Kurt at his typewriter in his study, so I took a long walk and returned to find him preparing a leisurely breakfast. When he excused himself to go back to his study, Jill and I had another conversation. I was touched and charmed when she confided their plans to adopt a baby and wanted me to see pictures. I felt warmed by her sharing, although I didn't share my concern about an adoption at Kurt's age. He would be sixty in November.

Edie and I went with her to shop for antiques and we returned just in time to leave for Three Mile Island and the Scholes's arrival.

Kurt and I drove to the harbor where we spotted Bob and JoAnn walking down the road toward us with a knapsack. It was a warm reunion. JoAnn, Bob's second wife, was a high school biology teacher, considerably younger than Bob and warmly deferential toward him. I could see they'd be compatible sailing partners. Bob had continued his prolific scholarship after moving to Brown and an impressive career. Despite his scholarly achievements and reputation, he was a down-to-earth and jovial man who loved good conversation, good wine, seafood, and, of course, sailing. He had written extensively on Kurt's work.

Back on the Vonnegut patio, we yielded to intense conversation and catch-up until Gloria Jones' partner, Kermit Love—one of the creators of Sesame Street characters—arrived on his bicycle with two parrots astride his shoulders, there for a previously scheduled camera shoot with Jill. (*And* demonstrations of his parrots' verbosity.)

Kurt wanted to go to the beach after lunch, but first, he'd promised to teach Bob and me Transcendental Meditation—something he insisted he'd learned from the Maharishi himself. He sat us down in the drawing room and with a reverent voice and slight smile, explained how this was like Christian dreaming and could replace naps. He even revealed his own mantra, which was supposed to be kept secret, and wryly gave both of us our own. We soon persuaded him we were "rested" enough for swimming. By then Jill and JoAnn had left for an apparent shopping trip.

Rickety bicycles stored in Kurt's potato barn were our transportation for the few blocks to the beach. Kurt pointed out Peter Matthiessen's house as we rode by, Kurt's friend and a writer I'd long admired. Later, on a long beach walk, he mentioned the stress Edie had coped with in past months and celebrated her now blooming health and productivity. She would soon be off to Chicago for a part in movie being filmed there. He agreed enthusiastically that I should visit Jane in Barnstable.

It was late afternoon when we all left for the home of Kurt's good friend, Sid Solomon, who was hosting a dinner party exhibition of his work. It was another big crowd, with the only recognizable person being one of my feminist heroines, Betty Freidan. Kurt immediately introduced me, telling her I was working on a book he knew she would find interesting, which of course put me into an initial state of speechless awe. The top of her head came about up to my nose, from which she stood about four inches, to question me intensely, and insist on books I *must* read immediately.

I could see our host in various clusters of joke-telling and boisterous laughs. His abstract art was hung throughout the house, and it wasn't too long before I was giddy with picture viewing, conversation with strangers, and knowing I had better eat before I was seriously drunk. Food was served in the nick of time. It was late when we left, and we all immediately went to bed, myself still in a daze of over stimulation.

The weekend had gone much too fast, and in the morning we were soon off to the marina. I was excited about the sailing venture, but not looking forward to saying goodbye. As we hauled our gear to Scholes's dinghy that would take us to the mooring of their boat, I heard Kurt say quietly to Bob, "Loree's a good salt," perhaps remembering that wild and lovely day in Key West, the only time I'd sailed with him. As we three paddled out to the boat, through tears I watched Kurt on the pier, hunched with his elbows resting on a piling. I have never seen another human being whose body language so vividly portrayed gravity.

We all would have loved him to join us for the sailing venture. Fortunately, my enthusiasm for sailing and two buoyant companions replaced the sadness of farewells, and we were off for a perfectly delightful week. By the time we sailed up Narragansett Bay past Newport, we entertained the possibility of racing two twenty-four-meter yachts flanking us, but wisely yielded and put in at the Providence marina. After a pleasant two days at the Scholes's home, I departed by a morning bus to Barnstable, there to finally reunite with Jane Vonnegut.

It had been fifteen years.

She had the same breathless exhilaration she'd always had, and seemed as excited or perhaps as nervous, at first, as I was when my cab arrived at the large shuttered Vonnegut house in West Barnstable. This was where she and Kurt had raised six children and he had produced his early work before I met him in Iowa City. I had to step over a suitcase inside the front door as I entered.

"Oh, sorry," she laughed apologetically. "I haven't unpacked yet from Colorado." With almost childlike animation she led me upstairs to a guest room. "Did Edie tell you the kids are here? China, Tiger's [Kurt's nephew, whom he and Jane had raised] baby, is sleeping in that room—she's such a darling. Mark's here, and Nanny. They're all at the beach."

Later Jane and I sat on a blanket in the shady yard where we could talk. Edie, of course, had told Jane I'd been visiting Kurt and Jill in Sagaponack. She wanted to know about Kurt's health and what I thought about their marriage. I measured my words carefully, still unsure of her feelings. I acknowledged they seemed happy, and that he was clearly pleased and proud of the house they were restoring. I brought her up to date on Bob Scholes and his new wife and recounted some of our sailing adventures.

What was dominating Jane's concerns about Kurt and his new marriage had to do with the way she felt it had split their family. And then she said rather abruptly that she had wanted to phone me when he was first living with Jill, to ask me to intercede. "I knew you would always want the children included."

I was taken aback. It was like Jane to be so naïvely honest about her feelings. Embarrassed, I reminded her that I was married by then and had a teaching job.

"Yes, I know. It was absurd of me."

My inability to respond was partly because I lacked information—I knew how much Kurt adored their children and how at a loss he'd felt when they began to leave home. And I knew nothing of Jill's relationship with them, except for Edie, which seemed good. I felt honored and, at the same time, humbled by her confidence about their children. It was a moment of forgiveness and trust I'll never forget, and for which I'll always be grateful.

Jane was also concerned about Kurt's recent book, *Palm Sunday*, which she perceived to be less than worthy of his talent. "I really do think he's a genius," she said earnestly, to which I agreed. She was worried about how the recent bad reviews were affecting his state of mind and described his obvious discomfort when attending a recent family celebration there at the Barnstable home, attended by old friends and neighbors.

"He sat outside by himself and wouldn't talk to anybody. . . . It was awful."

She didn't seem aware of his longstanding discomfort about what he felt was their neighbors' avoidance or disrespect for him as a writer when they had all lived here as a family. It also seemed possible that his present well-publicized summering with celebrities in the Hamptons probably didn't exactly endear him with the Cape Cod crowd. I finally did remind her that Kurt had seemed to me to have felt painfully ignored by some old Barnstable friends, if not offended, which seemed to surprise her.

What was apparent was that both Jane and Kurt had loved each other despite the strains on their marriage, and that healing was probably not fully over.

We continued to talk as the family beachgoers returned. Suddenly Mark appeared, carrying a tray of freshly cracked and iced crabs on the half shell, along with gin and tonics. He grinned awkwardly as I reached for his hand, moved by the sensitivity of his respect for our privacy and the generosity of the delicacies he had prepared.

Obviously, those in the house were purposefully giving us some time to be alone. Jane and I indulged in the lovely feast, and I was grateful when the conversation shifted to our children. After dinner Jane and her daughter Nanny took me to see the Barnstable Village Theater Jane had played such an active roll in developing and sustaining. It was Nanny who later told me about Jane's summer visits to the Aspen Institute where she led discussions in the humanities and had put together a substantial anthology on the history of Western thought and values.

Back at their house, Nanny recalled some of her memories from Iowa City where she and my daughter had been brief friends. She was tall and slender, bright as a penny, with eyes that reminded me of Kurt, but enthusiastic animation like her mother. She showed me a collection of her prints and photographs, which I found quite appealing, and asked if I might purchase one. She penciled in a title after some thought: "Israeli Aftermath." The picture had an interesting narrative quality of tiny figures suggesting a series of crises and resolutions.

The next day was a family picnic in the yard between the house and barn, behind which was the salt marsh and beyond that the bay. The jokes and conversation were *so* infused with playful humor that it almost seemed like we were back in Iowa City. When my friend

Solveiga arrived for our drive to Provincetown, I felt as though I were bidding farewell to family. I was most grateful to have reconnected with Jane, a woman of bountiful energy and unassuming talent.

Nonetheless, as we drove toward Provincetown, my mind was in overload as I reflected on the unlikely conjugation that had linked me with these two extraordinary and strikingly dissimilar women who had just shared their concerns about the complex man they both loved, or at least had at one time, a man for whom I, too, cared deeply. The happenstance of my role in their lives left me pondering and humble. I felt appreciative, but at the same time apprehensive about how everything would turn out. I knew Jane would always somehow manage to come through as a good sport. Jill's way of "coming through" was less familiar to me. Clearly I was in no position to judge, but I wished them both well.

* * *

It seemed altogether fitting, in this trip through the past, that I reconnect as well with the man whose decision had kicked off this strange chain of events: Verlin Cassill, who had endorsed my Workshop study so long ago, before abandoning his writing life in Iowa forever.

His summer home in Truro off a dirt beach road, had a studio workshop in back, which was where Solveiga and I found him, working outside on a clay sculpture at a picnic table. He was affable in a reserved or perhaps bemused way, and it was clear he was not about to be overly enthusiastic about my visit. I couldn't help feeling affection and gratitude for his mentoring and support that first year at Iowa, but I knew he considered I was among other Workshop students who had somehow betrayed him. A perceptive writer with superb ability to create fictional character, he had published several more novels while teaching at Brown, and was then at work on *After Goliath*, which would see print in 1985. Obviously he loved it here, as he should. I was happy to know he had a good place to work.

We went on to Provincetown and its rich history of nourishing the creative arts. Solveiga and I stayed at a B & B owned by an artist friend who shared bountiful information and connections. We ended the Cape stay with several days of sailing with friends living in Orleans.

Since I would be flying back to Iowa from Boston, I called another old friend and Workshop teacher, Dick Yates, to see if he might be available for dinner the night before my flight left. We made a date, and I waited at my hotel for him to arrive, but inexplicably he never showed up. I phoned him several times that evening with no answer, so figured I must have somehow misunderstood. Just before leaving for the airport the next morning I tried once more to contact him. This time he *did* answer: "Sorry sweetheart, but I'm lying here in a pool of blood waiting for the ambulance to come."

"What happened?" I gasped.

"The cops think I must have fallen or something. I'll be all right. Sorry to have missed our date."

"Do you have somebody to help you?" I asked.

"Naw, the cops are here. It's OK. I'll call you when I get out."

I was so concerned that I phoned Kurt in New York, hoping he might follow up on him, which he promised to do. We both agreed it was the continuing saga of Richard Yates and his lonely bad luck. A week or two after I returned to Iowa, Kurt did call to say Dick had recovered and was back in his apartment, still writing.

Kurt, too, was working intensely—on *Deadeye Dick*, a novel reflecting his morose concern about nuclear bomb weaponry and accidental catastrophes—which he finally had resolved by the end of the year. It was a celebration of that accomplishment that inspired his holiday trip to the Galapagos Islands in the spring of 1982.

On May 22 of that year, he sent a pep talk about my research project on *Earth Mother and Father Time*, which would be central to my study in France and England that summer. I was hoping to enhance my understanding of hunting-and-gathering peoples of the Cro-Magnon stone age period, especially how their perceptions of time and spirituality differed from later agricultural peoples. He said

You are already well into the heavy gambling, as far as time is concerned. A lot of us love and admire you, and I will dare to be their spokesman in saying this much, anyway: We would be very unhappy if we thought you were risking anything more than time. Promise us that, if you are for one reason or another unable to find the unified vision you seek, you yourself will feel that all you have lost is time, which would have gone out the window, anyway.

The caves of France seem exactly the right place to go next. They will give you all sorts of insights which you need at just this time. *Earth Mother and Father Time* is a stunningly suggestive title, by the way. You couldn't do better in encapsulating what your mind is like and what your book could be.

He closed by telling me,

I preach tomorrow morning at 11 at St. John the Divine, the Anglican cathedral here. My sermon is on disarmament. For the next ten Sundays, the pulpit is to be turned over to druids like myself—who supposedly have interesting opinions on disarmament and peace. I have busted my ass for a month, trying to find good things to say.

In the context of the accelerating arms race between the United States and the Soviet Union, the Soviet invasion of Afghanistan and the British defense of the Falkland Islands, his "ass-busting" speech was timely. "Fates Worse than Death," was one of the finest satires he ever wrote. In it he surveyed the misery humans have perpetrated upon one another and pointed out the irony he had observed on his recent trip to the Galapagos: "If we desolate this planet, Nature can get life going again. All it takes is a few million years or so, the wink of an eye to Nature." He left his audience with a motto borrowed from a robber baron to help humanity endure "all sorts of insults and humiliations and disappointments without committing either suicide or murder: 'Nothing is lost save honor.'"

When I offered my congratulations and asked about publication, he replied, "I was high as a kite—in a pulpit thirty feet above the congregation, and wearing crimson robes. My performance was pro bono publico, and anybody who wants to reprint it can do so without any sort of permission from me or anybody." The speech was widely published, including a version he illustrated for the University of Northern Iowa's *North American Review* (December 1982, vol. 267, no. 4). The central thematic kernel of humility in that speech eventually was fully developed into what would be his novel *Galapagos*, which would follow *Deadeye Dick*.

When I returned from Europe in August, Kurt's phone call welcomed me home with a double message. The good news was that he was sending me a galley proof of *Deadeye Dick*, which would be released later that month. The bad news was that Jane Vonnegut was under treatment for an advanced case of ovarian cancer. By September, after *Deadeye Dick* was out and the reviews were coming in, he seemed subdued and worried that Jane's violent reaction to the chemotherapy raised fears "the cure" might be harming her as much as the disease itself. I was relieved to hear from her in mid-October that her chemotherapy was "making a difference," even though she had more to endure.

As for *Deadeye Dick*, critics were having a field day. For me, it had remarkable depth and subtlety that grew with each reading. Beneath the multiple ironies and his usual way of satirizing characters, were old Vonnegut themes, but spun through the experiences of a humble protagonist whose behavior provides a model for decency and kindness.

I sent Kurt my lengthy review for the *North American Review*. He responded

> your essay on *Deadeye Dick* ... is an accurate and imaginative piece of work, and wonderfully flattering. . . . I figured I owed it to myself, if to nobody else, to look into why Dwayne Hoover's wife committed suicide. It was a serious thing to do. . . . It scares me some to see, with help from you and some others, how the boundaries between my books are vanishing, now that I have come this far. There is this great big puddle. (9/18/82)

That "puddle" was likely the power of accidents in life, a theme often reflected in his work. But the suicide event, which was new, reflected the inner misery of a beautiful woman who felt humiliated by how others responded to her beauty, a possibility I think very few men recognize. I wondered if it might have reflected the painful experience of his own mother and her suicide, but at the same time, another way of expressing Kurt's value of kindness and levity as a response to life's pain. I never found out.

Reviews of his and John Updike's new books both appeared on the front page of the *New York Times Book Review* on October 17, 1982, Updike for his *Bech Is Back*. Benjamin DeMott did not give *Deadeye Dick* a rave and acknowledged he understood "why some critics find Vonnegut vexingly soft on both the cartooning and preaching sides of his nature." He added,

> But I know that on some days this very odd writer is good medicine . . . on the day when, for instance, you hear that the shelling hasn't stopped, or the liveliest young mind in your acquaintance can't find work. . . . But gloating and meanness are excluded from the game, and the observing eyes are sad, humorous, kind.

DeMott's careful insights escaped those few others whose vitriol reflected an enigma that still puzzles me today. I'm tempted to think overly outraged critics were so angered by Kurt's seeing life as a cosmic game of chance that they failed to recognize his insistence on human awareness as uniquely creative and perhaps even sacred, even if not to be taken *too* seriously. Rudy Waltz, the accidental murderer learns this, and thus finds the preparation of tasty recipes a least offensive and kindest way of surviving. Allegorically, then, Kurt may have meant readers to see value in such a humble purpose.

That's a long way from speaking out of "rage and hurt and hate," as one critic had accused him. In *Deadeye Dick*, Rudy's purposeless scat-singing may have seemed an insult to heroes who represent exalting power and noble courage, no matter the consequences. But for

Kurt, lightheartedness was a useful substitute for exhausting efforts to transcend life's absurdities.

That he had actually been able to earn a substantial living by creating such stories was another one of life's happy surprises. But the very fact that this melancholic lived to the age of eighty-four and still loved to laugh may offer some confirmation of the value of his sensibility.

Ecce Homo, one of Kurt's "Enchanted I.O.U.s"

5

Celebration, Crash, and a Comeback, 1982–1984

Any leftover negative response to *Deadeye Dick* was transformed into a gala sixtieth birthday celebration for Kurt by his wife, Jill, with a black tie dinner party on November 11, 1982, at Michael's Pub in Manhattan. She had issued invitations the previous spring for festschrift submissions as a surprise gift for Kurt. I was thrilled to be invited and loved writing a short piece that compared Kurt's fictional visions to some I'd witnessed on my visit to ancient sites of Europe the previous summer.

Besides honoring Kurt, the event was a rare chance to identify if not meet his friends, who were listed on a dinner seating list that read rather like a *Who's Who* of America's creative elite.

The first familiar face I spotted at the celebration was that of Dick Yates, apparently fully recovered from the accident that botched our Boston date the previous summer. Still strikingly tall and handsome, he looked healthy if a bit graying since I'd last seen him. We had a happy reunion—it had been more than fifteen years! At the bar we ran into my sailing buddies, Bob and JoAnn Scholes. Bob was in the middle of an anecdote account to Tom Wicker about running into William Buckley at the Yale Club and baiting him about why he wasn't publishing more Vonnegut. (Kurt had actually sold his "Harrison Bergeron" short story to Buckley's *National Review* magazine while he was still at the Iowa Workshop.)

Scholes and Yates had been Iowa colleagues, but I knew the Yale Club reference would make Dick uncomfortable. Predictably, he edged me away and bent to whisper, "Sit next to me at dinner, sweetheart. I don't want to have to talk to Scholes. He hates my work. He's reviewed all of Kurt's stuff, but never me. Nothing!"

He led me toward table number six, where we'd been assigned. "Here, we'll just change you with this person." Obviously he'd been here early enough to familiarize himself with the seating arrangements. He replaced someone's name card with mine so I'd be sitting next to him. I was nervous about this, and told Dick so. "Naw, it won't matter. Nobody'll know the difference, anyway."

Suddenly Kurt arrived to warm applause, a bit shy but beaming, with Jill on his arm. It was the first time I'd ever seen him in a tux. He looked great, and I gave him a big hug when he came over to us.

"I know you," he grinned. "Be sure you come over to my place for coffee in the morning, OK? Edie and Nanny will be there, and they want to see you, too."

Hanging out with celebrities was not exactly routine for me, but I didn't falter when the chance came to meet John Updike and Norman Mailer. I asked Updike if he had ever taught at the Writers' Workshop, which he had not. Whereupon I launched into a celebration of Iowa and the Midwest. He liked New England just fine, thank you. When I mentioned to Mailer that I'd met his wife in Provincetown that summer, he asked, "Which one?" And I couldn't remember her name.

After that, I decided to hang with Dick Yates. I introduced him to Don Fiene, Kurt's friend from Tennessee. Don was a good drinker *and* he liked Dick's novels, so they hit it off. Don was also subject to depression, always a lively conversation topic they could share. Both of them were getting pretty sloshed.

I barely had time to say hi to Kurt's kids before dinner was announced.

At each guest's place was a slim red clothbound book with gilt-edged pages in a matching slipcase embossed by Kurt's signature in gold. It was his festschrift, titled *Happy Birthday, Kurt Vonnegut*, compiled and edited by Jill and published in an elegant, limited edition of five hundred by Dell. It contained unusually affectionate and entertaining tributes, a discerning appreciation of Kurt's work, his kindness and generosity, and his sense of humor. My contribution was a consciously subtle expression of gratitude and affection for his invention of harmless untruths that helped us all endure.

Dr. Mark Vonnegut provided a tribute to his dad as the dinner came to a close. I remember thinking what a bright kid he was and appreciating his dry wit and sincerity. He was his father's son all right.

After the cheers died down, Kurt stood with a boyish smile and proceeded to sing an old tune from the forties made popular by Perry Como, "I Wonder Who's Kissing Her Now." It was characteristic of him to proffer his gratitude with a little performance, something people our age were taught to do as children. (One of the things Kurt admired about Dick Yates was his knowledge of old ballads and show tunes from the forties and fifties. But Kurt knew them, too, as he proved that night.)

It had been a lovely evening and a deservedly great success for Jill.

Late the next morning at Kurt's brownstone, I was eager to make my appreciation clear. Jill was not to be seen, but Kurt and his daughters were having coffee. I was taken aback when Kurt rather abruptly asked me why I'd changed seats at my table. When I explained that Yates hadn't wanted to sit by Bob Scholes, he laughed heartily. Jill made an appearance shortly after that, and Kurt solemnly explained how Yates had insisted on the change and that I had not been responsible. I added my apologies, unsure why this was such a big deal, but it was evident Jill was not moved by my remorse and left the room without a word.

As other friends of Kurt's began dropping in, I was about to make my leave, but at Kurt's urging I stayed, drifting into the dining room with Edie and Nanny.

It was then that they quietly explained Jill had meticulously planned the seating arrangements to facilitate dinner conversations. Yates was to be seated by an editor who might be helpful to him. I felt truly sorry I'd been party to messing it up, but relieved my celebrations didn't have to be planned that way. I resolved to make further amends to Jill, but didn't see her again before I left.

Meanwhile, it was good to have some secluded time with the girls to hear their confirmation that Jane seemed stronger and was getting good reports about her cancer treatment. *And* to learn the cheery details about Nanny's recent marriage to Scott Prior and her new life in Northampton, Massachusetts. She scrambled to get photographs of some of her husband's paintings, which I agreed were stunningly impressive. "And so, how about *your* work?" I asked her.

She shrugged and smiled, "It's coming along. But you should see Edie's. She had a great show this fall."

"Are you finally going to visit my studio while you're here?" Edie asked. I wrote down her directions and promised I wouldn't miss it for anything.

After most of Kurt's other friends had left, we carried some snacks into the living room. The remaining visitor there was a tall, pleasant woman about Kurt's age. He introduced her as a cousin visiting from Indianapolis. I listened raptly as their conversation continued with humorous anecdotes about shared childhood experiences and Indianans with onerous conservative values. She had a warm sense of humor and their mutual affection was clear. After she left, Kurt sat quietly for a moment. "She's about the only friendly relative left in Indiana," he smiled.

I departed soon after that, pleased with the accord that seemed strong in his life and delighted to have shared in his celebration.

Before leaving the city the next day, I took a cab to the East Village and Edie's studio. She met me at the rickety elevator that opened into her space cluttered with shelving for ceramic pieces, work tables, tools, and paintings. She seemed to almost prance from piece to piece—I was struck again, as I always was, how like her mother she was in spontaneity and exuberance. Ceramic angel heads hung on the walls, along with paintings of voluptuous angels. At one table she demonstrated her newly devised technique for cutting tiles, a method that overcame her light body strength. She was elated about the good chance she had for the tiles' placement on consignment in a large department store. No wonder Kurt was so energized by her presence in the city and so proud of her artistic commitment. We parted with her promise that she'd keep me informed about her mother's health.

It was about two months later that I received a surprise in the mail from Jill Krementz—an announcement adorned with angel drawings by Edie—of the December birth of Lily Vonnegut. Kurt was now the father of seven!

I didn't hear from him until early in the spring, however, when he responded to my letter about the sudden death of the editorial cartoonist of the *Des Moines Register*. Frank Miller was an artist we'd both admired and whose work Kurt had followed when he lived in Iowa City. The *Register* was still, at that time, an independently owned paper, whose editorial stance had long been a liberal one. Frank Miller had been the cartoonist for about twenty years, following the famous J. N. "Ding" Darling whose environmental protection concerns were history-making. Iowa's populist readers had appreciated Miller's daily cartoons that continued the paper's liberal position and integrity. His unexpected death was widely mourned.

Kurt, too, mourned him:

> the disappearance of a first class political cartoonist leaves a terrible hole in a community. My own home town is so reactionary that it hasn't had a good cartoonist ever, maybe. He would have disturbed the peace. Like all the great ones, I notice, Miller pretended to be a wimp. He sure could draw. (3/3/83)

He was delighted about his new daughter, if characteristically brief as he usually was about his personal life: "The baby is enchanting. What seducers they are."

His newsy letter went on to note that he'd been lecturing at several universities in England the previous week and was cheered to find "that

sermon of mine" ("Fates Worse than Death"), on sale in booklet form
by the Bertrand Russell Foundation in all the bookstores. Russell, the
late writer, philosopher, and Nobel Laureate was one of Kurt's heroes.

Kurt said he'd observed John Irving's forty-first birthday the previous night, at a small dinner party prepared by John himself. Kurt
noted, "He has a very rich and clever and nice lady friend. He has become a grave elder statesman."

He also had news of another old friend, Andre Dubus: "I had congratulated him on a short story of his. He remains a great enthusiast
for that ancient form." By then recognized as one of the country's
finest story writers, Andre was about to publish his third collection,
The Times Are Never So Bad. It was pretty amazing, I thought, how
many gifted writers had come out of that prairie Workshop, and how
their affinity for one another persisted over the years. Andre was still
teaching at Bradford College in Massachusetts.

On May 6, Kurt's letter began with a report on the end of pilot
fear about breaking the sound barrier: "The barrier turned out to be
psychological. Flying faster than sound was as easy as pie." In February he had flown on the Concord to England: "Ever wash down
caviar with champagne on a Trailways bus, which has tiny portholes
instead of windows? That's what the Concord is like." This was his
lead-in for generous praise for a long article I'd published in the *North
American Review* about the Cro-Magnon cave paintings.

> you have easily pierced a psychological barrier that, for a
> thousand reasons, probably, scared you for years. I am
> congratulating you on your confident, authoritative, wisely
> passionate essay on Ice Age cave paintings, paintings you went and
> saw for yourself, by God.... I have known you for a long time now,
> and have seen you gum up the expression of your best thoughts
> with prose recommended by others—Verlin, me, academic
> bullshitters of many kinds. You are your own author now.

It was the strongest praise I'd received from him since giving up
fiction, and from that point on I felt reassured enough to regard myself as an essayist.

Best of all, was his happy news about the imminent conclusion of Jane's debilitating chemotherapy without which "the theory was and remains that she would have been dead by now, if she hadn't agreed to be poisoned . . . every month for the past year." A CT-scan had revealed no new tumors, and she would even be able to see her new grandson born to Tiger and Lindsay Adams.

> It may be that she does not have cancer any more, and that chemistry and prayer and faith healing and so on worked. Everybody sure hopes so. . . . Jane has behaved *so* well, and would have been so much worse off without religion. I have never recommended that people should do without it.

A month later (6/14/83), he let me know that her chemotherapy had indeed been concluded, and that she'd written him "a sweet, intimate and candid letter . . . the first such since our breakup so long ago. So we're close friends again." Obviously he was grateful her recognition of their deep relationship had survived the social turmoil of their parting and her struggle for life. It was like Jane to be able to rise above her own pain to let Kurt know that.

This letter also answered my question about the status of his next book, the germ of which had been hinted in his "Fates Worse than Death" speech at the Cathedral of St. John the Divine the previous year. In that "sermon" he said the strange creatures one could see on the Galapagos Islands had suggested to Charles Darwin that Nature could accomplish simply anything given enough time. Now, he was still

> hacking away at the last book I owe Dell. I bought a beautiful model of *The Beagle*, hoping it might help some . . . the real thing was only 94 feet long. Imagine going around the world in a little sailboat like that before there were any canals between the continents.

I could visualize him grinning when he closed with a recollection of our long ago sailing venture in Florida: "We damn near perished in the soupy waters off Key West."

In addition to "hacking" at the book, which would become *Gala-pagos* in another year and a half, Kurt said he had again hired an agency to organize and schedule his public speaking appearances. In November he wrote that although it had worked very well, the schedule had been exhausting with eleven "lucrative engagements" spread over fourteen days in the spring and again in the fall. "I lived and behaved like the great Willy Nelson, a dazed traveler when between manic exhibitions . . . it felt very queer indeed . . . disorientingly, it worked every time. . . . What the fuck was that all about? It was about money, I think. . . . So I will lie low for a while."

To accommodate this strenuous schedule, he had devised a kind of boilerplate structure for his speeches, entitled "How To Get a Job Like Mine," into which he could insert relevant updates, jokes, and political rants that always included attacks on President Reagan's policy for a nuclear arms buildup as a "M.A.D." (Mutually Assured Destruction) defense against the Soviet Union.

In December 1983, I made plans to fly to New York to attend the Modern Language Association annual meeting, plus a musical performance by Bonnie Koloc, who was anchoring Joseph Papp's new musical adaptation of William Saroyan's *The Human Comedy* at the Public Theatre. Bonnie was getting rave reviews. It was a lucky break I could combine a professional event with the pleasure of seeing my good friend appear in her first New York stage production. I let Kurt know I'd be in town and found to my delight he'd actually be speaking at the MLA on censorship and free speech, so we made a date for lunch.

Unfortunately, he had grim news about Jane. Her condition had worsened in late November, and exploratory surgery revealed new tumors that would necessitate further chemotherapy. "Never has anyone been less deserving of such agony," he lamented. "She always took such good care of her body." The counterpart was good news: His daughter Nanny was pregnant and would give birth in the spring, one of those incredible life ironies that nobody anticipates. We all dared hope that Jane would be around to see that baby.

The MLA was meeting at the Hilton in Manhattan, and I had decided to stay there instead of with Bonnie who had her hands full with nightly performances. One of the attractions of the MLA that year was the appearance of Jorge Luis Borges, the extraordinary Argentine fiction writer who was then eighty-four years old. I was thrilled to hear him speak, even though comprehending him was a challenge. That night I spoke with Kurt to confirm our lunch date at the Hilton after his morning talk. He'd invited Peter Reed from Minnesota to join us. I hadn't seen Peter since Kurt's UNI visit in 1977. I explained that I'd also invited a friend—Will Stone, an E. M. Forster scholar from Stanford, who had chaired an evaluation of our department the previous year.

The next morning I scrambled to find the large Trianon auditorium where Kurt would be speaking. I took a seat near the front, a bit nervous that he was nowhere to be seen. He'd told me it would be at 9:45, and he had only ten minutes to spare. Then I overheard—in fact was shocked to overhear—some professors near me complaining that he was late. "He's quite the drinker, you know," one of them said. "Probably's still sleeping it off." I was outraged at this unwarranted gossip, and stalked out to find a phone.

Kurt answered.

"Hey, Kurt! You know you're on in about five minutes?"

"Oh, shit. I'll be right there. . . . I'm only a few minutes away."

True to his word, he appeared shortly and immediately approached the moderator and shook hands. It gave me major satisfaction that he gave a brilliant lecture on the First Amendment, and nicely quieted the grousing academics who applauded wildly when he finished.

I waited while he took questions from a cluster of admirers who rushed the stage. Finally the crowd thinned and I approached.

"Thanks for that call," he grinned, giving me a hug. He guided me toward the restaurant. Peter and Will had already met.

I was still somewhat giddy with excitement and grateful to sip a glass of sherry and listen while the three men became more acquainted. Borges and Vonnegut all in twenty-four hours was a bit of an overload. Peter was obviously delighted to see Kurt, and when Will, the Forster specialist, learned Peter was not only British, but a longtime fan of Forster, the gathering became amiable and easy. Kurt seemed especially playful and cheerful.

After lunch Kurt and I caught up on family news. Edie's huge opening at the Dan Turk Gallery in Los Angeles the previous month had been a great success—and Jane had even been well enough to attend it, as was Edie's partner, John Squibb, and her cousin Steve Adams, one of Kurt's three adopted nephews and now a successful comedy writer in L.A. Nanny was due in the spring and happily content with her husband and their nice house with an expandable attic in Northampton. Baby Lily was an angel, although he didn't mention her mother. Kurt invited me to come by the next day to meet his new daughter, which I agreed to do before heading back to Iowa.

It was later that evening, during the intermission of Bonnie's play at the Public Theatre, that I had the total surprise and delight of running into Jane Vonnegut and Edie in the lobby! Jane looked a bit wan, but a lot better than I would have expected. I gave her a hug— "You look terrific!"

She grimaced, but said the holidays with her kids had really cheered her up, before facing the ordeal of new chemotherapy treatments in January. She was living in Washington with her partner, Adam Yarmolinsky, but had come up for the weekend because this show had had such good reviews. I informed her with some delight that Bonnie was my good friend from Iowa, and we agreed to connect after the play so I could introduce her. It was one of those serendipities for which one is always grateful. It would be the last time I would see Jane.

The next day I made a quick trip to Kurt's to meet baby Lily, stopping first at the Margo Feiden Gallery, which still carried some of Kurt's art work, but it was closed. When I arrived, I expressed my disappointment at not seeing his pictures. He was pleased to know the Koloc performance had been a success and reminded me that he and Jill had heard her when she sang at the Other End on Bleecker Street. "We'll catch the show before it closes," he promised. I told him what I'd learned from Bonnie the night before—that Joe Papp hoped to take the show to Broadway—plus the great surprise of running into Jane and Edie. He was obviously pleased I'd seen them, but his mood darkened as he lamented Jane's forthcoming chemo treatments, even though "she still believes in faith healing." Soon the nanny presented Kurt's new daughter: a darling, dark-haired one-year-old.

"No wonder you're in love with her," I teased Kurt. "What a sweetheart."

Soon I explained my unfortunate shortness of time and prepared to leave. Kurt started out the door with me, saying, "I'll get you a cab," just as Jill entered the room. I hadn't realized she was even in the house. It was then that I experienced a side of her I found somewhat incomprehensible.

I greeted her with warm congratulations for Lily, which she acknowledged with a brief "Hi" as she turned to Kurt and said, "Darling, I want you to see my studio. I have a new screen and it's going to work just fine." She took his hand and started leading him back into the house, explaining to me how they had bought the ground floor of the brownstone next door for her studio space. Kurt followed her in obedient silence, as did I—not quite knowing how to respond to her obvious indifference.

We all three looked in silence at the tall screen that hung from the ceiling and curved forward on the floor. "Very nice," I finally said, not knowing what else to say. "This is really great space."

"Loree has to catch a plane," Kurt said abruptly, taking my arm and guiding me back up the stairs and out the front door and down to the street. He said nothing, but his face was dark with anger. He summoned a passing cab and after a brief discussion with the cabbie, opened the door and gave me a quick hug. "This is a good cab," he assured me. "I'll send you some pictures."

That was it. I climbed into the cab and was gone. What the hell was that all about? I had no clue. Had I offended Jill? Maybe she was annoyed she hadn't been included at lunch the previous day? Or was she still miffed about my switching seats at Kurt's birthday party over a year ago? It didn't seem important enough to dwell on, and Kurt never mentioned it when I next heard from him. But then, he rarely referred to Jill in his letters unless perhaps it was to describe one of her a fabulous parties. Nonetheless, I hoped my brief visit had not upset their relationship. It occurs to me now that this was the last time I saw Jill in person.

In a few days I had a sweet letter from Jane (1/3/84), which celebrated our serendipitous meeting at The Public Theatre. I received a brief letter from Kurt written the same day:

Dear Loree—

It's always so good to see you. What a keen friend you are. I'm sending you in a mailing tube some pictures I made—which aren't so hot as pictures, but might be of interest as literary curios some day. Maybe you'd be well advised to keep them in their tube.

I made these on document parchment, the stuff used for diplomas and so on, to show a gallery owner the sort of stuff I did. He told me to make some bigger ones.

Love as always—Kurt

A couple days later, a beat up mailing tube arrived in the mail. Rolled tightly inside were eight large, wildly colorful magic marker drawings by Kurt, pictures I characterized as iconic parodies. (An artist friend of mine called them "colorful doodles.") I was thrilled with them, and managed to scrape up enough money to have them all framed. I even found space where they could all be together—lining opposite walls above the bookcases in my study. I wrote a Valentine letter to thank him and explain where they were hanging.

On Valentine's Day he replied, again briefly, that he was

glad the pictures look O.K. in frames. The art publisher, Harry Abrams, Inc., is at this moment considering about forty new pictures I've made—with the idea of making a book. There will be no story to go with them. There is no story. Tomorrow morning they will let me know if they will go ahead with the project. (2/12/84)

I was eager to know if Abrams really would publish them—forty pictures! But I heard nothing for another month. And then came his shocking letter, dated 3/14/84, which began

Dearest Loree—

> I will tell you in confidence, since you are one of my closest friends, that I am no renaissance man but a manic depressive with a few lopsided gifts.

To my dismay, I realized the purpose of his letter was to inform me Harry Abrams had declined to publish his pictures, following which he had committed himself for "acute (all but terminal) depression. . . . So I was there for eighteen days, under lock and key, and have been sprung now."

He went on to explain that he had not had the classic symptoms of depression, but nevertheless was treated chemically with antidepressants, although now he was only being treated with talk therapy by a Catholic psychiatrist.

"I am glad he is a Christian. That means I can talk to him about all sorts of things a non-Christian might find tiresome and irrelevant, such as my atheism." He added that his family had been supportive and that he had started writing again and felt better, "although nothing has really changed." I took it as significant that he also added "I'm O.K. now." As if to assure me of this, he concluded that he would be the keynote speaker at a P.E.N. meeting in Tokyo in May. "I hope to speak moderately—neither too high nor too low."

I recalled again that he'd been among a number of Workshop writers and poets interviewed some years earlier by Dr. Nancy Andreasen about the relationship between psychopathology and creativity in artists, a study she eventually expanded to an historical perspective. Her book titled *The Creating Brain: The Neuroscience of Genius*, published in 2005 by Dana Press, gives a fascinating and readable account of that research. She now directs the Mental Health Clinical Research Center in the University of Iowa's School of Medicine, where the emphasis of her research is the development and use of novel neuroimaging tools in the study of cognition and major mental illnesses.

When Kurt gave me his painful news about his own hospitalization, I was struck by the preponderance of mood disorders in his family, beginning with Kurt's mother's suicide, of course, but also with Jane's apparent schizophrenic symptoms prior to the death of Kurt's sister.

Then Mark's horrendous experience in Canada, and now Kurt. (He did not specifically tell me until later that his hospitalization had been precipitated by a drug overdose, the same thing that had killed his mother.)

I was terribly concerned, but helpless to do anything—as if "anything" could have helped. Instead, I wrote frequent supportive letters. I pondered whether his reference to his atheism might be related to his own skepticism or to concerns about Jane's belief in faith healing. To say nothing of his distress about the agonizing chemotherapy she was submitting to. And because of Jill's abrupt coldness on my last visit, I worried some about their marriage but was reassured by Kurt's statement that "the family has all gathered around to help me." and that he'd started writing again.

In frustration, I even sent Kurt a copy of a satirical speech I'd given at a writers' conference equating the Reagan foreign policy to George Orwell's *1984* concerns, thinking it might cheer him up. His response was almost a formal letter, lacking his usual witty energy, letting me know he had forwarded my Orwell essay to Victor Navasky, editor of the *Nation* magazine. (Mr. Navasky returned it, with a polite letter, asking me to send something else if I thought it appropriate.)

And Kurt didn't write again that year, although he resumed public speaking. At the Japan P.E.N. meeting he discussed, "Why do we write in the Nuclear Age?" According to the Japan *Times,* his answer was "We write because we write. That's the kind of animals we are, that's what we do best, and that's all there is to it"—a motif about the imperative of creative drive that would appear in his *Galapagos* the coming year.

He called a couple of times, but usually just to tell me a funny story and then quite abruptly, say goodbye. He obviously didn't want to discuss his health or life, although he did report that Jane's health had improved somewhat. Even so, he was pessimistic about her recovery. I let him know I'd be on an extended trip in Alaska over the summer and would write to her, which I did.

Back by August to prepare for teaching, I had a cheery letter from Jane written from the Cape, saying she'd been there for two months, getting stronger, that all the children had been visiting over the summer. Besides that good news, she and Adam Yarmolinsky would be married in October. She was at the moment babysitting for Maxwell, Nanny's four-month-old son. I was elated!

I wrote Kurt, celebrating her new vitality, and in return he let me know he was reading proofs of Dick Yates' new novel. "This makes two of us who have been in a nuthouse. He went to a snakepit, though, and I went to a Catholic country club. As always, you get what you pay for."

In December, a belated marriage announcement from Jane arrived with a description of her October wedding to Adam Yarmolinsky, with all nineteen of their combined children and seven grandchildren in attendance. It was good to know that both she and her family were elated with her new status, especially after what she called her "fourteen years of recovery." I hoped that would bring some joy to Kurt as well.

In January 1985, a package from him arrived, containing a slim, ninety-nine-page, staple-bound volume with the title *MATKA NOC*. "Kurt Vonnegut, Jr." was on the cover under an image of the Nazi eagle and swastika. He said it was "a copy of *Mother Night* published by the underground press in Poland. It has a special introduction I wrote for this edition and no other. . . . Any nut who tries to collect all my stuff surely won't have this one."

He explained this underground edition had been sent to him by "a stranger in England who had just come back from Poland." A year previously, he had been visited by "a very young Polish exile here in New York," asking him to write a new introduction for that edition, which he did. He now felt especially honored because they would also be publishing *1984* and *Darkness at Noon*. It had been nearly twenty years since Kurt's Workshop students and friends had celebrated that book's hardback reissue in Iowa City.

I phoned Kurt shortly after that to congratulate him and was relieved to hear his jaunty voice. I asked whether he knew anything about our mutual friend from the Iowa City days, José Donoso. A troubling news report indicated he'd been arrested in Chile, where I assumed his political position would be hazardous. Liberals in Chile were in even worse jeopardy now with Ronald Reagan's second presidential term and far right forces gaining political strength.

Kurt wrote on February 15 to say he'd looked into the Donoso question and found he was OK: "He was hauled in for questioning by rural cops, and then let go again as soon as it was discovered how famous he was. The cops had busted in on a dinner party on some remote island, thinking it had to be a conspiracy."

He also mentioned that Dick Yates had recently phoned him:

> I told him I had written the *Times* saying that Broyard should be fired for his review of *Young Hearts Crying*. . . . Yates replied that he hadn't been bothered much by the review . . . he was trying with some success not to be paranoid any more, and I warned him that he was overdoing it.

This referred to the devastatingly personal trashing of Dick's book in the *New York Times Book Review* by his former friend, Anatole Broyard. Unfortunately, Dick was in such desperate health from alcohol abuse that even his publisher was losing confidence, and many of his friends were avoiding him.

Kurt closed with an especially good piece of news about himself: his new book, *Galapagos*, would be out in October.

> I am a free agent now, having fulfilled a five book contract with Dell. I really don't feel much like signing up for even one more book just now. The state of the union is making me low as hell. I never expected my beloved country to be ruled from a country club men's locker room. I used to caddy, you know. I know how those guys talk and think.

I was relieved. He sounded like his old self again.

THERE ARE
ORGANIZING PRINCIPLES
IN THE UNIVERSE
WHICH WE CAN NO MORE
UNDERSTAND
THAN MY DOG CAN.

HI, LOREE: THIS ONE IS ABOUT INTELLIGENT DESIGN. LOVE, KV 4/28/06

6

Darwin Revisited, 1985–1986

Galapagos, Requiem, International P.E.N.

The year 1985 became an unusually good one for Kurt, despite the political scene. The relief from being out from under his Dell book contract had an elevating effect, and of course the generally rave reviews to come for *Galapagos* didn't hurt. In March he and his friends Bill and Rose Styron were sent by American P.E.N. to Eastern Communist-dominated Europe—Poland, East Berlin, and Czechoslovakia—"to find out how our fellow artists were," since the Polish government had dissolved the old P.E.N. chapter and set up a new one, which, Kurt said, "we decline to recognize." He returned in April to report artistic productivity flourishing widely, even though "most hate Communism and Capitalism equally, and hate the either-or-ness of their political situations." Having met Lech Walesa in Gdansk, he said, "He is like a Tibetan holy man, dreamy and ignorant of many practical matters. He can't understand why everybody isn't a Roman Catholic" (4/5/85).

Pursuing what he called his own "aggressive agnosticism," Kurt was inspired earlier that spring, at the premiere of a requiem mass by Andrew Lloyd Webber, to write "nicer words to go with" the beautiful music so many had composed. During the Webber concert he'd been "following in English the words sung in Latin, and I was appalled."

By April he had actually commissioned a professor of Latin, Jack Collins, to translate his new English version into Latin to make it "legitimate." It would later be performed by musicians of the Unitarian Universalist Center in Buffalo, New York.

Essentially his text replaced the traditional agonizing cries for God's mercy with milder pleas to the "Cosmos." And instead of beseeching Divine Judgment to grant eternal life, Kurt's requiem simply asked the Cosmos for an eternal nap: "Let ashes remain as ashes." He seemed especially pleased with his achievement and delighted when it was set to music.

That spring of 1985, he was back on his two-week speaking circuit, hitting college campuses, plugging his forthcoming *Galapagos,* and doing his best to take the Reagan administration to task for policies in South Africa and Saudi Arabia, plus incursions into Nicaragua. He continued to praise the bravery of artists behind the Iron Curtain, but at the same time decried the fact that forty million people in our own country could not read or write, insisting on the need to reduce class sizes and pay teachers decent salaries.

By the summer of 1985, he was ready for a slower pace in Sagaponack, to have more time with his young daughter and enjoy some leisure with old pals like Joe Heller and John Irving.

Absent from the Hamptons that summer was Dick Yates who, Kurt informed me in September (3), had had "another crackup, followed by the usual shaky, unbearably solitary recovery." Nonetheless, he said, Dick was finishing another novel.

Kurt was anticipating prospects for his own *Galapagos* whose celebratory reviews would come later that month. He had enjoyed a dinner party that summer at John Irving's, a gathering that included Gail Godwin, another of his Workshop students whose novels were also doing well. He said

John then expected to ride at the very top of the best-seller list for a year or so [on June 16 his *Cider House Rules* was Number One on the *New York Times* list], and I told him to be gracious when I knocked him off. He promised to be nice about it, but we were both ignoring the fact that this was the Age of Reagan, during which we can both expect to float somewhere around the middle for just a little while, and then be shipped off to the remainder shops. (9/3/85)

Kurt was right: neither he nor Irving had a lengthy stay at the top, although both of them rode it for a while. Yet the reviews for *Galapagos* were consistent raves, with many suggesting this was his best book since *Slaughterhouse*. I agreed. My analysis in the December 1985 *North American Review* said *Galapagos* exemplified something Kurt had once told me: that he could draw a representational picture quite easily, but that he preferred to complicate and tinker with his drawing. His tinkering softened the edge of how serious he was "about the damage done by humanity's insistence on taking itself too seriously."

In *Galapagos* his usual humor masked his concerns about the fate of humanity by identifying "the only real villain in the novel as the oversized brain of human beings, an accident of Natural Selection," surely a flaw in Darwin's evolutionary theory. (A major theme in the novel is the blatant exploitation of the poor by powerful corporate entrepreneurs who try to sustain the illusion that money entitles them to any behavior, since "survival of the fittest gives them scientific justification for their actions.")

To correct this error, Kurt created a hapless group of people fleeing a missile attack on Ecuador and becoming shipwrecked on a little island where they ironically survive over the next million years as the forebears of "a race of people with small-brained, sleek skulls and flippers who learn to live compatibly with the mild, blue-footed boobies that supply them with eggs."

The more I read *Galapagos*, the more awed I became with the symmetries imbedded in the story. The most obvious was the cruise of the "Bahia de Darwin" (paralleling Darwin's voyage) captained by Adolph Von Kleist whose ship is ransacked and occupied by starving escapees from Peru's bombing of Ecuador. Pondering the resemblance of the captain's German name with Vonnegut's, I learned the real Heinrich Von Kleist was a nineteenth-century German writer with uncanny parallels to Kurt. Both had crafted unusual literary forms to express the absurdly chaotic nature of reality. Both were haunted by man's inhumanity to man, had served in the military, spent time in Dresden, and were largely rejected by the traditional literary establishment. Like Vonnegut, Von Kleist perceived that the irony of tragedy taken to its extremes is stunningly close to comedy.

So both the fictional Bahia de Darwin's captain and the historical Von Kleist seem to be *doppelgangers* of Vonnegut. As they inhabit his head as he writes, so the story's narrator, Leon Trout, receives messages from his deceased father, none other than Vonnegut's old standby *doppelganger*, Kilgore Trout. These four "doubles" provide the opportunity for the story to easily range over a million-year period and add to the thematic density and coherence of the novel.

My review concluded that "Vonnegut's humbling message is . . . that the human race has muddled its way to such splendid and horrific achievements because [its randomly evolved] brain does not seem to comprehend the danger of its own arrogance, and that how we perform the dance of life is largely a matter of luck and genes, whether the critics like it or not."

I never asked Kurt if my perception of these parallels was correct, but he did write to thank me:

> for the glowing review of *Galapagos* and for taking seriously my entire output. This is an era of short and jittery attention spans and empty memory banks, so that a person is only as good as his or her last microsecond. There is nobody with the patience to examine a lifetime as a whole. The most exasperating case in point is the attention given to the bottle cap in the throat of Tennessee Williams' corpse. Who was he? He was the man who choked on a bottlecap. (10/8/85)

The latter referred to the 1983 headlines that seemed to celebrate the bizarre cause of Tennessee's death rather than the significance of his remarkable contributions as a playwright, something that had disturbed Kurt immensely. By then I had decided to attempt a serious critical biography of Kurt, which I hoped would transcend "post-modernism," then all the rage in academe.

I figured a good way to start was to attend the International P.E.N. Congress in New York City that January, which Robley Wilson had asked me to cover for UNI's *North American Review* magazine. Kurt had told me Donald Barthelme had "dreamed up" the themes: "The State in the Imagination of the Writer and The Writer in the Imagination of the State." He even offered to help me get interviews with writers, "surely the most remarkable assemblage of world class writers in this century." I was thrilled about this assignment, and felt lucky to know Kurt was there to open doors if needed.

I was also excited a couple weeks later (11/12/85) by his letter indicating he had begun a new novel whose protagonist would be Rabo Karabekian, the maverick artist from *Breakfast of Champions*. He would appear as "one of the founders of the Abstract Expressionist school of painting [who] looks back on his long life and realizes that he has spent almost all of it painting pictures of nothing."

Two years earlier Kurt had written a lively celebration of Jackson Pollack and his abstract expressionist paintings for *Esquire*. I felt both Kurt and Pollack shared the unusual craftsmanship to transform their skills as representational artists into less conventional and more fanciful forms of art.

Meanwhile, the press credentials Kurt sent would get me into any P.E.N. sessions I chose, and I arrived at the Essex House hotel the morning of January 13 in a state of awe, trying hard to pretend I was a seasoned reporter.

I had missed the big excitement the night before at the New York Public Library, where Secretary of State George Schultz had tried in vain to welcome the largest gathering of international writers ever to assemble in the United States. In addition to inadequate space and an ineffective sound system, security checks had kept many people standing outside in the street. Meanwhile, protesters inside were harassing Schultz and the Congress chair, Norman Mailer, for refusing to read a protest statement from the U.S. delegation against Schultz's presence.

Mailer called the opening session to order that morning by scolding P.E.N. members for "silly bad manners," which heightened the tone of political controversy for the rest of the week. Most writers were quick to reflect their profound unhappiness with the "imagination of the state" as represented by George Schultz, whether they were U.S. citizens or not. Some 150 of the world's top authors and political leaders had gathered to discuss this topic. Kurt had once told me young writers regarded the P.E.N. organization as "a bunch of Rotarians," and that politics were rarely discussed. Now, midway through the Reagan era, the opposite appeared true.

As Kurt had anticipated, West Germany's Günter Grass was among the first to vent his outrage against U.S. foreign policy and the nuclear threat hanging over Europe. He cast his own pall over the Congress on its first day by suggesting that the only thing left to the writer was "hellish laughter" in the face of the Kafkaesque power of the state. Late in the week he kicked off one of the livelier dialogues when he questioned Saul Bellow, who had called for a calmer view, concluding that writers' alienation is simply a longing for higher spiritual values.

Political frustration near despair was palpable in those who rose to question Bellow, among them American Sol Yurick who insisted alienation "is not just a mental construct" when authors are being tortured in many countries. Günter Grass sarcastically asked whether American democracy had given food and shelter to people in the South Bronx, adding that "freedom and plenty in many parts of America are based upon the lack of freedom in other countries, such as South Africa."

This drew South African novelist Nadine Gordimer, a tiny woman with remarkable authority in her quiet voice, to the questioner's microphone to insist that the writer's spiritual concerns cannot be divorced from the political. She reminded the audience of how Günter Grass had purged the German language of political garbage after World War Two.

I looked around, hoping to see how Kurt might react, but he was nowhere in sight. I knew Nadine Gordimer was a friend and that he'd never seemed overly fond of Bellow.

But it was Salman Rushdie, the Indian-born British citizen and novelist, who best summarized two views of America coming out of the P.E.N. talks. One was from American citizens, but the other was from non-Americans who wanted to know "why have Americans abandoned their responsibility to write about how America behaves in the world?"

I was able to catch Kurt's appearance on the last day of the Congress: "The Statesman's View of the Imagination of the State." But he said virtually nothing, deferring to Peruvian author Mario Vargas Llosa, who had moved toward a more conservative stance and later made an unsuccessful run for the presidency. Most on the panel—a virtual "who's who" of political leaders and writers—also deferred and were mobbed afterward by the disappointed press.

The final session concluded with a near riot by feminists led by Meredith Tax and my heroine, Grace Paley, protesting that only sixteen of the 117 speakers present had been women. Through it all, Norman Mailer was stalwart—somewhat bloody, but outrageously unbowed. Unfortunately, it seemed a cynical and disappointing conclusion to the creative idealism I had expected to crest by then.

I pushed toward the Essex House bar to meet Kurt and Vance Bourjaily for a farewell drink, eager to hear their reactions. The place was crowded with writers by the time I arrived, some wondering what went wrong, but others, like young Ishmael Reed and friends, celebrating with considerable gusto. In a darkened corner booth I glimpsed Czesław Miłosz, the Polish poet and Nobel Laureate, who leaned fervently across the table to speak with an awed and attractive young woman. These were all stories that cried out for writing that day.

It had been years since I'd seen Vance, who was by then remarried to a former Workshop student, and teaching at Louisiana State University. As I joined them, Vance was speaking with animation about the Congress-sponsored galas he'd attended since arriving in New York. This was his old stomping grounds, the town where he and his former wife, Tina, had lived after the War, and whose Sunday afternoon Greenwich Village salons had been a favorite for writers of that era. He ordered refills and a drink for me, but Kurt declined. Vance soon left to join his wife at a dinner party at the Met, disappointed that Kurt didn't wish to join them.

Kurt seemed concerned about his old Workshop colleague but was a bit subdued, especially when I asked him a few questions related to my study of his work, now underway.

"You're going to find it very tedious being a Vonnegut scholar," he said.

"No way," I assured him. "It's a nice excuse to re-read you. This is all Klinkowitz's fault, you know. He's been bugging me for years to do this." I tried to treat lightly the fact I was working seriously on his opus, not wanting to embarrass him. In fact he was quite shy, and I recall him grinning and mumbling something innocuous to several of my questions that afternoon.

"But you *will* do a big story on the Congress for *The North American Review*?" he insisted, changing the subject. "The great *New York Times* sure hasn't done anything very significant."

I gestured toward the crammed notebook in my book bag and admitted I'd been pretty awed by the whole thing—the political significance of it, the feminist controversy, and the impassioned eloquence that afternoon of writers like Isabel Allende of Chile. I'd been intimidated at times, such as by young Salman Rushdie, who'd seemed unnervingly sarcastic when I had the chance to interview him in a small press conference (and who eventually would serve as president of P.E.N. American Center and continue as an eloquent purveyor of the importance of international writers to American readers).

Kurt agreed Mailer had upset quite a few people, adding "but nobody could get away with inviting Schulz!" I remembered Mailer at Kurt's birthday celebration, and especially that Jill and Mailer's then wife were close.

"So how," I asked, "are *you* doing, and how is your darling Lily?"

"She's an angel," he replied with a smile. "Have you seen the book Jill did on her?" I hadn't. And then, quite abruptly, he said he needed to get home to take care of his daughter. As usual, he deplored making small talk, especially about himself.

I took the train back to Queens where I was staying at a friend's apartment—in something of a blur over the week's incredible events, mixed with puzzlement about Kurt's withdrawn mood. He looked fine, but he wasn't his usual buoyant jokester. I surmised he might be on medication, or perhaps just felt a new parental responsibility because of Lily. Nor did I exclude the possibility he was consciously more reserved in recovering his emotional health.

Back in Iowa again, a while after that visit, I received a one-hundred-page manuscript from him, a play titled *Make Up Your Mind*. It seemed strange he hadn't mentioned he'd been working on a play. It was a comedy with a cast of four; the primary character was twenty-eight-year-old Roland, who was a badly educated quack therapist purporting to help indecisive people achieve free will. I read it eagerly but was disappointed before getting very far into it. It seemed like an effort in which his comedic way of coping with a serious theme simply wasn't working. It occurred to me it might even be reflecting his own effort to shake off something related to his recent psychological struggle, about which I certainly didn't want to speculate.

Instead, I reluctantly responded with something inane like "It doesn't quite work" to Kurt and was frankly relieved when he replied that his daughter Edith didn't like it either, "considers it weightless and possibly a threat to my reputation. So it's O.K. if you feel the same." Nonetheless, he said it had been optioned by a Broadway producer, although "I am now thinking of scrubbing the enterprise"—a pity, really, because more than anything, Kurt wanted to write a great comic play. He once told me he envied Molière and longed to write a book like *Candide*. I surmised he might even have been playing with the premise of Molière's *Doctor in Spite of Himself* in *Make Up Your Mind*.

Apologetically suggesting that I "must be sick of being a Vonnegut scholar by now, what with all the crap I send you," he included in this letter a copy of his new preface to the Russian edition of *Mother Night*. The preface was a revelation to me, in that it explained the novel's protagonist, Howard W. Campbell, was actually inspired "by a real non-German, pro-Nazi propagandist, William Joyce, who had broadcast in English from Germany during the Second World War under the pseudonym 'Lord Haw Haw.'" Kurt explained that Joyce had been born in America of Irish extraction but grew up in England and was hanged there as a traitor because he'd sought an English passport as proof of his loyalty. In the preface, Kurt explained that he'd heard Joyce's humorous broadcasts when he was in high school and college, and that the "grotesque follies and outrages of the British class system were then and remain today a rich, bubbling sludge for the delectation of black humorists." He conceded, however, that "he was less funny in his hatred for democracies and Jews and Slavs and Gypsies and so on."

While Kurt had invented Campbell as the *American* traitor in *Mother Night*, he added that letters he received "indicate that there was a genuine need for such an invention. Young people want very much to hear from me that he was real."

His letter closed with positive news about Jane. Some large tumors had been removed and "it appears that she can look forward to another summer at least. Her treatments from now on will be with hormones. . . . She isn't to be poisoned along with her tumors any more" (2/17/86). He was especially pleased that she would likely be alive when their daughter Edie's baby was due in mid-April.

In the next few months Kurt sent mostly copies of speeches or new introductions he'd written. I marveled at how adept at such tasks he had to be and still manage his own considerable fictional output. For example, he'd celebrated Dr. Elena Bonner, the pediatrician wife of Andre Sakharov, Nobel Laureate physicist and Soviet dissident who was then exiled in Gorky. At a New York banquet for her, Kurt had reminisced about parties in Leningrad and Moscow where he'd been pleased to learn scientists are regarded as artists because of their playful imagination, something he loved repeating, whenever possible. He said Dr. Bonner and her husband had "achieved the worldwide majesty of Tolstoy. Thank goodness you are on our planet in these awesome times" (2/11/86). Indeed, Sakharov, who died three years later, was credited as one of the major agitators for democratic reforms of Soviet governance leading to perestroika and the end of Communist's constitutional monopoly on political power in 1990.

One of the most endearing of Kurt's tributes that spring of 1986 was a preface he did for a reissue of Nelson Algren's *Never Come Morning*. In the draft he sent me, he recalled that no matter how famous Algren became as a writer, "he remained a poor man living among the poor, and usually alone"—even as he had been in his last years, when he lived in Sag Harbor near Kurt's summer home. He recounted how Algren "was bitter about how little he had been paid over the years for such important work, and especially for the movie rights to . . . *The Man with the Golden Arm*," for which he had received no share in the profits, something Algren had revealed back in the Iowa City days. Kurt recalled hearing Algren say, "I am the penny whistle of American literature."

In the mid-twentieth century, when Algren was at the peak of his powers, Kurt noted he had been the first recipient of The National Book Award for Fiction, and that "only a few years before his death the American Institute and Academy [of Arts and Letters] had given him its Medal for Literature, without, however, making him a member." Reflecting that Algren's "response to the medal had been impudent," Kurt had phoned to urge Nelson to come to New York, all expenses paid, to receive the medal at a "big ceremony. . . . His final statement on the subject to me was this: 'I'm sorry, but I have to speak to a ladies' garden club that day.'" The Institute and Academy finally did award him membership, but only a few weeks before his death, and I suspect Kurt was instrumental in assuring the reversal of that earlier oversight.

Kurt's preface compared Algren's characterization of persons dehumanized by poverty, ignorance, and injustice with "those in the works of social reformers like Charles Dickens and George Bernard Shaw." He wrote that Algren refused to "soften his stories, as most writers would have," but instead his penchant for truth "shoved him in the direction of unpopularity . . . with his dismaying truthfulness" about down-and-out people who deserved respect just for surviving.

I found this especially revealing about Kurt, who, of course, wrote about the same kind of people, but did so with caprice. In Iowa City I had found Algren intriguing but also somewhat daunting with his biting satirical disregard for social conventionality. His penchant for the social underbelly of Chicago was outside my experience, but Kurt had an inherent respect and compassion for the underdog with utterly no apologies. He was always completely at ease with Algren, as well as genuinely respectful of his literary achievement.

And even though Kurt's Indiana experience hadn't made him all that familiar with his own down-and-out characters in *God Bless You, Mr. Rosewater*, I can imagine his delight in celebrating Elliot Rosewater's friendships with impoverished citizens of an Indiana-like Central City. In Kurt's several public tributes to Ida Young, the African American woman who served his family during his youth in Indianapolis, one can surmise the benevolent respect she nourished in him. But Kurt knew Algren never had that kind of care in his upbringing, and had gained his humane concerns through his own personal experiences of Chicago's squalor. It was Algren's passionate admiration for the gifts of its survivors that honed his unique contributions to fiction.

*   *   *

My 1986 summer Vonnegut study was interrupted by the shock of a phone call from Dick Yates about the horrific accident our friend Andre Dubus had suffered. Andre had closed down a bar in the Boston area and was on his way home when he stopped to help a downed motorcyclist on an interstate. Assisting a victim, Andre was struck by a speeding car that crushed his legs. At that moment, it was unclear if he would walk again, or even live. He did live, but with the eventual loss of one leg and severe damage to the other—a stunning blow that transformed his life, to say nothing of the writing he eventually resumed.

At least there was happier news from Kurt that summer, despite his shared concern for Andre. Edie gave birth to a healthy baby son, who was celebrated by Grandma Jane. He also reported Yates had "finished another good, if again depressing, book [*Cold Spring Harbor*]. He did me the honor of dedicating it to me."

That June of 1986, Kurt sent a copy of the Ware Lecture he had presented to the Unitarian Universalist Association in Rochester, New York—the first such lecture I'd seen by him that took to task the violence historically perpetrated by Christians in the name of love. Written during the presidency of Ronald Reagan and the rise of the "Moral Majority," his lecture condemned "the ethical pronouncements of leaders of the so-called religious revival going on in this country, including those of our President" which nonetheless resulted in attacks against other countries. Kurt was especially distressed when Reagan authorized bombing attacks against Libya, resulting in the death of President Muammar al-Kaddafi's baby daughter. Kurt had phoned me after this event, aghast about the child's death, his outrage likely heightened in the context of his own young daughter.

In the Unitarian lecture, Kurt also launched his diatribe against television, asserting that "you live in a time when killing is a leading entertainment form" and noted the thousands of TV murders children would see before they graduate from high school, after which "they are supposed to feel grateful to the corporations, our Federal Government among them, which put on such shows." Since Christianity "stopped taking the Sermon on the Mount seriously . . . it joined forces with the vain and rich and violent." This was the increasingly insistent message he continued to give in lectures across the country.

Nonetheless, midway through his autumn speaking tour in 1986, he told me he was giving up public speaking for good:

> I realize I am too old or jaded or something to tolerate the empty hours on planes and in motels and nightmare airports anymore. . . . The exhibitionist phase of my life is over. At least I tasted the mania of life as a standup comic. I don't have to guess about it. . . . Among other things, I found out more about the State of the Union than is nice to know. It serves us right, maybe, that

our Hitler would be a machine rather than a person: One nation, one people, one TV set.

Although his vow to end his twice-a-year speaking tours was short-lived (perhaps he truly did miss the lift from entertaining audiences), his hatred for how television shaped American values and attention spans never subsided. For a time he poured his enthusiasm into his poem "Requiem," which was then being set to music by Edgar Grana, "the composer I met on jury duty." He was elated that Atlantic Records was interested in recording it and that Grana believed he could arrange a symphony premiere in New York.

On a darker note, Kurt let me know Jane had been released from the hospital to spend a few days on the Cape (where she could enjoy Edie's new baby) and that nothing more would be done for her medically. He later chartered a plane to take her back to Washington, where she lived with her husband Adam. He said the family hoped she would enter an excellent hospice "where two close friends of ours died peacefully." She felt too weak for him to visit her, but he felt everything had been settled well between them.

He closed with a poignant

hope that Andre's suffering, at too high a price, God knows, will buy him some profound and beautiful reflections on life of use to us all. That seems likely, given what a fine artist he is. When I was in Czechoslovakia, the hideously oppressed artists I met pitied all the people who were going through shit without even being talented. (10/25/86)

Indeed, many old Workshop friends agreed Andre Dubus did us all proud in reflecting another side of life from the one we had dreamed of back in those optimistic Iowa City days twenty years ago.

There was, of course, *not* some way out of this for Jane. A letter from Kurt written at midnight on December 19 (1986) let me know she had died at eight o'clock that evening in a Washington hospice with Adam at her side. Kurt said he had returned with Lily and Jill about ten from a Christmas party to find a message to call his son Mark, who gave him the news. Personally, he felt deeply grateful that Jane had come out of a coma about five days earlier and had asked Edie to get him on the phone so they could say "everything which should have been said."

The following week, in a Christmas Eve letter, he described her "jam-packed funeral" in Washington, which he had attended, as had his brother "and shoals of young and old friends from Washington and Cape Cod." He was gratified to know that José and María Pilar Donoso had been in the Washington, DC, area during the past month and that María Pilar had also been nearby when she died. Kurt didn't speak at the funeral, but her husband Adam did, as did Mark and Steve Adams and Nanny. He noted that "Nanny is nine months pregnant and a little more. Her baby will be the next big news." Edie would take Jane's ashes back to Cape Cod where they would be scattered "in some kind of Druid ceremony when springtime comes. . . . I miss her so. . . ."

The following May, Nanny described to Kurt the Cape Cod memorial service in a letter he shared with me. The Vonnegut and Adams children, along with beloved Barnstable friends, celebrated Jane's life in a beautiful ceremony that "went exactly as she would have liked it."

I mourned her loss from a distance, grateful to have shared in the brief but rich renewal of our friendship.

Perhaps, one of Kurt's "Enchanted I.O.U.s"

7

Renewal Out of Chaos, 1987–1989

Bluebeard

The year 1987 marked a high point in Kurt's writing career, even as he reached the age when most of us consider retiring from our more conventional jobs. That January (16) he wrote that he'd be leaving his Dell publisher after the final book in his contract, which would occur in the next month or six weeks: "I'm not mad. I just didn't want to be sold to Germans, who are buying up Dell and Doubleday." However, he had no intention of retiring. Writing was as much a survival behavior for him as breathing. His new contract with Putnam would take him into the future. Certainly he was now distinguished as a man of letters, both here and abroad, and sought as an illustrious public speaker who never failed to pack an auditorium. All his books were in print and most could be found in translation throughout Europe, South America, and Asia. *Slaughterhouse-Five* was among the sixty top U.S. novels named by The Book-of-the-Month Club in celebration of its sixtieth anniversary. His opinions on art, music, religion, and politics were widely esteemed as were his contributions to the world of theater, music, and television. He had even written a "requiem with cheerful words," which had been set to music for a premiere performance (in Latin) the following year in Buffalo, New York. He was an avid defender of the freedom of speech guaranteed in the

Amendments to U.S. Constitution as well as of "The Sermon on the Mount" preached by Jesus in the New Testament.

Nonetheless in 1987, *Bluebeard,* his final book with Dell, turned out to be one of his more challenging and vilified novels, even though it was one of his most significant. I say this because of its complex structure and its reflections on the function and value of the arts but especially because it clarified *Kurt's own* ingenious artistic vision.

That spring he sent a copy of a letter unearthed by the Indiana Historical Society that he himself had written as a twenty-two-year-old army veteran newly released from a prisoner of war unit in Dresden. Addressed to his Indianapolis family from a Red Cross repatriation camp in LeHavre on May 29, 1945, it satirically narrated his P.O.W. experience from December 1944 until his release that spring of 1945. That forty-two-year-old letter reflected both the experience and the style that now resonated with his newly completed novel, *Bluebeard,* whose protagonist, Rabo Karabekian (a minor character from *Breakfast of Champions*), was an army camouflage artist during World War II.

Bluebeard was released in October 1987, offering a fictional view of America's controversial gift of abstract expressionist painting to the world of art and history. Purporting to be the autobiography of Rabo Karabekian, the novel provoked more than its share of spitefulness just as Kurt was to celebrate his sixty-fifth birthday. In an October interview with Steve Paul (*Kansas City Star*), Kurt said his novel was "a history of my own idiosyncratic responses to this or that" rather than "a responsible history" of abstract expressionism.

It did, however, point to possible origins and the historic significance of that artistic movement. It had been some forty years since the Museum of Modern Art in New York City had launched the spectacular post–World War II visions of America's abstract expressionists into worldwide view, making the United States a major art center. So I puzzled that fall, as reviews appeared, why critics from papers like the *New York Times* or the *Village Voice* seemed at special pains to regard *Bluebeard* with near vindictiveness. None seemed to recognize the cultural and political significance of those artistic departures from the conventional he celebrated in the novel.

In early November I sent Kurt a birthday gift: a *faux* painting made up of colorful liquid pressed between two sheets of framed glass, so as to resemble an abstract painting, one that could be transformed by standing the frame on its side or upside down. I meant it to be a teasing reflection of *Bluebeard* that might lighten some of the critical nastiness. In response, came his November 12 letter thanking me for the "swell birthday present," which he said was

> perfectly attuned to the mood of BLUEBEARD. Like all paintings, it is a friendly joke on that part of the brain which deals with information received by the eyeballs. A lot of critics have been infuriated by BLUEBEARD. Take a look at this week's *Village Voice*. What makes them so mad, I think, is that I say art is child's play, and can be discussed in playful, simple language. I am like a doctor who speaks to patients in words they can understand, thus angering other doctors, who imagine mystery and pomposity to be major components of their power and self respect. (11/12/87)

Indeed, the *Village Voice* review by the poet and columnist, John Ash, was especially acrimonious. Its (11/17/87) headline read "Paint Misbehavin" with a sarcastic subhead, "Kurt Vonnegut Knows What He Likes." (The only other time Kurt had ever mentioned a negative review to me was when John Ciardi had attacked his *New York Times Book Review* satire on summer workshops for writers.) The Ash critique seemed to me a general misreading, insisting Vonnegut was "unsettled" by the absence of the "figurative" in abstract expressionism and that the character of Rabo Karabekian betrays aesthetic principles "in a final scene of truly revolting sentimentality." It suggested this reviewer, like some others, not only misinterpreted the book, but also chose not to take seriously the author's attempt to portray quite explicitly what it was like *for a writer like Kurt Vonnegut* to be a nontraditional artist.

It was four years earlier (December 1983) that *Esquire* had published Kurt's insightful essay about the controversial Jackson Pollock titled "Jack the Dripper," who clearly resonates with the fictional Rabo Karabekian. While Rabo had his first appearance in *Breakfast of Champions*, in this book, Rabo's paintings reflect those of the actual artist, Barnett Newman. *But most especially as a character, he reflects some of Kurt's real life experiences.* While this was not all that unusual for him as a writer, in many ways this character is a deep, unexamined reflection of the unusual complexity of Kurt Vonnegut as a man and artist.

For both Kurt and the fictional Rabo, the financial calamity of their early careers put a strain on their work as well as on their family lives, but when both became part of "artificial extended families," their creative work, at least, achieved new energy and insight. For Rabo that family was a group of abstract expressionist artists in New York City following World War II; for Kurt it was the community of writers and artists in Iowa City and now in New York. As he has noted frequently, these "gangs" helped him make major inroads into his twenty-year effort to resolve his World War II experience of the Dresden firebombing into *Slaughterhouse-Five*, the novel that rewarded him with sudden fame, and financial security.

Both Kurt and Rabo were revitalized by their new creative environments to find ways to express the undifferentiated chaos and absurdity of their war experiences. Kurt's accidental survival of the tragic Dresden firebombing provided new, creative insight into the bizarre powers of chance. Likewise, Rabo's artistic vision was reborn through abstract expressionist art and its ability to reveal the contradiction that "birth and death are always there" (p. 84). In such paintings, "nothing is hidden." Both artists transcended their personal and demoralizing experiences of absurdity and death by creating powerful and elevating new forms of art out of horror.

Both also recognized that their previous experience of life's painful incongruities had been "camouflaged" by comforting cultural traditions of order, purpose, realism, and meaning, thus providing a useful, if dulling sense of security. But *Bluebeard* portrays Rabo's new awareness of *time*: "Life, by definition, is never still. Where is it going? From birth to death with *no stops* on the way" (p.84, emphasis mine).

This experience is celebrated by Rabo and his muse, Circe, when they view his final triumphant painting hidden in his potato barn studio—a secret room that, unlike Bluebeard's room of death, reveals Rabo's transformed manifestation of life's ironic capacity for renewal. The painting reveals the *simultaneity of both life and death* and the impossibility of any reassuring "truth" separate from that mysterious paradox. However, its renewing power (called "revolting sentimentality" by John Ash) is available only to viewers who comprehend it as *active participants* in the light-hearted, nonlinear process created by the painting, and only thus can *experience* the "pure *essence of human wonder"* (294)—which is clearly what Kurt believed the best abstract expressionists had achieved. This last painting of Rabo's, "Now It's the Women's Turn" was meant to reveal not only a significant moment in the history of art, but also the powerful, creative principle of life articulated by Goethe as the "eternal feminine."

In an autobiographical sense, Kurt's description of this painting in *Bluebeard* is a literary expression of the "head-on collision" he himself experienced on VE Day in Germany after he was "reborn" out of his Dresden underground meat locker at the end of the war. After the bombing, his guards had moved the prisoners to a schoolhouse near the Czechoslovakian border. On VE Day (May 8, 1945), Kurt walked out of the schoolhouse and discovered his German guards had suddenly vanished.

In a May 8, 1976, letter to me exactly thirty-one years later, he described what he had seen: "There were lunatics out there, and prisoners from every land, and remnants of the Herman Goering Division—still armed. It was so beautiful. The Russians would not show up for a week. Hi ho."

This personal epiphany transformed into *Bluebeard's* fiction expresses the resolution of Rabo's painful life and war experience in his sixty-four-feet-long painting, "Now It's the Women's Turn," locked away in his East Hampton potato barn. Its central view from the front shows what Kurt himself recalled in 1976: exact images of those hundreds of exhausted soldiers from many nations, both Axis and Allied, along with civilian survivors. Added to the painting was the bloated body of a dead gypsy queen from whose mouth flows not maggots, but a fortune in rubies and diamonds. However, the painting takes on a dramatically different aspect when viewed foreshortened, from the far end of the potato barn. When Rabo leads his muse, Circe, to this perspective, she sees "what the painting was all *about*": a big *fence* "every square inch of it encrusted with the most gorgeous jewelry" (289).

Consider the paradoxical power of the fence image echoing that of Friedrich Nietzsche in *The Birth of Tragedy*, which revealed the irony that the art of the Greek *tragedies* functioned as a revitalizing "living *wall*" against the assaults of life. Rabo Karabekian (and Kurt's) "fence" painting does the same thing. It suggests that even in the face of exhausting war and despair, life's multiple perspectives offer new access to creative and renewing possibilities for those willing to engage. Recall that Circe (the mythic "fate-spinner") insists that their participatory experience of this painting was like a celebratory dance with Rabo. She represents his vital feminine aspect that integrates and helps renew his creative powers.

* * *

Alas, critics insistently accustomed to regarding Kurt as a lowbrow seemed unwilling to take this scene, or his book, seriously. Kurt later sent me a copy of his preface to the 1987 Franklin Library Edition of *Bluebeard,* which reflected some of his personal regret about this. In it he described the "dismaying power" of third parties to hold up to ridicule professional picture painters who, as grownups, continued to play what, as children, might have been called games of "intoxication with the Universe." Such critics were, he said, "that part of society which does not paint well, usually, but which *knows what it likes* with a vengeance" (my emphasis).

Kurt was not an elitist educated to become a gentleman intellectual. He had no reservations about celebrating intoxicating epiphanies, even if they came from stand-up film comedians like Laurel and Hardy or radio stars like Bob and Ray, whose artistry he admired immensely. In a (12/27/87) letter to the filmmaker, Robert Weide, who was preparing to do a Vonnegut documentary, Kurt said Laurel and Hardy were so successful at comic artistry because they were capable of "opening a window on a wintry night and . . . [making] love to everybody on the planet." In that letter Kurt acknowledged the difficult challenge writers had in creating a similar epiphany. This was why he said he had always advised his students instead to make love to only *one* person in their writing.

Knowing his regard for stand-up comics, I felt pretty certain that to laugh in the face of loneliness or death had considerable influence on why he continued his lecture circuit at colleges and universities. It was not to provide stuffy intellectual critiques on the arts or humanities, although he understood and cared deeply about them. His way of teaching was not as an intellectual, but as an entertainer. As arduous as it was to entertain an audience into new awareness by laughing, it was something he did effectively—and that gave *him* a lift at the same time. It was a comic artist's way of "making love" to lots of people at once.

Nearly every time he made a phone call to me, he began his conversation with the gift of a joke. One time I'd written him about the mess a roofing crew was making of my yard and house. A couple days later my phone rang.

I answered, and without even a hello, he said, "You know the major flaw in human character, don't you?"

I obediently said "No," and he returned, "Everybody always wants to *build* and no one wants to do *maintenance!*" His long, wheezing, coughing laugh followed. (I later shared his joke with my roofers, who loved it.)

So it was no surprise that his Franklin Library preface for *Blue-beard* included a profound expression of his personal credo when he addressed "all my friends and relatives in Alcoholics Anonymous" to "say that they were right to become intoxicated. Life without moments of intoxication is not worth a nickel." He spoke of children who could "get smashed for hours on some strictly limited aspect of the . . . Universe. . . . The child teaches the Universe how to be a good playmate, to be nice instead of mean." Speaking of painters, he said "the most satisfied of all painters is the one who can become intoxicated for hours, days, or weeks, or years with what his or her hands and eyes can do with art materials, and let the rest of the world go hang." (Painting and drawing, in fact, were something he himself began to practice quite seriously once he gave up writing.)

He was aware, however, that such "adult intoxication," when taken *too* seriously, could be risky. Jackson Pollock, whose playful work was "goofing around with spatters and dribbles of paint on canvas," soon began more overtly "to trust his intuition to control his hands so as to show . . . how mysteriously whole and satisfying such pictures might be." That became his downfall when the abundance of critical response grew into "hellish noise to a person as shy and innocent as Jackson Pollock" was. Kurt might have been a little shy, but he was not innocent. He loved the stage and he trusted his intuition as a performer. Public speaking and his later work as a visual artist offered Kurt alternate ways of teaching the Universe how to be a good playmate. Neither became his downfall; in fact they helped sell his books.

By the fall of 1987, I completed a draft of my own critical study of Kurt's work, a treatise I called *Myths and Melodies for a Turning Century*. I sent it to Kurt, who, after he read it, warned (10/6/87) that I'd likely have trouble finding a publisher because "there are few people well enough educated to understand what you are saying. . . . Ignorance is the new Black Death." He returned the manuscript, which he called a "wise study" with his characteristic humility:

It sure has made me thoughtful. It has externalized, has held before my eyes, machinery which I have not examined until now, and which I have been content to call my intuition. I acknowledge that the machinery is as you depict it. What you have done is what only the greatest critics can do with the creations of another person, Sartre with those of Genet, for example. I am admiring and grateful, but, as I say, autumnally thoughtful, too, as the leaves fall and fall. Last year an organization gave me a medal for lifetime achievement. In my acceptance speech I said, "Does this mean I can go home now?" (10/8/87)

I had argued that his intuitive vision as a writer resonated with that of some of the most profound of our Western philosophers. Even though *he* didn't take comfort from that recognition, I wanted to explicate the richness of his inherent knowledge to scornful critics who read his work as fluff. Still, he was taking something of a beating on his hard won *Bluebeard,* and I could well understand why he might feel tired and "autumnally thoughtful." But I knew there was no "going home" for Kurt Vonnegut. To idly meditate on the nature of the universe would drive him crazy for sure.

Thus it seemed an especially serendipitous irony as 1988 rolled around, that he was cheered up by a requiem! That is, by the public performance of the *Requiem* he'd been inspired to write three years earlier after attending the Broadway premiere of the Andrew Lloyd Webber *Requiem.* The Vonnegut *Requiem* not only had cheerful words, but it had acquired a Latin translation and been set to music by Edgar David Grana, a composer he'd met by chance during jury duty. In January 1988, Kurt wrote that the Unitarian Universalist Choir of Buffalo, New York, accompanied by four synthesizers, would perform his work on March 13, with the composer present to discuss the music. Kurt would speak, with lecture funds going to support the professional musicians. He was thrilled.

And there was more: His film-documentarian Bob Weide had arranged to have a private car added to the Amtrak Maple Leaf train for Kurt's private transportation to Buffalo from Grand Central Station. This would be a real production. Bob had visited Cedar Falls the previous fall to consult with Jerry Klinkowitz and me about his plan for a full scale Vonnegut documentary. The Pullman car would become the studio for a leisurely interview with Kurt and his dear brother Bernard, who would board the train at its Albany stop. Weide and his crew would remain in Buffalo to film the *Requiem* concert.

Kurt adored his big brother, the SUNY professor and researcher "who'd become such a big shot at G.E. that they gave him his own private laboratory where he could perform all kinds of experiments."

In the train interview, Kurt told a story about Bernie's lab, adding the anecdote that, "When the safety officer came in, he found the biggest mess he'd ever seen." Bernie's reply, barely managing to control his laughter, was, "If you think this is a mess, you should see what it's like up here" (tapping his head). He added, "But the most creative part of a scientific experiment was actually a practical joke on nature."

Kurt loved to boast about his brother's brilliant achievements, and often had credited Bernard and his colleagues for helping him understand technology and its influences. In this interview, he revealed, "All the crystology stuff in *Cat's Cradle* is what Bernard was working with at G.E."

Weide was a boyish prankster whose own wit masked his unusually successful career as a filmmaker. As a Vonnegut fan since his teens his sense of humor played perfectly with Kurt's and Bernard's. The whole Amtrak filming enterprise was deemed a success by all accounts. Excerpts I saw of Kurt and Bernard's conversation were charming.

As for the *Requiem* concert in Buffalo, Kurt sent me a taped cassette, but later, under the title "Stones, Time and Elements" the *Requiem* was again performed with new instrumentation by the Manhattan Chamber Orchestra and the Magic Circle Opera Ensemble. Its CD, released in 1994, is still available, and includes a Vonnegut solo reading, unfortunately the only discernible part of the text. For my taste, the music was jarring. Kurt agreed, but never mind: in a phone call he told me "everyone involved had a swell time."

(As a footnote to this venture, a quite splendid new musical adaptation of a portion of the *Requiem* text was composed later by Seymour Barab and recorded under the title "Cosmos Cantata" by the

Manhattan Chamber Orchestra and soloists. In 2001 it also was produced as a CD by Kleos Classics. Kurt loved it.)

At midsummer 1988, he wrote that he was trying to get started on a new novel and by fall would be out on another speaking tour. While I marveled how he could keep that pace and still write, he obviously wasn't going to forever. So when he said he'd agreed to do a major series of talks at four colleges in the Davenport, Iowa, area the following spring, I asked whether he'd consider adding another Iowa visit to Cedar Falls as well.

He said he could swing it, so I talked with English Department colleagues, and we booked him for our annual "Reninger Lecture," the highlight of our state-wide writing competition for high school kids. He would definitely draw a substantial crowd on April 7, 1989.

As the new year arrived, I had a rather gloomy greeting from him (1/7/89), informing me our friend "Dick Yates is up to his neck in shit as usual, and Andre [Dubus] has a lot of money his ex-wife is trying to get away from him, and on and on." (Andre, now operating from a wheelchair, had been awarded a $310,000 MacArthur Genius Grant. He was being sued by his former wife, Peggy Rambach, whose divorce from him had followed his accident.)

The story on Dick was his desperate need for a job or money, with his health deteriorating badly. He'd been hired earlier by his former Iowa Workshop student, David Milch, to write for the highly successful NBC television series, *Hill Street Blues*, but Kurt said, "Unfortunately, they've had a falling out and Yates has asked me to write a letter of recommendation for him so that he can get a teaching job somewhere, anywhere."

His February 20 letter was more cheerful. He said he was "starting to go on the road again like Willie Nelson" with his schedule beginning the next day taking him from Texas to Maryland. "By the time I get to Cedar Falls on April 7, I should be pretty well shot. . . . Make cocoa."

He concluded with a fascinating account of the book he was working on:

I am running a terrific risk of long duration now, and especially
risky since I, as was the case with my father, am getting dumber all
the time. It is a novel which acknowledges chaos as the matrix for
life. We are particles ungoverned by laws which require us
absolutely to be doing such and such a thing in such and such a
place at such and such a time. Talk about liberty! Talk about
anarchy! It could turn out very easily that nobody can stand to
read such a book. Where are the coordinates?

So much for being "autumnally thoughtful!" I knew that restless
mind of his could never go into neutral with any degree of comfort.
Finding creative ways to transform chaos into artistic vision was his
forte.

His April Quad Cities appearance was identified as the "Vonnegut
Symposium." Since I'd been asked by the program coordinator to
write an evaluation of the two-day event for the state Humanities
Board, I soon learned the symposium was a biennial occurrence, a series designated as the "Super Author Program." It was likely called
"super" because in only two days, Kurt was to make six appearances
in four communities (located on both the Iowa and Illinois sides of
the Mississippi River).

Our mutual friend, Peter Reed from Minnesota, had invited a
group of Vonnegut scholars from across the country to present academic papers in conjunction with Kurt's appearance. Peter would also
attend Kurt's Iowa Workshop and Cedar Falls programs.

Bob Weide would film Kurt's Workshop gig, as well as his UNI
speech. He flew in to the Waterloo/Cedar Falls airport to visit Jerry
Klinkowitz before driving with me to Davenport. When I picked
him up the morning of April 3, he was dressed in a bulky knit
sweater as his only hedge against chilly weather. It was typical of
Iowa to delay springtime with early April snowstorms. Bob kept me
laughing for the entire three-hour drive to Davenport. (His comic
sense still serves him well in his ongoing career via cable television
and film.)

We were both booked to stay at the Black Hawk Hotel where Kurt and Peter and his scholars also had reservations. As we walked through the lobby, Bob suddenly made a point of taking my arm, and just as we approached two elderly ladies he whispered loudly, "Remember, it's *MR. AND MRS. BROWN!*" It was the kick-off for a weekend of laughs and pranks.

So as a Vonnegut coterie gradually gathered in the hotel bar late that afternoon, I began to connect with a group of people who cheerfully evolved into a *Cat's Cradle* type *karass* by the time the week was over. Asa Pieratt was the librarian bibliographer from Delaware I'd met previously by phone—a huge fan and collector of Vonnegut books and memorabilia. Some had presented scholarly papers earlier in the day. Peter would later collaborate with young Marc Leeds, then from East Tennessee State University, to edit two major collections of critical essays on Vonnegut's work. Leeds would eventually put together the huge compendium, *The Vonnegut Encyclopedia*, which cross-references just about every character, place, and event in Kurt's opus up to 1995. It was a delightfully congenial group.

Kurt was to arrive that night (Monday, April 3), but our newly bonded group waited in vain, hoping to welcome him. Nor was he in evidence the next morning when we gathered at 10 a.m. near the front row of an auditorium on the Augustana College campus in Rock Island, Illinois, across the Mississippi from Davenport. By then, Peter had convinced the Augustana officials to reschedule his appearance in a larger hall than the small discussion room originally chosen. The auditorium was already filled to capacity. Soon it was announced that Kurt's previous evening flight had been cancelled due to bad weather, so he was being flown in from St. Louis this morning by private plane.

This does not bode well, I thought—he likes time to get collected. When he did breeze into the auditorium about fifteen minutes late, he looked downright dapper in a sporty soft cap and herringbone jacket. Since he'd been scheduled to discuss the relationship between his work and modern society to a small group, he seemed taken aback to find himself instead before an audience swollen to at least four hundred. But it didn't take him long to sense the audience and link his discussion of the historical context of Augustana with his own descent from German "free-thinkers" and their commitment to solving social problems. He warmed to the enthusiastic group, identifying his concerns as adult illiteracy and loneliness, environmental abuse, and irresponsibility in government and corporations. He concluded with the importance of preserving the Bill of Rights, the freedom of expression always one of his most adamant concerns.

It was one of those times he let his love for America and its historic origins and values rise spontaneously, without comic enhancement or framing. I was glad students had this brief opportunity to experience the basic clarity of his knowledge. He once told me realistic drawing was too easy and tedious. Rather, he loved to complicate the image into something engaging or challenging. "Anybody can tell a story or draw a picture."

Well, maybe not everybody. I thought again about his *Bluebeard*, and the historic depth underlying its story and intent.

*   *   *

We only had a quick chance to say hi before he was rushed on to his next event back across the Mississippi for lunch and his talk on "The Writer and Nationalism" at Marycrest College, in Bettendorf. There a capacity crowd heard him identify nationalism as a cause of wars and argue that high military budgets deprive schools of funding and cheat students out of classes small enough for real learning, a cause he raised whenever he could.

I greeted him after the talk long enough to hear his explanation of his wild trip and the confusion of the night before. He figured there'd be some time after his evening lecture for a drink and a chance to greet the aficionados I told him were eagerly awaiting him.

The speech that night, his standard "How To Get a Job Like Mine" adapted to the capacity crowd of two thousand, was a rollicking, almost vaudevillian presentation laced with jokes and anecdotes to soften his usual political and social criticism. He'd perfected that speech since I'd last heard a version on the UNI campus a decade ago. The audience was in the palm of his hand, and he obviously had a good time, closing with his "chalk talk" graphing of stories to illustrate how narrative plotting reflects a given culture's view of life's meaning. And as usual, his treatise culminated with the horizontal line plot of Shakespeare's tragedy of *Hamlet*, and its profundity of life's unanswered questions.

A wild standing ovation testified the audience's appreciation.

By the time we devotees returned to the hotel and settled around a table in the empty bar for a nightcap, it was ten o'clock. After Kurt's intense day, I wondered if he'd show up, but he did, at least long enough to enjoy a Scotch and thank the group for being there. "Those empty hotel rooms get to look the same after a while," he grinned. Then he sat down and proceeded to entertain *us* with his magic. It had always impressed me how generous he was with his admirers, certainly the case that night.

The next day's schedule was considerably lighter, with Kurt slated to read from work in progress and to receive an Intellectual Freedom Award at a dinner meeting that night, prior to the showing of the film *Slaughterhouse-Five*.

He began the morning gig with *ad lib* responses to the morning paper to demonstrate "the planet is a work in progress. . . . This is why I'm having trouble writing these days—stories like these make any story I'd write simply irrelevant." He eventually did read something of his own work, which would become *Hocus Pocus*.

Of particular interest in his afternoon discussion of humor (including a standup performance as illustration) he spoke at length about Dr. Nancy Andreason's study that indicated fiction writers often appear to be monopolar depressives from families of depressives. His point was to suggest that his use of humor is a way of dealing with his own chronic depression—which led nicely into his personal account of his survival at Dresden and his struggle to write about it.

Although this small group of students had been crammed uncomfortably into a tiny, overheated auditorium, they obviously left awed by what they had heard.

At dinner that evening with organizers, participants, and teachers, I was touched by what an energizing experience Kurt's presence had been for them. They spoke of his courage and wit and of the humane values he espoused, and how inspired they were by his regard for the importance of teachers and their commitment to the arts and humanities. Later an overflow crowd of more than two thousand appeared at the Adler Theatre to hear Kurt introduce the *Slaughterhouse* film by expressing his high regard for George Roy Hill's production, and Stephen Geller's screenplay adaptation. As always, he acknowledged the film's integrity as a work of art independent of his novel, adding in mock shyness, "*I'm* not in it."

The next day I drove Kurt and Peter to Iowa City, dropping Kurt off at the Workshop office, which by then was located in the new English and Philosophy Building. (I'd never quite become used to the fact that the Workshop was then housed in such an institutional edifice. Nor had I found it comfortable that the old Workshop Quonsets had been replaced by a gargantuan, frosted aluminum building for laser technology.)

Kurt was a longtime friend of the new Workshop director, Frank Conroy, a man he'd nominated for the position two years earlier in 1987. The plan was that he'd dine with Frank, speak informally with Workshop students, and then drive with Peter and me to Cedar Falls, where he'd speak the next day.

Meanwhile, I gave Peter a campus tour, and after dinner we connected with Weide who was setting up his film crew at the small Shambaugh Auditorium in the university's main library. Shambaugh was a traditional venue for visiting writers' appearances, a frequent benefit for the writing program. While we waited, I entertained Peter with a Workshop anecdote I'd heard from the late Mary Engle, the first wife of the Workshop's titular founder.

Known for her generous use of alcohol as well as her stories, Mary had once confided her personal responsibility for the existence of this auditorium, which honored a deceased English Department director. Her story was that her husband Paul had invited the great novelist Thomas Mann to speak at the university and asked the director, Dr. Shambaugh, to introduce him. Unfortunately, his introduction was unbearably long and the audience restless. Paul was outraged, Mary said, and she was bored silly. Paging through one of Mann's novels in her lap, she suddenly realized Shambaugh was actually reading the words of Mann himself. She was so incensed that she put a hex on him, then and there! (She considered herself especially skilled at this dark art.) "It worked!" she had explained triumphantly. "He died about a week later, and his memorial became the Shambaugh Auditorium."

The evening became almost as bizarre. The audience was young and noisy, and not overflowing as I had expected. When Kurt walked in with Frank, it stayed noisy until Frank actually stepped up to the lectern and asked for quiet so he could introduce Kurt. The applause was moderate, a puzzling contrast with the Quad Cities.

Kurt launched into his talk by asking abruptly, "What are we going to do about television?" There was silence and a few titters of laughter. Kurt looked around and then asked, "Should writers be concerned that their audience now has at most a twenty-minute attention span?"

Still no reply. He softened somewhat and told a few humorous anecdotes to warm them up, but it was evident he was not going to get a dialogue going. He read from his *Hocus Pocus* manuscript and, finally, he and Frank parried back and forth a bit until Frank asked if Kurt would take questions. The audience warmed, but soon it was obvious Kurt had had enough. His wish for a writer-to-writer dialogue hadn't happened, and he was tired of answering inane questions.

I gave Weide last-minute driving instructions to Cedar Falls and then went outside to find Kurt backed into a dark corner at the top of the library steps, sheltered from a brisk wind. He was surrounded by a crowd of students and autograph seekers, with a bemused Frank watching from the side. Flakes of snow were beginning to swirl. I signaled Frank to get him down the steps to my car.

Underway with the heater blasting and snow diminishing, I assured Kurt we'd have a more eager group of students at UNI. I was relieved when we got to town and had him safely ensconced in a motel near the campus.

When I picked him up the next morning, he seemed remarkably refreshed. By the time we got through a lively afternoon press conference, he clearly had warmed to the task. He handled questions ranging from the Islamic *fatwa* called against Salman Rushdie for his new book, *The Satanic Verses* ("Interesting, but only mildly interesting in the States because of guarantees of free expression"), to newly elected President George H. W. Bush's involvement in Ronald Reagan's Iran-Contra deals ("Acting as go-between, with Reagan's knowledge"). In the afternoon he sat with Klinkowitz and me for an informal question session from a large group of students (considerably more engaged than the Iowa City group). Finally, I smuggled him away for a break before his evening speech. He wanted only a light dinner at the motel, and we agreed I'd call for him at seven for his eight o'clock gig.

As I waited with him later in the Green Room of our newly remodeled auditorium, I reminded him that he'd spoken here twelve years ago. Then my faculty friends and I had spent days preparing students and event venues to assure an informed and well-attended audience. This time, however, no audience preparation was needed. Technicians had prepared for remote telecasts to accommodate an overflow crowd. Additional college and high school students from a number of Iowa schools would be in the audience as participants in the annual Student as Critic essay competition that weekend. Kurt was pleased with the professionalism of the staging and the pleasant jazz music being piped into the room, while I paced, nervous about my plan to impersonate a made-up Vonnegut character when I introduced him.

A standup comic I was not, but I introduced myself as "Eloise" Rosewater, a "philanthropist" from *Breakfast of Champions*, here to present Kilgore Trout (Kurt), who had hitchhiked all the way here from Manhattan on semi-trucks. I said,

•

Mr. Trout learned a lot about the Midwest by the time he crossed the Mississippi at Davenport: Passing through his home state of Indiana, he was told that Vice President Dan Quayle thinks Roe versus Wade means two different ways to get across the Potomac River!

(This joke hadn't been heard by the audience yet, so it got a laugh.) I continued,

His trip was not without hazard, however: When he paused for a nap under a bridge in Iowa City, he was mugged by a fifty-three-year old graduate of the Writers' Workshop, who was enraged because "Kilgore" hadn't taught him how to write TV dramas about displaced pinball machine players.

That was funny only to those who knew about the Workshop. So maybe it wasn't a rave performance, but I got to conclude with a for-real statement that, "Kurt Vonnegut is an extraordinarily wise human being whose respect for all life is a model of courage, wit, generosity, and kindness. . . . He has enlarged my life beyond measure, and if you listen carefully, he might enlarge yours, too."

The standing room crowd greeted him wildly and obviously loved him, from his explanation about why it was snowing in April (the Midwest has *six* seasons: March-April is the "unlocking" season, and spring doesn't come until May-June . . .) to a bumper sticker he saw in Texas: "Guns don't kill people, the NRA kills people," to what will happen if we don't start taking care of the planet: "Someday the flying saucer people will land, look around, and say 'What the *hell* happened here?'"

He gave an impassioned plea for smaller class sizes in public schools: "We're becoming one of the dumbest nations in the world because we overwork our teachers and give them classes of thirty-six students and more to teach." He insisted the first qualification for a writer is passion rather than technical skill or having read great literature. "Write from passion, and people will read you."

As a colleague and local newspaper columnist, Scott Cawelti wrote later:

> Vonnegut chided, cajoled, sermonized, one-linered, admonished, and cautioned a thousand or so of us and had us in the aisles as well. . . . His humor grows out of his own shock and pain about what's happening to our world, environmentally, politically, economically.

I was thrilled with Kurt's speech and his standing ovation. Later, a last *karass* gathering at my house was brimming with love and elation for his success. He was high, too. It had been a great week.

When I drove him to Cedar Rapids airport the next morning he was markedly quiet. I knew he detested goodbyes and small talk, but I *couldn't* just drop him and leave. I insisted he buy me breakfast, hoping somehow to prolong the fun we'd enjoyed over the past few days. But he had shifted gears. He was quiet and solemn and withdrawn as I walked him to the dining area. So I gave him a quick hug, said "Thanks for everything"—and split.

In a brief letter written a day later he said his Iowa visit had been "a major event" for him. Another major event was the news that his daughter Edie had given birth to her second son, Buck. But unexpectedly, he said he'd told his lecture agents not to book any more speaking engagements until further notice. "Cedar Falls may have been the grand finale of my speaking career. What place could have been more suitable for that, since I was all jazzed up." Jazzed up or not, this was another sign of his waning energy, and I was not happy to have confirmation of it.

A few days later a package arrived in the mail—a bronze replica of the actual Rock Island Railroad locomotive that once had steamed along the Mississippi through the city of Davenport. It sits to this day in a case in my sunroom, along with the Long Island locomotive replica he'd sent years ago. Above them hangs one of his later silk-screen print posters that reads

GOD ALMIGHTY
HIMSELF
MUST HAVE BEEN
HILARIOUS
WHEN PEOPLE
SO COMBINED
FIRE, IRON AND
WATER
AS TO MAKE A
RAILROAD TRAIN

On "VE Day" (May 8) Kurt wrote to explain the locomotive's Quad City origins: "[It] was a Rock Island model, I felt you had to have it. It really runs, you know. I told the salesman I didn't care."

He included a letter he'd received from Bob Weide celebrating the "great time we all had in Iowa . . ." to which Kurt agreed "it really was an enchanted five days in April. We all believed in Fairies. There really are such times."

6/11

8

Life as a Yo-Yo, 1989–1992

Hocus Pocus

When Kurt returned to New York, he faced a dilemma of his own making he was determined to remedy:

> Nobody but my typist had seen the manuscript I read from in Iowa City. Now my new publishers, Putnam, have two hundred and twenty-five pages in hand, and report that they like it. It is so fucking depressed, but they say that's O.K. with them. I'm not so sure it's O.K. with me.

It was his draft of *Hocus Pocus* that was troubling him, but later that fall, he wrote that although Putnam was after him to "get any kind of book as soon as possible," he'd decided to put it through another revision. "Having spent three years on it so far, I think I understand at last how it should go. So now I'm back at the beginning, but with some confidence this time. This could be my last book so I want it to be a good one" (9/6/89).

Especially after his demoralizing reviews of *Bluebeard*, I appreciated his concern.

Meanwhile, Kurt's exhilarating love for theater had definitely not been put to rest. He'd never given up on his play *Make Up Your Mind*, and that fall of 1989, it had a chance for a New York opening the following year. "With the help of good actors who read for us, and God love them, we revise and revise. It's really working awfully well now." In August he sent reviews of its successful East Hampton reading at the John Drew Theater, and by September he said it "will open for four weeks outside of London within the next year, and then move into the West End if all goes well. Jonathan Miller says he wants to direct it, but can't say exactly when he'll have the time to do so."

So far as I know, that didn't happen. I knew it had to be a major disappointment for Kurt, but he never said anything more about the play.

Nonetheless, the summer had been a good one, and in October he would be off to Mozambique! He explained he was traveling at the request of CARE, an organization involved with emergency relief that was desperately needed because of the horrific civil war going on there since 1977, just two years after achieving independence from Portugal. CARE's administrators were hoping Kurt's visit could draw attention to the growing disaster and desperate need for financial aid.

Early in November he sent proofs of the article he'd managed to place, at CARE's request, in *Parade* magazine—the Sunday weekly news supplement with a distribution of more than 34 million at the time. Although he wasn't sure they'd actually print it (since it had "so little to do with sports, TV, or Hollywood") his article did appear in January 1990—a dramatic account of the mindless terrorism being conducted by the RENAMO organization that had slaughtered thousands in the past two years, including at least eight thousand children under age five. For five days, Kurt and several reporters from the U.S. press, had been flown in a small Cessna aircraft "from one refugee center to another" where they witnessed "starving children with eyes as big as dinner plates, adults with chests that looked like bird cages," and the "new twist" of "purposely mutilated people . . . who had their noses or ears or fingers or whatever cut off by hand-held sharp instruments."

When I asked how he had dealt with such horror, he wrote

About Mozambique: I have seen or thought about so much starvation that I feel almost nothing about it any more. When Vance and I came home from Biafra, I cried so hard I barked like a dog. When I came home from Mozambique, where about a million and a half farmers have been driven off their land and are now starving to death with their children in refugee centers which can only be supplied by air, it was as though I had walked into a pet shop and then walked out again. I talked to a high school friend about this at lunch yesterday, and he said the same thing happened to him when he was in China for the Signal Corps at the end of World War Two, setting up radio stations. He saw cartloads of people who had starved to death day after day, and after a while scarcely noticed them.

CARE (no longer C.A.R.E., since that acronym spoke only of relief to Europe) wanted the widest possible publicity about the Mozambican tragedy caused by nothing but war. So they asked me to try to place a piece with *Parade*, which I did.... Mozambique, incidentally, is twice the size of California, has plenty of rainfall most years, and is under populated. It has half as many citizens as Tokyo. The only trouble is a guerrilla army first trained and supplied by white South Africans and Rhodesians back in 1976, when the country was only one year old. In the past two years alone, according to our own State Department, it killed 100,000 unarmed civilians. It doesn't govern or farm areas it overruns. It just kills and loots and burns down every sort of man-made structure, and then runs off into the bush again. (11/6/89)

Love as always,

K

The headline for the actual *Parade* piece (in Kurt's view about "a Garden of Eden . . . as beautiful and habitable as California") was "My Visit to Hell" (1/7/90, pp. 16–17). Kurt's prose style, always tight and graphic, explained that the RENAMO was an organization that may originally have been supported secretly by our own government because of Mozambique's earlier Marxism. Now, however, only unknown nongovernmental sources were supplying "roving gangs which have become a crippling or fatal disease, unreasoning, existing for their own sake and nothing more."

As I read it, I pondered again his extraordinary discipline as a writer and as a humanitarian. He had come off his spring speaking tour exhausted, with a growing sense of malaise and concern about his novel. Not only had he returned to work on his play, and traveled to Africa to write brilliantly about the impending Mozambique tragedy, but he also resumed life as a celebrity, a husband, and father of a young daughter, to say nothing of contract pressures from Putnam bearing down for completion of a novel in his two-book contract.

In addition, the present political scene did not make for Kurt's light-heartededness. Ronald Reagan's far right presidency had yielded to that of former vice president, George H. W. Bush, who had ordered U.S. troops into Panama following the murder of a U.S. Marine. That misadventure had culminated in the arrest of Panamanian leader Manuel Noriega on drug trafficking and other charges. Meanwhile, tensions within the Communist Party in the Soviet Union were causing considerable unrest, as were power moves by Saddam Hussein in the increasingly volatile Middle East.

In short, I was very worried how this was affecting Kurt's state of mind.

I didn't hear from him again until after the first of the year, when he wrote

I'm sorry I wrote you such a crazy letter. I hope it didn't upset you too much. I go off my nut sometimes.

This is February 2, and it now appears that I will finally finish a book which has cost me 4 gruesome years before the Sun goes down. It is called *Hocus Pocus*.

I have again nominated Paul [Engle] for a medal from the American Academy which is supposed to go to people who have helped a lot of other artists, not just themselves. . . .

Again I apologize, and send love as always. (2/2/90)

In April he wrote again to say he had just heard from Peter Reed, who had "checked in with me, making sure I knew we were experiencing an anniversary of an outing which evidently meant a lot to him. Meant a lot to me, too" (a reference to Kurt's Iowa visit the previous April). He continued that he'd been revising *Hocus Pocus*, "which is supposed to go to the printer right away. It is very slow going, since a copy editor has loaded it up with hundreds of queries. . . . There's a whole lot wrong. I am embarrassed."

But he was very pleased that Paul Engle would indeed receive the award for which Kurt had nominated him. It was duly bestowed that May, which Kurt reported with some delight:

Paul enjoyed the considerable and enviable honor bestowed upon him by his peers tremendously. What a contrast to Nelson Algren! Cocktails were served from noon until one, during which time Paul was reunited with several world class poets who had spent time in Iowa City. He thought he had left his acceptance speech in a taxicab, but eventually found it in one of his twenty pockets. The speech was a majestic lulu, delivered after lunch to a packed auditorium which is used for only three hours a year.

I took him and Hualing and five old friends to supper at Elaine's, the closest thing we have to a literary restaurant. Jill was working out of town. (5/24/90)

But in the interim before the release of *Hocus Pocus*, on April 22, an unusually grave piece by Kurt appeared in the *New York Times Book Review* (p.14). It was about a "world . . . too grim to be funny." Titled "Notes from My Bed of Gloom: Or Why the Joking Had to Stop," it amounted to a kind of apology for the darkness of his forthcoming book. He wrote that American humorists "become intolerably unfunny pessimists if they live past a certain age," which he believed included works by authors like Mark Twain and himself. "So guess what: my next novel, *Hocus Pocus*, to be published next September, is a sardonic fable in a bed of gloom."

I found his essay worrisome. It suggested what I'd fretted about earlier, that he'd been pushing himself to a point of exhaustion since *Bluebeard*, and was now uncharacteristically apologizing for writing a book that wasn't going to be sufficiently entertaining. I feared for him if he really meant what he wrote: that he had truly reached a point in his life and career as a writer when he felt he could no longer successfully create humor as a comforting survival technique—for himself *or* for his fictional protagonists. There it was in his *Times* article: "Mark Twain finally stopped laughing at his own agony and that of those around him. He denounced life on this planet as a crock."

Despite his assertion that all American humorists "have clear images in their heads of what American citizens ought to be," he said he had called upon Mark Twain's *Huckleberry Finn* as his guide. Even so, Twain could find no way to let his readers "off the hook." And that book was written before the great wars "and all the rest of it," when Huck is young and resourceful and knows he can "light out for the Territory" as a fallback. In short, Kurt was announcing that now there *was* no territory left to light out for. That was as close as he could come to letting his audience off the hook in the spring of 1990, to prepare his readers not to expect magic relief from *Hocus Pocus*.

But he was in for a surprise.

I was away much of that summer and returned in August, to learn, among other things, that Kurt's dear friend and war buddy, Bernard V. O'Hare, had died the previous month. That would be tough enough, but in addition our government was preparing for another war. Hundreds of thousands of U.S. troops were being flown to the Persian Gulf in response to Iraq's invasion of Kuwait. I could just imagine Kurt's frame of mind. Then I found a package from him in my backlog of mail. It contained the proofs of *Hocus Pocus.*

I read it eagerly. It was GOOD! He wasn't going to take a beating, I was sure of it. In fact, it was uncanny at one stage to read about the fictional U.S. 82nd Airborne flying troops to Mohiga Lake in upstate New York. The reason for the troops? To rescue rightwing trustees of Tarkington College taken hostage by the Black Brothers of Islam escaped from the Maximum Security Prison run by the Japanese across the lake at Athena. Absurd symmetries like these resonated uncannily with current actualities: the *real* 82nd Airborne at that moment hauling thousands of U.S. troops to Kuwait, to protect U.S. corporate investments in Persian Gulf oil from Islamic Iraq. Actual parallels with Kurt's new book were dazzling, even as they also echoed historical contexts. He'd done it again.

But no wonder it had taken him four years! The fictional prison (a Japanese corporation interring only African Americans) across the lake from the elitist college in Athena (for learning disabled offspring of millionaires) set up the satiric parallels of the whole novel, a socio/economic and political set of opposites, supported by dozens of historical timelines, institutions, and events. I was elated to be able to phone my delighted congratulations and insist Kurt had no cause for concern.

The reviews soon confirmed my zeal. Readers were widely dazzled. By the time I left in early October of 1990 for a visit with friends in the Samoan Islands (with U.S. commercial planes still hauling our militia to the Gulf), it was clear Kurt's book was a success . . . a hard-earned one, for sure. It would either be perfect preparation for winding down his career, or a great jump start for his next novel. He had signed a two-book contract with Putnam, so he had one more yet, if he was thinking about retirement.

When I returned toward the end of the year, he was in high spirits, although gravely concerned about the Persian Gulf situation.

Our military, backed by an international coalition, was poised for an imminent attack if Iraq did not withdraw its forces from Kuwait by January 15.

On January 8, 1991, Kurt wrote: "All life is on hold now . . . and all eyes are on the President. What a slick way to make people ignore another Great Depression. My brother says that if he were Saddam Hussein he would launch an attack during the Super Bowl." (The Washington Redskins were to play the Buffalo Bills there on January 26.) I phoned Kurt a few days later, an indulgence just to vent my anxiety. His response could only confirm his surrender to impossible quandary: "I tell you what I tell my daughters—'It's all right, it's all right.'"

Of course, it wasn't: President Bush *did* launch the horrific bombing of Baghdad, which was dramatically broadcast live by CNN from the top floor of a downtown Baghdad hotel for a worldwide audience. And that rapidly "victorious" war was just a forerunner of what the second President Bush would launch a decade or so later.

Meanwhile, Kurt had found a temporary solution to his two-book Putnam contract: a collection of earlier speeches and essays connected by autobiographical material into a collage somewhat like *Palm Sunday*. It would be called *Fates Worse Than Death* with examples drawn from those suggested by his sermon of that title at the Cathedral of St. John the Divine. That sermon, he said, "described what the Soviet Union would do to us if we let down our guard. They were almost all things we had already done to ourselves."

He added that "business was good for him at the moment, even though it was lousy for practically everybody else" and cheerfully announced that

> Showtime Cable and a Canadian film outfit called Atlantis are dramatizing a series of short stories I wrote many, many decades ago. They shoot on soundstages in Vancouver. The first three are done, and they are a lot more grownup than my stories were. Other people write the scripts, and I thank them effusively.

This cable television series launched later that year was hugely successful. Despite his complaints about television, he was adapting to the electronic age. And a traditional film was also likely: Klinkowitz and I had just read and given feedback to Bob Weide on his *Mother Night* screenplay adaptation, which we both thought was promising. Weide *and* Kurt both were on a roll.

The following month (Feb.15) Kurt sent an elegant promotion folder for the *Welcome to the Monkey House* cable series along with a jubilant letter. He was

> back from five days solo in Monaco, where the Canadian outfit Atlantis and I were hustling a TV series to European networks....
> We were a class act there, and everybody bought. Everybody else had schlock....At Monaco we were after enough money to make ten more episodes. I think we got it. I am so stimulated that several of the episodes will be brand new stuff.

(Although more episodes were not produced, the first three were successful enough for a run of several seasons on the Showtime network.)

His high spirits were somewhat dampened in March when he sent an update about Dick Yates, for whom he and several other friends had set up a rescue fund because of Dick's illness (emphysema, among other things).

He sent Dick's address in Tuscaloosa, where he had a teaching job at the University of Alabama and was finishing a "great big book . . . about Bobby Kennedy . . . which could be a hit and solve all his financial problems."

He told me George Starbuck, from the Poetry Workshop staff back in the sixties, was also teaching at Alabama and had helped Dick get the job. Alas, George himself was ill with Parkinson's and would die in 1996 at the age of sixty-five. His wife, Kathy Salyer Starbuck, who had been the Workshop secretary, co-edited a splendid collection of George's poetry after his death.

I wrote to Dick, and soon after had a phone call from him celebrating the fact he'd managed to get a portable oxygen machine that
freed him to be ambulatory.

"You quit smoking, didn't you?" I asked.

He laughed and coughed extensively before he managed to reply,
"Of course not!" His wheezing was evident as he pleaded in that typi-
cally romantic voice of his: "We had some good times back in Iowa
City, didn't we baby?"

God, I thought, Dick wasn't going to make it. Why bother to quit
smoking?

Dick had said nothing about his Kennedy book in that phone call
but did express hopes for a film version of his novel, *Easter Parade*,
something that did not materialize. I had the distinct sense that I'd
likely not hear from him again.

Another farewell occurred that month: the Iowa Writers' Workshop had *its* end-of-chapter moment when the renowned and longtime director, Paul Engle, died March 9, 1991, of a heart attack at
O'Hare Airport on his way to accept yet another meritorious award.
Kurt faxed a tribute to Iowa City for the April 14 Memorial Service. I
was among those gathered that Sunday afternoon on the tree-shaded
patio of the splendid Law Library Building on the university campus.
Kurt's elegantly personal statement said in part:

There wouldn't be Writers Workshops worth a nickel here if Paul
Engle hadn't committed his whole body and soul to their creation. . . . His *World Symphony* is the enormous body of literature
created, and which is still being created, by men and women who
gained or regained self-confidence as artists right here in River
City. . . . I was rescued by Paul Engle's Writers Workshop in the
mid-1960s', and he didn't know me, and I don't think he had ever
heard of me. He didn't read that kind of crap. But somebody else
out here did [George Starbuck], and assured him that I was indeed
a writer, but dead broke with a lot of kids, and completely out of
print and scared to death. So he threw me a life-preserver, which is
to say a teaching job. . . .

Paul Engle should get a posthumous medal from the Coast Guard for all the lives he saved.

No writer in all of history did as much to help other writers as Paul Engle. . . .

One last thought: To hundreds of writers all over the world now, Paul Engle wasn't merely an Iowan. He was *Iowa*!

It was a fitting tribute.

But the next message from Kurt a few weeks later was completely in a different key. He was alone in Sagaponack when he called in a rage with the shocking news that he'd left his home in the city because his wife wanted a divorce and had asked him to leave. Most especially, he was concerned about their seven-year-old daughter.

A couple times in the past few months he'd mentioned concern about the number of different nannies they'd employed over the years, and how Jill's career required her frequent absence. But this was different.

The few friends who'd expressed past concerns about his marriage had always respected Kurt's privacy as did I. It was rare for him to share family matters. This day it was understandably painful for him to acknowledge that mutual friends had apparently been aware of his wife's intentions for some time.

We spoke several times over the next weeks. He was coming out to Chicago to speak at a book fair and wanted to get together in mid-June. We could connect in Chicago or he'd fly to Iowa. Since I'd be back by then from my grandson's graduation in Tennessee, I suggested a little road trip to Minneapolis for a visit with our friends, the Reeds there. Kurt and I could take a leisurely drive north along the Mississippi and have time to talk. I agreed it would be good for him to clear his head and have a few days away from New York.

He told me to rent a nice convertible. "We can put the top down."

I was determined to provide a calm and cheerful interlude, a time-out space of Midwestern balance—even though I realized extended calm could easily bore him into frustration. Laughs were essential.

He arrived, unexpectedly buoyant with a big hug.

"You look great," I said, grinning up at him, shocked as always by his unexpected height.

"I have a present for you," he beamed as he retrieved his luggage.

Walking to the parking lot, I confessed my failed effort to rent the convertible he'd requested. "There's just no such rental in all of Iowa."

Never mind. He was brimming with enthusiasm about Chicago's healthy vitality and creativity. "Have you seen the new Washington Library? Splendid! They've done all the right things to make that city just what it should be on that beautiful lake . . . it was a treat to be back." He gave me another hug. "It's good to see you!"

We got to my house and he immediately gave me his gift, which he insisted I put on at once: a Kurt Vonnegut T-shirt!

He'd been honored with the Harold Washington Literary Award at the kickoff event for Chicago's annual Printers Row Book Fair. And yes, they'd liked his speech OK. "So go put on the T-shirt," he teased. I did and then insisted *he* get the charcoal grill started so we could make dinner. I showed him the nice fillet of salmon I'd marinated.

It was as though the whole divorce episode had never happened. Why not, I figured. We'd just relax and have a happy time and talk about it later.

I had teasingly invited Kurt earlier that spring to fly out to go canoeing on one of Iowa's wild rivers, a favorite way to celebrate the end of winter, along with a traditional search for morel mushrooms in the woods. Our old University of Iowa friend, Bob Scholes, had been here earlier that spring for a science fiction conference, and we'd done a challenging canoe trip on the Wapsipinicon in northeast Iowa.

Now I suggested that the Mississippi offered a substitute opportunity, to which he agreed enthusiastically. So we headed out the next day to drive toward Minneapolis, tracking the river and watching for canoe rentals.

At some point we crossed over to the Wisconsin side for a lunch break at a little roadside diner that served fabulous root beer floats. There we picked up a mimeographed anthology of poetry and stories by locals, which I read to him as we sat outside in the sun by the river.

"Just think what some Wisconsin farm kid would say if he knew you were reading his story," I said.

Driving on, we found a sagging boathouse next to a bait shop that offered rental canoes. The elderly man who outfitted us seemed a tad reluctant—we didn't exactly look like the roustabout crews that work the Mississippi. (Or maybe we did!) But we *did* know something about boats and made that clear to him with a rather snappy departure, Kurt paddling stern with me in the bow.

"Just try not to swamp this boat like you did in the Keys," he joked.

"Hey, this is a piece of cake," I yelled back at him. "Whaddya mean, anyway? You had the stern on that little romp, and you still do. Pay attention!"

All went well for an hour or so, on our meandering Huck Finn venture through several slow loops in the river. It was a beautiful day. Suddenly I spied some floating loons ahead of us, my favorite water bird in northern Minnesota.

"Nah, those are cormorants," Kurt said.

"No way! They're loons—we're in Minnesota!" I insisted with authority.

We paddled hard, figuring to catch up with them, working up a good sweat. The birds were still far ahead of us.

"We *are* going north, aren't we?" I finally questioned, resting my paddle. We continued to drift ahead at a good pace, but so did the birds.

Kurt began to laugh. "Maybe it's north, but we sure as hell are going downstream. Not a chance we could catch up with them." He laughed some more. "You didn't tell me your Mississippi flows backward!"

We bade farewell to the elusive river birds, reversed direction, and began the pull back to the boathouse. Upstream all the way. So much for Huck Finn! We'd forgotten how river bends could play with your sense of direction. The slanting sun's rays confirmed our bearing, but we were supposed to return the boat by five—a challenging trip ahead.

By the time the bait shop was in sight, it was obvious everything was closed up. The rental guy had probably gone home to report a canoe robbery. Laughing breathlessly as we pulled up to the rickety pier, we both leaned back on the thwarts, coasting into the shallows to catch our breath and cool down.

"That was some cormorant rout for a couple of pros," he chuckled.

"Loons!" I protested feebly.

We opened lukewarm bottles of water and rested there, laughing and talking by that shaded beach, rocking gently in the wakes of occasional barge traffic, and catching up with all that had happened. As we gradually eased into his marital dilemma, he grew increasingly angry about his wife's abrupt intentions and how apparently everyone in New York but himself had expected this. He felt certain of his legal advantage, "but I just sank a hundred grand into remodeling . . . and now the locks are changed." He lit a cigarette and took a long drag.

He would stay in Sagaponack until he figured out how to proceed, "but it's Lily I'm concerned about."

"It's tough on kids," I agreed, feeling like I was quoting a counseling textbook. "You could get custody?"

He sighed and lit a cigarette. "I dunno . . . she wouldn't want to come out to Sagaponack without her mother."

"Think of all your friends. No matter what, they'll help." Of course I knew that was utterly inane. He wanted his kid, not his friends.

He shook his head. I felt angered, too, by the unfairness of his being thrust into a humiliating situation.

Finally there was no more to say. He seemed lighter.

"C'mon, you loony babe," he said, tossing me a sponge. "Get this craft bailed out."

There was no need to hurry. We dutifully moored the canoe tightly to the piers of the dock before leaving the deserted bait shop to follow the river north, or whatever direction it was going.

The fun continued in Minneapolis the next day, when I showed Kurt some of the surprising architecture of that city, especially the

Walker Art Center, its gardens, and the adjacent Guthrie Theatre. As we strolled through the flower-filled greenhouses, he told me about the major landscape gardening he'd been doing around his house at Sagaponack, and the lily species he was cultivating. Later, in a tour around the city, he was impressed with the old mill sites on the Mississippi at St. Anthony Falls, the city's first enterprise center and now a gradually thriving cultural area.

That evening was our dinner date with Peter and his wife Maggie, a high school English teacher. We had a delightful time recalling the laughs we'd shared at Kurt's Quad Cities appearances a year earlier. Peter brought him up to date on his and Marc Leeds' plans to bring out an anthology of critical essays on Kurt's later fiction, works grown from presentations at the Quad Cities conference. He hoped it would be in print in the next year or two, although it didn't actually appear until 1996 (*The Vonnegut Chronicles*, Greenwood Press). I was working on a piece for that collection which would argue that Kurt's novels after age fifty were marked by the new appearance of muselike female characters who played significantly mellowing roles in his work from *Breakfast of Champions* on.

Our conversation rambled pleasantly, interrupted by laughs at Kurt's occasional one-liners and his sarcastic references to Norman Schwarzkopf, the infamous general then commanding coalition forces in the ongoing Gulf War. On a lighter note, Kurt was charmed by Maggie's anecdotes about her teaching experiences and impressed by her inventive methods of getting kids to write well. I surmised her examples would give him compelling new samples of good teaching for his speeches.

Later we shared after-dinner drinks in an outdoor garden near the river before saying goodbye. Gazing into the water, Peter, a wild animal advocate, noticed turtles swimming about. He and Kurt stood to lean over the guardrail and peer at the wildlife navigating this concrete-sided, urban part of the river. Kurt wondered if they were snapping turtles, still a mystery.

Peter recalled boyhood experiences of England during World War II. He'd been working on a story reflecting his memories of nighttime bombings, a long way from that quiet evening. He took the opportunity to query Kurt about German military figures from that war. It always awed me how sharp Kurt's memory of history was. As usual, he came up with names and roles immediately.

It had been a delightful interlude. After we bade them goodnight and returned to the hotel, however, Kurt's mood shifted. We talked as he smoked cigarette after cigarette. He was understandably troubled about how a divorce would affect his young daughter, with growing rage and impotence to imagine any alternative that could ease its impact. It was a long and restless night.

On the ride back to Iowa the next day, Kurt was quiet, often nodding off as we headed south. He hadn't wanted to take the wheel during this visit, and I wondered if his vision might have been bothering him. We stopped at my favorite highway shop and found a special on ice cream floats made with homemade root beer, his favorite. Before we left, Kurt browsed at the souvenir counter and made a guarded purchase, which he presented as a surprise when we got to the car. It was a ceramic coffee mug with the image of a mother loon swimming beside a baby chick. It brought to mind the old china mug he'd given me long ago, to commemorate our Stone City visit in Iowa.

I gave him a hug. "I told you they weren't cormorants."

I'd arranged for Jerry Klinkowitz and his wife Julie to join us that evening before Kurt flew back to New York the next morning. Fortunately the conversation grew cheerful as we settled on the backyard patio of my house to sip a nice wine at dusk. Kurt was most comfortable being outside, where he could smoke without bothering anyone. He was fond of Jerry, who had published ample books about Kurt's work. They shared stories and concerns about mutual friends, like Jerzy Kosinski, whom both had admired despite his turbulent career, and who had died by suicide a few weeks earlier. Kurt would later write an especially compassionate tribute to Kosinski in which he spoke of his fragile tolerance for life, a fragility I felt Kurt understood intimately at that time.

Fragile or not, it was a pleasant evening. Because I lived near the university, the occasional voices of students alternated cheerfully with the sound of someone practicing a guitar from the steps of a rooming house across the yard. Now and then, the chiming of campus carillon bells was a pleasant accompaniment. Kurt especially loved the ancient box elder tree in my backyard, certified to be the largest and oldest in Iowa. Its comforting gnarled and leafy presence made a latticework of the moon's light in the growing darkness. He seemed more at ease and it cheered me to hear him laughing again.

The next morning I brought coffee out to that same patio. He'd been up since early dawn, and was impatient to leave. Having exhausted every viable coping scenario for his dilemma, we drove to the airport in silence. The weight of his despair about the future was a black cloud isolating him. We both knew there was nothing I could do to help.

Kurt promised to call from the "country" (Sagaponack) where he would reside alone. He'd phone as soon as there was news. I wished him luck and assured him of my love. There was no more to say.

What details he shared during the months that followed left no doubt that the summer was a rocky one. To make things even worse, he suffered a painful compression fracture of a vertebra during an August horseback outing. In September, in considerable pain, he traveled alone to Salerno, Italy, to receive the prestigious Premio Mondello literary award for *Galapagos*. He made a point of telling me, upon his return, that the gracious Italians had been shocked he was without a female companion while being regaled for this rare honor, "the only international prize to come my way" (9/17/91).

His sense of aloneness was nearly palpable in his conclusion to a letter in the fall: "[Sagaponack] remains my residence, where I live alone and rootless, going into the city maybe once a week on business, and to see my darling Lily for an hour or two" (10/29/91).

For his sixty-ninth birthday in November, I sent him a relic I'd found from his past, a 1953 *Colliers* magazine containing one of his short stories. In a letter that followed on December 19, he seemed charmed by the recovery of that story, calling it "flotsam rescued from the wake I've left," and reminisced that "there must have been a celebration in our little house in Osterville, Cape Cod. Daddy got paid!"

But his letter contained the news that his wife was suddenly now fighting against "the divorce she once wished me to expedite." It was a dreary letter, except for the closing bit of cheer that he had "quit smoking for a month, and felt fine except that I couldn't even write a letter. Now I have lit up, and I have written one. Who knows, I might even write a book next" (12/19/91).

That was my hope for him as I departed for a holiday visit with my daughter in Florida. But to my surprise, when I returned in mid-January, a letter dated 1/5/92 contained his announcement that Jill had fired her lawyer, and Kurt had decided to end litigation: "It now appears that I will be married to Jill for the rest of my days. . . . She is the sun and the moon to Lily."

He added, "I am out here in the country alone, except for my cat, and writing all day long as a distraction from having been sent to the end of my string and then brought up again like a yo-yo."

I worried some about his being there alone all winter. As lovely as it was, that house could become pretty bleak through a solitary off season. We stayed in touch by phone and letters. He did accept a few speaking gigs and continued to make regular trips into the city to visit Lily. Later in January he seemed more energized and wrote that Lily, "who is the whole show," was talking more about spending time alone with him in Sagaponack. Best of all, his letter closed with the announcement that "after hacking out garbage on my IBM Selectric for nearly a year now . . . I have gotten control of enough of it to make another novel. It is called *Timequake*, and, like this country, should be completely finished by the end of 1992" (1/5/92).

Good news indeed, at least for his book! His reference to the country reflected his disgust over the recent savings and loan scandals, the Gulf War, and the desecration our bombers were making of Iraq and innocents there. He was especially outraged about the unfairness of massive U.S. bombing of civilian as well as military targets, contrasting this with the more decent contest of hand-to-hand battle he and thousands of others had experienced during World War II. Dresden still haunted him, as it would for the rest of his life.

My phone conversations with him were frustrating in that I could offer little if any comfort for his obvious distress, even though he rarely dwelt explicitly on his personal feelings. A February news account of his campus lecture at Duke University was worrisome. The Duke *Chronicle*'s February 19 headline was "Vonnegut wanders through discussion of life," and suggested that his rambling speech to a packed auditorium had "shifted gears" and lacked coherence. Changes of pace and topics marked his usual campus style, but I winced at the concluding quote in the article: "'It was the most conservative audience I have ever spoken to,' said an exhausted Vonnegut afterwards."

It wasn't surprising he was exhausted, pushing himself reluctantly through lectures, even though he'd reduced their frequency. But if his exhaustion was visible and he wasn't connecting, he was obviously off his stride.

In March he wrote of continuing domestic strain. Nonetheless, all was not gloom: his stray cat had recently been photographed for the following year's Purina Cat Chow Celebrity Calendar! A delegation from St. Louis and Los Angeles had even come out to Sagaponack to do a celebrity photo shoot of Claude and donate $3,000 to a charity of Kurt's choice: "I gave it to the Gutman Institute, which sends X-ray vans into poor neighborhoods to give anybody who wants one a free mammogram. Good choice?" The following year, he said Claude would be "the cat for December, since that is when Lily's birthday is" (3/31/92). He also sent a copy of a new introduction to an Italian translation of *Breakfast of Champions*, which would be published as *La Colazione Dei Campioni* in Milan. Perhaps the best possible news was that he was continuing to work on *Timequake*.

I was away again for most of the 1992 summer, and heard from him only rarely. By fall he was lecturing on campuses again, one of those gigs being Winona State University in Winona, Minnesota, a community to which my daughter had recently moved after her husband changed jobs. When I suggested we both could reconnect with him there, he urged us to do so. Meeting his plane on October 29,

I was relieved to find him looking fit and cheerful. At his press conference, I ran into a former student, Lynn Olson, who then worked for the nearby La Crosse, Wisconsin, *Tribune*. She had taken several of my courses on Vonnegut, and I knew she would not write a dreary story like the one from Duke. Kurt had arranged for Leslie and me to attend a faculty dinner prior to his lecture and promised Leslie would be seated next to him, which she was, much to her delight.

His speech later that evening was met with cheers from a packed house. Afterward, he joked and conversed warmly with a select reception of students and faculty. They were obviously thrilled with his solicitations.

When the crowd dispersed and we strolled into the hotel bar to catch up, he seemed a bit subdued but enthused about seeing Leslie again. "I'm astonished at her courage," he said, "moving back to the Midwest from Florida. And then giving birth without [her husband]. You were with her for that event, yes?"

I nodded. "He's a beautiful little boy."

"She's a beautiful woman," he said. "Like her mother."

"And now she lives right here on the Mississippi."

"So which direction does it flow here?" he asked with a grin.

"Probably west," I shrugged and handed him a package. "It's an early birthday present . . . in commemoration of the river." It was a CD recording called *New Age Loon Music*.

We talked a bit about his *Timequake* progress. "Slow, but it's coming."

"And your marital situation?" I asked. "Unresolved," he said with a shrug. "But Lily's doing well." I left him with a continuing sense of wonder, if concern, at his ability to maintain the pace and presence he did, despite his apparent energy drain. He would be seventy in November.

He called about a month later, for an entirely different concern— to tell me Dick Yates had died on November 7 of emphysema, in Birmingham.

I was honored to send a personal statement for Kurt to read on my behalf at the memorial service. Andre Dubus also called, in tears—Dick had been his major mentor in the Workshop, and especially supportive following Andre's accident. I told him of Dick's concerned calls to me when Andre was hospitalized and how much he wanted to be a "good dad" to him.

Kurt phoned with an account of the memorial attendees—some of the country's finest writers. I loved it that Art Blakey's "For All We Know" was a musical interlude—one of the songs Dick loved. In Kurt's remarks, he said: "The happiest I ever saw [Dick] was when he was singing all the words, clever, witty, ironic, silly, sweet words, at a party."

He continued that Dick had

yearned to live as F. Scott Fitzgerald lived when Fitzgerald was rich and famous and young, to jump into the Plaza Fountain with his clothes on. . . . I submit to you that he was a more careful writer than Fitzgerald, and one who was even more cunningly observant. . . . Unlike Fitzgerald and Hemingway . . . he did not and could not run away from middle-class life in America. So that is what he wrote about. And like another outsider, Tennessee Williams, he celebrated the utterly unglamorous gallantry of Americans who had not and could not amount to much.

Later he wrote that the "service was delightful. It was by invitation, and only people in the book trade who adored good writing were there. Sam Lawrence intends to publish a little booklet of what was said or read . . . you should get a copy in a few months."

Kurt and Loree, Winona, Minnesota, 1993.

9

Triumphs of a "Celestial Calamity,"
1993–1999

Timequake

Early in January of 1993, his marriage still unreconciled, Kurt sent a package from Sagaponack, the New Year's Purina Cat Chow calendar, with his stray one of the celebrity features. He wrote

> I guess I am finally on track on the book I have owed Putnam
> for so long, meaning I at least have some glimmering of what my
> deeply submerged intelligence wishes I would talk about. Jesus,
> I have now lived much longer than Steinbeck or Hemingway. This
> will be my last book, and what a relief that will be.

He reported that he had spent all of Lily's Christmas vacation with her, his words echoing the remorse and loneliness he felt for this little girl who had turned eight in December:

> We went to Puerto Rico for six days after Christmas, and Lily
> and I rented a tandem bike. There was a swimming pool one mile
> long. It was in the form of a river, with pools connected by
> waterslides, and there was a stiff current, so you didn't have to
> paddle and kick if you didn't want to. Crazy.

By late April (26), his sense of isolation in Sagaponack seemed even more pronounced, with a letter reversing his optimism about being on track with his book:

> To the dismay of my publishers, Putnam, I have started my long-overdue novel, *Timequake*, all over again. It was a hopeless jumble, which I now think I can straighten out. I want my last novel to be a good one, whereas Putnam thinks they can sell it whether it's good or not.

He said that in his lectures he'd been expressing "what is really on my mind these days . . . the terrible vulnerability of so many Americans because they don't even have a rudimentary extended family, people willing to help when something, anything, goes wrong." Understandably, he worried about Lily.

> They're both . . . so alone, despite a teeming city around them, and their frequent expeditions to parties and plays and museums. There should be twenty people in that house, where I myself stay maybe ten days each month, and it would be comforting to know that a lot of them would still be there ten years from now.

He noted his daughter Edith and her family had visited him that weekend: "They are on Cape Cod, in what used to be Jane's and my house, in a darling village. But they have no gang. And neither do the people in the cozy houses all around them" (4/26/93).

In hindsight, his words seemed not only the expression of his own loneliness but also his regret at not being the husband and father he'd always wished and vowed to be.

I sensed a turning point in his effort toward a satisfactory resolution to their living situation. In fact, Kurt's May 22 letter seemed infused with new vitality and clarity. Part of that new energy was related to the successful premiere of his new libretto for the Igor Stravinsky work, *L'Histoire du Soldat*, performed earlier that month by the New York Philomusica Chamber Ensemble in Lincoln Center's Alice Tully Hall. He wrote

It was a one-night stand [May 6], and worked like a dream,
although not in the opinion of that majestic gate-keeper institution,
the New York Times. Other orchestras have expressed interest in
doing it. It's about the only project I've managed to complete in
the past two or three years. Talk about a lost weekend!

Kurt had been approached by his good friend George Plimpton to
write this new text, one that was more in keeping with the perspective
of the 1990s. Kurt had agreed, saying (in the program notes):

I cannot understand how Stravinsky, in exile from his native Russia
but of military age when he wrote the music, could have found ac-
ceptable words which were so unresponsive to a war then going on
in which 65-million persons had been mobilized and 35-million
were becoming casualties.

So what Kurt's new libretto offered was a soldier facing real challenges of war, basing it on the actual story of Private Eddie Slovik during the last days of World War II, the only American executed for
cowardice since the Civil War. It likely also reflected an America recently victorious in "Desert Storm," but now plagued by a faltering
economy, deficit spending, and increasing inner city violence. The
newly elected Bill Clinton had just taken over the country's leadership.

Kurt had also been cheered a few days earlier by his reconnection
at Stanford with Bob Weide, who'd come up from L.A. to hear him
speak: "He still thinks we'll finally have a movie of *Mother Night*,
which can't possibly be a hit, given its subject and attitude. Another
moral victory." Weide, whose sense of humor (to say nothing of talent) was attuned to Kurt's, was always an upper for him.

Kurt also reconnected about then with his old Workshop pal,
Vance Bourjaily, who was in New York to receive an American
Academy of Arts and Letters "citation and check for seven thousand
dollars for being a good writer. Better late than never." At that event
Kurt had been pleased to present the Strauss Livings prize to his former Workshop students Joy Williams and John Casey, providing
them each fifty thousand dollars a year for the next five years.

His letter concluded with an assertion now pointed more toward firm determination than desperation: "I have started my book *Timequake* all over again. I couldn't stand it, the way it was."

*   *   *

By midsummer in 1993, he was again hosting his youngest daughter alone in Sagaponack. Knowing his love of extended families, I sent some photos taken in my backyard of a reunion of my family, most of my kids, their spouses, and a growing number of grandchildren. He replied that he'd shown the pictures to Lily who

> went absolutely bananas over them. I was very touched as she asked me who this or that person was, and how they were related to the others. And she learned most of the names. Little kids are tremendously interested in families anywhere, and no doubt recognize them as ideal survival schemes. (7/20)

By fall, however, I had to share with Kurt the news that my daughter, a mother of three, would be ending her marriage. His 9/22/93 reply was a comfort to my concern. Referring to the new preface for the forthcoming twenty-fifth anniversary edition of *Slaughterhouse-Five* he'd just completed, he said

> I mention Steven Hawking's mystification about why we can't remember the future, and I reply that we only have to grow old to find out what will become of our children and all our friends and enemies. As my late beloved sister (who would die at 41) used to exclaim, "Soap opera! Soap opera!"

Along with his letter came the gift of a new work of art he'd recently finished, in partnership with the artist, Joe Petro III. Because *Timequake* was ostensibly to be the end of his novel writing career, his playful love of doodling was becoming seriously intentional, giving him a more immediate creative outlet. Joe was a talented and amiable silkscreen artist he'd recently met, whose studio was in Lexington, Kentucky. They had formed a professional affiliation: Kurt would create a painting on acetate with India ink and send it off to Joe, who would transform it into colorful screen prints, each one unique.

The quality of their cooperative venture was evident from the artist's proof Kurt had sent. Elegant and mischievous at the same time, it was titled "Two Madonnas," and enhanced my longtime collection of goddess figures. It offers two perspectives: viewed upright it appears as a clownish mask, but turned on a side, suggests reflected images of a Madonna and child. (Knowing of my goddess collection, Kurt recommended hanging it sideways.)

In November he visited Lexington, Kentucky, partly to sign screen prints at Joe's studio, but also to help his old G.E. pal, Ollie Lyon, a board member for nearby Midway College. Bob Weide joined them to film a long documentary interview with Kurt as he signed prints and discussed how the creative aspect of painting was a relief from his long struggle to get *Timequake* right. Bob also filmed conversations between Kurt and Ollie about their jobs at General Electric following World War II. Especially impressive was their pride about the useful products GE created and how that pride soured as computerized automation came to replace human labor. In that interview, Kurt revealed his inspiration for his first novel, *Player Piano*, came from witnessing computer punch cards replace men at G.E.'s tooling machines.

As 1994 arrived, I heard less often from Kurt. Although that sometimes happened, it especially concerned me then because of his solitary life during the dreariness of winter in Sagaponack. But fortunately, by spring Weide continued his documentary work, this time filming Kurt's visit to his childhood haunts in Indianapolis. These included the splendid Illinois Street brick home his father had designed and built, where Kurt and his brother and sister grew up. Here he recalled his German family's immigration to Indiana prior to the Civil War to escape German militarism. Included was footage of the 1940s' home where the Vonneguts moved after the Depression forced them into more modest housing.

A cheerful account of the Indiana visit came from Kurt's daughter, Nanny, who had accompanied them, including their drive to Culver and the family summer cottage in a sizeable ancestral compound on Lake Maxinkuckee. There Kurt recorded wonderful reminiscences about his extended family he so loved as a kid.

In June, the twenty-fifth anniversary edition of *Slaughterhouse-Five* arrived unexpectedly in the mail on my birthday, and I was moved by the inscription: "For dear Loree, whose influence over the mood of this book was at least as significant as that of Mary O'Hare" (5/19/94). Nearly thirty years had passed since Kurt and I had met in Iowa City.

My thank-you was dated June 27, 1994:

Dearest Kurt,

Guess what came floating in today? Your twenty-fifth anniversary edition of *Slaughterhouse-Five*! ... Gosh we were excited about that book twenty-five years ago.... And we still are. Congratulations, dear....

Thirty years ago next month I arrived in Iowa City and moved with my two small children into an apartment that cost twice as much as I had ever paid before. I was scared to death, not only because I had no income—but because I secretly wondered if maybe my parents were right about my being foolhardy and irresponsible in wanting to be a writer. Well, look what happens when you pretend otherwise. A year later I found myself in your workshop class.

It was all worth it. Thank you.

Meanwhile, I was readying myself for another venture into the unknown later that summer—a trip to Greece where I would join five other women chartering a bareboat for an all-female sailing cruise in the Cyclades Islands. I'd agreed to contribute my knowledge of the Cycladic and Greek mythic sites as a supplement to my meager sailing skills. I returned unscathed and enthusiastic, eager to report on the venture to Kurt, a far more seasoned sailor than I. My account included our successful effort to escape disaster after running aground off the coast of Mikonos. He replied with a funny story:

October 29, 1994

Dearest Loree—

It is so natural for me to feel close to you that I feel that I too have been to the Greek Islands and back, having taken the helm from time to time. About taking the helm under seemingly serene conditions: A neighbor of mine on the Cape was once the youngest skipper in the Merchant Marine, and one day he was serenely following a ship in the distance. The only trouble with that was that there was a great big shoal between him and it.

As for how I am: I'm OK, although not wanting to write much anymore, and comforted by the knowledge that Brahms got sick of composing by the time he was 54. He wrote one short piece for a remarkable clarinetist after that. I worry about my kids, and I remember what a clerk in a curio store said when I asked if some sacred object from an alien religion might bring bad luck to me. She said, "That will depend on how many hostages you've given to Fate."

I hate the idea of the Information Superhighway, which will almost certainly turn out to be a narrow thoroughfare with lots of cops and tollgates. I attended a symposium about its prospects a few days ago, with nothing but good people taking part, but all vested interests. One man, an old friend, as it happened, and in charge of planning Time-Warner's participation in the Highway, said with some shrewd sadness, "We have to say it is going to be good because it is in any case inevitable."

Love as always,

K

It wasn't only the Internet he was dreading; it was the approaching fiftieth anniversary of the end of World War II and inevitable requests to help commemorate it. Kurt shared his polite but negative response to a technology magazine editor, which concluded

> World War Two was nothing but a second all-out effort by Western civilization to commit suicide by the most efficient means its universities and research organizations could provide at the time. Here is a Top Secret for you: Western Civilization finds being alive embarrassing.

His letter (2/6/95) to me concluded just as grimly: "A raccoon with a lump of sugar washes and washes it until it disappears. The same thing keeps happening to my novel *Timequake*, which has to do with the disappearance of the America I tried to write for."

He had turned down all requests for appearances observing the war's end that spring, except one: he spoke at the Rochester Arts and Lectures Distinguished Author Series in Rochester, New York, on May 4, to a sold-out crowd at the downtown United Presbyterian Church. The special reason for his appearance was clarified in a front page story from the "Inside" section of the May 3, Rochester, New York, *Democrat and Chronicle*. He had come to honor a fallen comrade from the war, Private Edward Reginald "Joe" Crone who, he made public for the first time, was the inspiration for his character Billy Pilgrim in *Slaughterhouse-Five*. He sent me the paper on May 12, with a short letter:

> Dear Loree—
>
> I sure do miss you. Mark was 48 years old yesterday! . . . I send you stuff from the yard sale at the end of my career. It is ending much like *A Handful of Dust*. Instead of reading aloud from Dickens I devote my full attention and treasure to a twelve-year-old. She is awfully nice, and extra-bright in unusual ways, so, thank goodness, she is clearly worthwhile. I never had a kid who was a dud, and neither did you. Having a dud kid must be horrible.

I am in the process of gathering my papers from all over the place, and hope to sell them to a library, ideally the Lilly Library at Indiana University. I wish now I'd been more of a packrat. I never thought I'd amount to a hill of beans.

I visited Joe Crone's grave in Rochester. I spoke affectionately to his tombstone, and that finally closed out World War Two for me.

Love as always,

K

The poignant newspaper account of Private Crone's life and death was compiled by staff writer John Reinan from testimony by locals, along with a phone interview with Kurt and excerpts from *Slaughter-house-Five*, for a particularly moving story. The few who remembered young Crone described him as a shy and gangly kid, the son of a wealthy businessman and protective mother. An engineering student at Hobart College when the war began in 1941, he enlisted in the spring of 1943, and was sent to advanced engineering school at the University of Alabama. Crone had just turned twenty-one in 1944 when he arrived in Europe as an infantryman for the final push of the war. That's how he ended up being captured two months later along with Private First Class Kurt Vonnegut, in the Battle of the Bulge.

Kurt's Rochester appearance was a serious thing to do. When I visited the Lilly Library at Indiana University a decade later to study Kurt's archived papers, I noticed that early versions of a first chapter suggest different takes on the P.O.W. narrator, who eventually becomes the protagonist Billy Pilgrim. In one version Billy visits the mother of a deceased buddy, apparently derivative of Private Crone. In one account this buddy is shot at the stake, in another shot by a firing squad, and in another he dies of starvation.

In another folder, written the year I met him in Iowa City, the book is titled *A Comedy of Manners*. And getting closer to the final version is folder number 24 in the tenth box of the archived material, with a significantly changed (and final) dedication, this time "for

Mary O'Hare and Gerhard Muller" with a statement that adds "What made Billy [so happy] was his belief he was going to comfort so many people with the truth about time."

This time statement is significant. Many have pondered Kurt's sense of narrative, since he made such a point that "Billy Pilgrim has come unstuck in time" in *Slaughterhouse*. As recently as May 30, 2006, in a public radio broadcast of the BBC World Book Club, Harriet Gilbert of the BBC World Service and Leonard Lopate of WNYC interviewed Kurt with a live audience, with others calling in from around the world. When someone asked whether Billy Pilgrim was really time traveling, Kurt's reply was: "That was really me, too, getting relief from a really black story—and to give the reader a break." Nonetheless, when one questioner brought up the related question of free will, it triggered an unusual response. Speaking of his actual war experience, Kurt replied, "I think my life had to be pre-ordained. We count on time as if we know what it is. We don't! I can remember leaning up against a tree, and I think I knew everything that was going to happen."

I had never before heard him make such a statement.

As for Billy Pilgrim's premise that people never die, one questioner asked Kurt how he felt about the fact that many readers feel his novel has given them a great sense of hope and comfort. He answered charmingly: "How lucky I am!"

Kurt scored another bit of luck in 1995. He appeared in the June 26 issue of the *New Yorker* magazine for the first time ever with previous omission a considerable sore point with him for years. However, this inclusion wasn't for fiction, but rather, a reproduction of the picture he had created as an Absolut Vodka ad! (He told me he and Lily had been particularly fond of those ads. After collecting them for months, Kurt playfully had done his own version and, to his delight, had sold it.) His picture was of a curly headed Vonnegut-like cartoon figure whose large hands played the string game, "Cat's Cradle." The image of an Absolut Vodka bottle sat on a table in the foreground. Its caption, in large, bold type at the bottom of the full-page ad read: "ABSOLUT VONNEGUT."

About this momentous coup, Kurt observed in a June 28 letter to me:

My Absolut Vodka ad was in the special fiction double issue of the *New Yorker*, June 26. I didn't know that was going to happen. I have never before appeared in the *New Yorker*, and was not invited to submit anything for that issue. But, by God, the boldest, biggest typeface in it says Absolut Vonnegut! Remember me?

The other coup for that year was the final shooting of the Weide film adaptation of *Mother Night*, which had been taking place in Montreal. Kurt continued to think Bob's enthusiasm was overly optimistic and had seemed strangely uninvolved (even though he had a great cameo scene toward the film's end).

In a November letter, Kurt enclosed an October 23 fax from Weide reporting on the film's progress and inviting him to the November 9 wrap party. He replied: "I will not be at the wrap party, where I would be a ghost among the living. I have had no part in the Montreal adventure."

His year's end correspondence was a full-page clipping from "The Glass Onion" supplement of the University of Washington newspaper, the *Daily*, headlined: "*A Post-modern Pierrot Kurt Vonnegut arrives at the UW.*" It was a review of Kurt's opus as part of a notice of his lecture appearance that night (Nov. 30) at the university. It was the first time I'd heard him associated with Pierrot, the nineteenth-century French pantomime, Jean Gaspard Deburau, a charming clown whose ever hopeful, always disappointed essence as a lover was portrayed with delicate pathos. Scrawled across the bottom half of the paper in red Sharpie ink was "Merry Christmas" with his characteristic signature.

The year 1995 had not been a cheerful one for Kurt. Nonetheless, it seemed apparent he was spending more time in the City, and gradually finding ways to re-accommodate his marriage and more time with his daughter. I was a mom and a grandparent, too, and I knew how he felt.

Early in 1996, I asked Kurt for Andre Dubus' phone number and received an update on Andre as well: Kurt had just written a blurb for Andre's new book, *Dancing after Hours*, which would be out later that year. His observations were more grim than usual: "He is famous because of his disability, which may give him wryly awful satisfaction. Jesus! So many real life stories have such muggy endings." He went on to add his concern about how fellow fictionist William Gaddis, like Andre, had "wound up high and dry now that his MacArthur has stopped."

Kurt was not hurting financially, but the question of money still was one he spoke of frequently—in his speeches and books as well as in concerns for fellow artists and writers. Early on he'd acknowledged effects of the Depression on his parents, and how that had influenced his writing and political concerns. I think he was always a bit incredulous, if grateful, that he'd been able to make a substantial living as a writer.

In a letter written February 20, he clearly was not in a cheery mood about anything, especially the recent poor sales of his and Joe Petro's silkscreen art endeavor: "The print business turns out to be no business at all, and I am feeling waterlogged by the enterprise." Although they'd been producing many new prints, he said, "I am still trying to recover the cost of framing the old ones." Despite their café exhibition then hanging in the huge Barnes and Noble store near his Manhattan home, the bookstore did not sell pictures as expensive as his, so his buyers had to visit the nearby Phyllis Lucas Print Center for purchases. Few were making the short trip to do so. "Most people don't understand why silk screens have to be so much more expensive than posters run off on a printing press."

He was also pessimistic about Weide's *Mother Night* film, a rough-cut of which he'd just received. "It is faithful to the book, which means it will never be a big hit. It is what it is." Kurt was right that it wasn't a big hit, but I daresay most viewers, despite its limited release, liked it immensely—perhaps because it *was* so faithful to the book.

Meanwhile, I was closing down my career at the University of Northern Iowa. I hadn't anticipated the difficulty of saying goodbye to colleagues, which became painfully clear at a gala retirement party held at the home of my longtime friend, Scott Cawelti and his wife. I'd known him since his student days and now, as a full professor, he was a specialist in literature and film. He was eagerly awaiting the film premiere of *Mother Night*, which he planned to teach in conjunction with the novel.

It was a great party. Among presentations was the gift of a colorful new Vonnegut artwork Kurt had sent, representing a wide-eyed figure gazing at a "star." Under the image, he had written: "Abstraction of a person made idealistic by the interdisciplinary lessons of the great teacher Loree Rackstraw at the University of Northern Iowa, presented at her retirement party May 10, 1996." He also had written a moving two-page letter, which had been framed, and was read aloud by my daughter Leslie who, along with my son Rob, had secretly traveled here for this event.

* * *

Kurt was at that time in Indianapolis presenting a graduation speech at Butler University, a delightful one, but which I learned about only in late August, after returning from a holiday trip with my friend Solveiga on Cape Cod.

This outing had given me an excuse to visit Kurt's two Massachusetts daughters, Edie and Nanny. Edie's husband, John Squibb, had transformed the barn on the old Vonnegut family property into a home for his and Edie's two young sons—Will, who at the time was ten, and Buck, seven. The beach cove nearby provided great summer recreation and must have been delightfully reminiscent of her growing-up years. A bonus was a spacious studio John had recently added, where I found Edie when we arrived. She was preparing for a large show in Boston, "Heroic Women"—magnificently whimsical nudes, most of them images of mothers protecting infants from hazards like a blazing sun or sharks at a beach. Some were later collected in a publication titled *Domestic Goddesses* and published by Pomegranate Communications in 1998.

She showed me antique frames she'd gathered from rummage sales, explaining how she created canvasses to fit them, saving an otherwise huge expense. Clearly, this was a trick her dad hadn't learned! After admiring the pet mouse Willy and Buck had recently domesticated, we made sandwiches for a picnic lunch at the yacht club to watch the boys perform spectacular dives off the pier. I loved seeing her, and I enjoyed the antics of her happy sons and their pals.

We drove on to Nanny's home in Northampton that afternoon, my first visit to that community and home of Smith College. Nanny, a tall and slender woman favoring both her parents, welcomed us for a stay of several days. As a painter, she delighted in satire and cartoon-like settings. It was the first time I'd met her husband Scott Prior, another painter. Nanny had recently sent a catalog from one of his exhibitions—oils of lush realism, what one critic called "beyond realism." Not surprisingly, their home was filled with art and artifacts throughout, along with treasures of their children Max, Ezra, and four-year-old Nellie, with whom I immediately fell in love. (She bore a remarkable resemblance to her grandmother, Jane.)

Our visit included a trip to the Berkshires and the home in an extensive wooded area of one of Kurt's Adams nephews, for the annual family potluck and variety show called "Slab Knob." All three nephews and their families were present for this celebration, as was Kurt's beloved brother Bernard and one of his sons, along with a hundred or so other friends and acquaintances.

It was an unexpected treat to meet Bernard, a wizened figure of a man then suffering from lung cancer. Bernard clearly wanted to talk about his brother. He was carrying a letter Kurt had written to friends who'd attended an operatic adaptation of *Slaughterhouse-Five* in Munich earlier that summer. He insisted I read Kurt's appreciative letter in response to their extended critique of the Munich performance, which they obviously considered to have been quite unsatisfactory (and also performed without permission from Kurt). After reading their review, I suggested he or they might consider submitting it to a journal like *Opera News*. Bernard grinned proudly, especially when I recounted some of the warm big-brother stories Kurt had told me about him. Kurt's celebration of Bernard's prestigious rain cloud achievement was well known, but less so was his single parenting of several sons. Their mutual admiration was evident, and I well understood why Kurt loved him so.

Altogether, the "Slab Knob" variety show was the day's culminating experience, one that likely reflected the general character and camaraderie of the growing-up years of the Vonnegut family in Barnstable. But first, young families took turns cooking at a grill on a rock ledge and sat at picnic tables or blankets to devour shared food. Kids squealed in joyful terror on a tall slide attached to a boulder and scrambled gleefully about on an enticing tree house structure. It was a kids' forest enchantment. The festive informality reached full peak around dusk with the variety show performance on an elevated stage at one end of the lawn, complete with bed sheet curtains. What's more, the curtains were suspended by wires attached to sturdy posts with stage lights. This was no middling production about to unfold!

I'd observed Nanny and Edie's boys rehearsing their all-cousin skit in Nanny's yard before we left. Obviously, they were seasoned and eager troupers. Blankets were spread out and chairs lined up for the show. As it grew darker, colorful luminescent wands were passed around to add to the children's enthusiasm. As acts progressed, it was evident that the final clowning performances by the three Adams brothers, who had lived with Kurt and Jane, were the *piece de resistance* the kids had been waiting for, a family in love with ham acting. The Vonnegut drama genes definitely had been passed on.

The next day Edie and Nanny and I had a lunch date alone. It was the only time the three of us had had a private time together since their mother died. It gave me a chance to share my view of how painful her death had been, to me, and especially to their dad. I was sure Jane had shared with them the mutual respect she and Kurt had exchanged in her last days. But I summarized his early concerns, plus the bereaved letter he'd written to me the night of her death, a letter

I later copied and sent to them. As a parent, I felt it was important they knew about his continuing sense of loss.

It was on our lunch date that I shared memories of Iowa City and discovered Edie and Nanny had not known I'd believed Jane and Kurt to be estranged those many years before when I was Kurt's student and he and Edie were living alone. To this day, I don't know why the family hadn't all arrived together that fall of 1965. Nor had I ever asked Kurt why he'd been negligent about informing me only a day before Jane and Nanny's arrival in Iowa City that spring. I suppose I probably just didn't want to face the possibility back then that he had been having a fling—before our relationship got way more involved than either of us had intended.

We talked some about my gratitude to Jane for her generous invitation to visit in Barnstable before she became ill and how appreciative I was that she had made it possible for us to reconcile our friendship.

Back in Iowa, I wrote Kurt a long letter summarizing my visit with his daughters and meeting his dear brother, as well as my own daughter's struggles with her new divorcee status. He wrote back (October 1), sympathizing with Leslie and "the harrowing plight of single mothers without extended families. Mission impossible."

Kurt had just returned to Sagaponack from Chicago and the Steppenwolf Theatre premiere of *Slaughterhouse-Five* adapted for the stage. He said, "Peter Reed came down to see it. It makes sense only to people who know the book, and can't make it to New York or into the Samuel French catalog because the set is too complicated and the cast too big." He closed by noting that "[Weide's] *Mother Night* premieres in New York City on October 21, as a fund-raiser for P.E.N. Weide and Nolte and I will be there."

It was clear from the terseness of this letter that Kurt was not exactly chipper, but he provided little clue as to the reason. I figured it probably had to do with either his personal life or the bog that *Timequake* had become. Or both. I did talk with him after the P.E.N. fund-raising premiere of *Mother Night* and decided I was right about "both," plus he hadn't been thrilled with the reception of Weide's film. I'd come not to trust his discernment when he was in a dark mood and felt justified in that when I finally saw the minimally distributed film several months later. Peter Reed and I saw it together in Minneapolis, and we both thought it excellent.

Kurt called in December to be sure I knew about the death of his old Workshop colleague José Donoso in Chile. Kurt had kept tabs on him, in part because his critical views of the rightist Chilean President Augusto Pinochet had put him at some risk over the years, but also because of Kurt's ongoing friendship with María Pilar, José's wife. His somewhat grim mood at that time was echoed by the Christmas greeting he sent: another photocopy of that letter he'd written to his Indianapolis family from France, after his 1945 P.O.W. release from Dresden. It was signed, "Seasons Greetings 1996."

In January (1997), however, he wrote in lighter spirits from his Manhattan home that "Donoso got an utterly respectful obit in the *New York Times*." He said he had called María Pilar after his death and learned from her that Donoso had lived "seven years longer than his doctors thought he could," adding, "Curiously, as close as we were, he never gave an indication that he had read a word by me. To a Jamesian like him, I think, I appeared to be writing in the fourth dimension."

Kurt left to the end of his letter the following brief message: "Turns out I will have one more book. I am still revising. It should be and will be ready for press by March." He also included, without comment, the notice of an exhibition of his artwork in two galleries, the first in Paterson, New Jersey, and the second in Stamford, Connecticut. Things were looking up in his screen print collaboration with Joe.

A few days later, a package arrived in the mail: a photocopied manuscript of *Timequake*! I dropped everything to read it. And loved it. He said he'd sent copies to a number of other literary friends, noting that because his publisher had not been positive about the work, he was asking for feedback, something he'd never done before, so far as I knew. I fired off a letter of congratulations and then reread the manuscript, making careful notes. Included in my second statement was the following:

> *Timequake* is not only a sermon about generosity and humility desperately needed by persons facing the next millennium, it is a brilliant and inventive and hilariously seductive commentary about the nature of the literary arts and the paradox of language and human intelligence. It provides a model of how humanity might respond creatively and nobly to the terrors of ubiquitous violence and greed.

And in case he showed my response to his editor, I added

> (And if this novel is being taught in an academic setting, the professor will require students to purchase previously published novels by the same author, so as to puzzle out for themselves what might be going on here. Hey presto! More books sold!) It even celebrates family values, so Republicans won't be afraid to read it!

He wrote back, on February 6, enclosing the January 30 fax his editor had sent him, at the top of which was a note he'd penned to his agent: "A HEARTBREAKER. . . . PLEASE CALL." Essentially, what the editor had said seemed, to me, not only condescending, but appeared to have misread the material, suggesting it was not really fiction, but rather just "simply" telling the reader about what he'd tried to do in writing this book. I found it puzzling, partly because she had worked with him through a number of other books, but also because she seemed to have missed the irony of *re*-writing a book about a book about the illusion of free will.

A heartbreaker indeed. *Timequake* had been scheduled for publication several years back, but he had looked hard at it and insisted it be withdrawn. And once again, he started all over. Now he was understandably incensed with this response to his seasoned life work. (The few other readers to whom he had sent the manuscript all had similar enthusiastic response.) In the long run, it didn't matter. Kurt told me his agent had immediately notified Putnam they could find another publisher, and "Putnam . . . promised to publish it as submitted. The event was a lot like the moose poop story in the book." He added that it would be out in hardcover on September 22 of that year (1997), saying, "With *Timequake* finished, I feel as though I've been fired from a job I needed but didn't like very much. I sure don't want to start another book. What next? Nothing" (2/6/97).

Of course what followed was hardly "nothing."

He maintained his speech-giving schedule and occasional essay commentaries, to say nothing of his artistic enterprise with Joe. Never mind that he was the seventy-five-year-old father of a thirteen-year-old. Nor did he ever cease his proactive support for fellow writers and other contributors to the American cultural scene. In that same letter, for example, he expressed his concern for Hualing Nieh Engle, Paul Engle's aging widow in Iowa City, who was trying to put a book together to honor her late husband. Kurt felt it was

> exasperating that the University sees no reason to celebrate this man, who did more than anyone I can think of to make it world famous. At least he is immortalized in the archives of the American Academy of Arts and Letters. When he won that honor [the membership for which Kurt had nominated him], he commented that he was the first person living west of the Mississippi to receive it.

I found it touching he would think of Paul at this time, and significant that he mentioned the American Academy of Arts and Letters, which plays a distinctive role in *Timequake*.

Kurt's *Timequake* editor not only relented but, he said, within a month assured Kurt she found it gratifying that everyone was "falling in love" with the manuscript as it made its way around the Putnam house. She likely was even more gratified when the celebratory reviews began coming in the following fall.

But first, Kurt would need to cope with the death in late April of his beloved brother, Bernard. It was characteristic of him to celebrate his brother by sending, on April 13, a multiple mailing to friends that retold the practical joke he and Bernard had attempted to play on their rather proper Uncle Alex fifty years earlier. At the time, both brothers were employed by General Electric in Schenectady—Bernard as a celebrated research physicist and Kurt as a publicist. In this mailing he explained he had just returned from his weekly visit with his dying brother in an Albany hospice, where Bernard had given him the original of a fake letter Kurt had written in 1947 to fool their Uncle Alex, shortly after Kurt had joined the G.E. News Bureau. (See letter on facing page.)

It was only two weeks later that Bernard died of lung cancer. Kurt sent me his obituary from the April 27 *New York Times* and later, his own lengthy tribute to his brother that appeared in a December 1997 *New York Times Magazine* under the title "Lives Well Led." Kurt would say many times that year, he "no longer had anybody to show off for anymore."

At the end of May, he wrote a somewhat nostalgic letter from "out in the country alone," to report he had just witnessed the "sensational success onstage" of his darling daughter Lily performing as an "Ethel Merman–style singing comedienne" at her boarding school, and added that his son Mark had turned fifty that month, and "I gave him a soprano saxophone."

He also celebrated the achievements of fellow writers, as in a moving statement honoring Allen Ginsberg he had faxed for presentation at a Los Angeles tribute following Ginsberg's death in May. In it, he recalled how both he and Ginsberg had been installed into the American Institute of Arts and Letters in 1973. When asked by a reporter what he thought about "'two such outsiders being absorbed by the establishment, he had replied, 'If we aren't the establishment, I don't know who is'" (5/31/97).

Kurt was often called upon to honor fellow writers but was increasingly saddened, as he aged, by the fact that so many of them

GENERAL ⊛ ELECTRIC
COMPANY
GENERAL OFFICE SCHENECTADY, N. Y.

1 River Road
Schenectady 5, N. Y.

November 28, 1947

Mr. Alex Vonnegut
701 Guaranty Building
Indianapolis 4, Indiana

Dear Mr. Vonnegut,

Mr. Edward Themak, city editor for the SCHENECTADY
GAZETTE, has referred your letter of November 26th to me.

The photograph of General Electric's Dr. Bernard Vonnegut originated from our office. However, we have no more
prints in our files, and the negative is in the hands of
the United States Signal Corps. Moreover, we have a lot
more to do than piddle with penny-ante requests like yours.

We do have some other photographs of the poor man's
Steinmetz, and I may send them to you in my own sweet time.
But do not rush me. "Wee bit proud," indeed! Ha! Vonnegut!
Ha! This office made your nephew, and we can break him in a
minute -- like a egg shell. So don't get in an uproar if you
don't get the pictures in a week or two.

Also -- one dollar to the General Electric Company is
as the proverbial fart in a wind storm. Here it is back.
Don't blow it all in one place.

Very truly yours,

Press Section
GENERAL NEWS BUREAU

Guy Fawkes:bc

had predeceased him. One of his most painful experiences was putting dead friends "to bed," as he phrased it, something he had never expected nor wished to do.

In July, another Sagaponack letter arrived from Kurt, reporting his return from a month-long celebrity cruise in the Mediterranean aboard the QE II with both Jill and Lily. Now Lily was enrolled in an immersion language camp in Spain, near Barcelona, a city in which he said he had "often thought of Pepe [Donoso] who lived there in exile for several years." On a more cheerful note, he could report that "*Timequake* is now going out to reviewers as uncorrected bound galleys. I will see that you get one. The publication date is September 22."

I think it's fair to say that although many reviewers were moved by his announcement that this was his last book, the end of his writing career was not the only thing that prompted their widespread praise. *Timequake*'s premise that "a sudden glitch in time" in the year 2001 had caused everyone in the world to repeat the previous decade became a well-appreciated allegory whose complexity sparked largely positive responses. In Canada's *Globe and Mail*, Jim Bartley recognized the book's warning that "humanity is blindly coasting on capitalistic autopilot," while John Barron of the Chicago *Sun-Times* wrote that it demonstrated the robotizing effects of TV, computer technologies, meaningless work, and just plain human carelessness. I especially liked *Newsday* jazz critic Gene Seymour's celebration of Kurt's style of repeating phrases such as "hey-ho" or "So it goes" as jazz-like riffs that function as "a background to the lead melody."

Although the *New Yorker* had never published any Vonnegut fiction, James Atlas opened its "Talk of the Town" commentary on October 6 with an account of Kurt's book-launching appearance at the Barnes and Noble flagship store:

> By six o'clock, the place was full; hundreds of disappointed fans, some of whom had traveled from other states, were being turned

away. According to Dennis Wurst, a Barnes & Noble coordinator for national events, it was "the biggest such event Barnes & Noble ever had anywhere for a writer."

Reached later by phone in South Carolina where he was giving a lecture, Kurt was not regretful about this being his last book and was quoted by Atlas as saying, "I can look back on my life's work. I'm completely in print. I don't see it [*Timequake*] as a freestanding novel, but as the last chapter in one long book." Atlas concluded, "He signed off with a terse, Kilgore Trout-like benediction: 'Go with God.' And he meant it" (p. 43).

Jerry Klinkowitz adroitly described it as "the autobiography of a novel," the story of a celestial calamity described by Kurt's oft-used doppelganger, Kilgore Trout, as "a cosmic charley horse in the sinews of Destiny."

That the celestial calamity ended on February 13, 2001, may well have been intended as a gentle reminder of that same date in 1945, when the World War Two Allied fire-bombing of Dresden began. In fact, I'm now convinced that he really *did* believe humanity's potential was limited by "a charley horse" he bluntly called laziness. He would give his fictional and real friends a celebratory clambake party at the end of this book, but he really did not have much hope for humanity's ever transcending that charley horse.

He may have offered some solace, however. He has his dear Kilgore Trout writing endless little stories during the fictional timequake and then systematically tearing each one up and tossing it into a waste can in front of the American Academy of Arts and Letters. It was about then Kurt began to tell his audiences: "When you return home, sit down and write a poem or story; then tear it up without showing it to anyone—just to enjoy the harmless pleasure of doing something creative." By 1997, he was concluding with this admonition in all his public speeches.

He even gave advice about the value of "farting around" to teenagers. The previous May, for example, Kurt had addressed the ninth grade graduating class of his grandson Max. Aside from the fact that they loved the anal humor, the kids' written appraisals obviously showed they were delighted and moved by his words.

With *Timequake* behind him, early in 1998, Kurt wrote that he'd been making trips around New England with his talented fifteen-year-old daughter ("an Ethel Merman who is hopeless at math"), interviewing for her next boarding school. He also was, at the time, mourning the untimely death of his forty-eight-year-old nephew, whom he was "nuts about." Terry Vonnegut, his late brother's "sweet son," had just died "in the same hospice where Bernie died of the same disease, cancer, ten months ago." He added, "As I've said elsewhere *ad nauseum*, one trouble with living longer than F. Scott Fitzgerald is seeing some of the bad things which happen to younger loved ones" (2/4/98).

He was also involved that month in recording a series of whimsical ninety-second interviews for WNYC's public radio station in New York City, posing as a reporter just outside a fictionalized "state-of-the-art lethal injection execution facility in Huntsville, Texas." Perhaps only Kurt Vonnegut could have dreamed up such a ploy to satirize the death penalty enthusiasm of George W. Bush, then the governor of Texas. It was also a way to applaud the efforts of Dr. Jack Kevorkian in assisting terminally ill patients with humane suicides. (Kevorkian was by then in prison for this offense.) In Kurt's contrived radio interviews, he purported to have been given a controlled near-death capability by Dr. Kevorkian, so he could interview famous heroes such as Eugene Debs or William Shakespeare. The setting for these interviews was the "vacant lot between the far end of the blue tunnel [to the afterlife] and the Pearly Gates."

On February 9, Kurt sent a copy of "the last of twelve reports on the afterlife" he had recorded for WNYC. This was his fictional conversation with "Karla Faye Tucker, the born-again murderer of two strangers with a pick-axe" following her actual execution February 6. (Governor Bush had repeatedly denied her pardon after several years of highly publicized appeals, including one on CNN's *Larry King Live* and another by the well known Catholic nun, Sister Helen Prejean, author of *Dead Man Walking*.)

Kurt's edited radio reports, with some others, made a collection of twenty-one, which were published in 1999 by Seven Stories Press under the title *God Bless You, Dr. Kevorkian*, the same year Kevorkian was found guilty of second-degree murder. Kurt said the book was "to be given as a bonus to heavy donors to WNYC." (In January 2000, he sent a copy of the letter of gratitude he'd received that month from Dr. Kevorkian, inmate No. 284797 in Lakeland Correctional Facility in Coldwater, Michigan.)

By April Kurt had moved from the city, back to "the country," where he expected to host visits from most of his grandchildren during the summer. He seemed a bit wistful when he wrote that he'd been in touch with his dear friend Vance Bourjaily who was also retiring. On the other hand, he was pleased that some of his former students like John Casey and John Irving were raking in National Book Awards. In a phone call, he mentioned somewhat offhandedly that he would be the "graduation speaker at Rice University on May 9." Since that would kick off a month or two jammed with his professional and personal appearances, I teased him a bit about his life of "retirement." Later, he forwarded copies of personal letters he'd received from President George H. W. Bush and his wife Barbara, celebrating his Rice speech and its positive effect on the Bush sons and grandchildren. (I could imagine his ironic grin as he posted those copies.)

Later that May he was in Chicago for a new performance of Stravinsky's "The Soldier's Tale," using Kurt's text based on the story of Eddie Slovik. It was performed by a young ensemble called Orchestra X at the Steppenwolf Theatre.

Kurt also experienced the loss that month of two valued friendships dating back to his World War II days: Tom Jones, "a close *Slaughterhouse-5* buddy," and Mary O'Hare, to whom *Slaughterhouse* had been dedicated.

Apparently lacking a typewriter, Kurt printed in longhand his letter about these deaths on yellow, lined tablet paper:

DEAREST LOREE —

WELCOME HOME, WHENEVER THAT'S GOING TO BE. IT'S JUNE 2ND HERE, AND THE GARDEN, 20 YEARS IN THE MAKING, IS (TO ME) A SPECTACULAR SUCCESS. THIS HOUSE APPEARS ON A MAP IN 1740, A FULL CENTURY BEFORE MY FIRST ANCESTOR BECAME WHAT THE BRITS CALL "A YANK."

OTHER DATES IN HISTORY: MAY 4TH, 1998, TOM JONES, A CLOSE SLAUGHTER-HOUSE-5 BUDDY, DIED OF CANCER, AGE 73. MAY 2?, I SAW TOM BURIED WITH FULL MILITARY HONORS, SIX SOLDIERS IN ARMY DRESS BLUES FIRING BLANK CARTRIDGES, AND "TAPS," AT ARLINGTON. BETWEEN TWENTY AND THIRTY WAR HEROES ARE BURIED THERE EVERY DAY.

ON MAY 28TH I DECIDED MARY O'HARE SHOULD HEAR ABOUT TOM'S GLAMOROUS FUNERAL. HER PHONE RANG AND RANG. NOBODY HOME. MAY 29TH: HER DAUGHTER CALLED TO SAY MARY HAD DIED THE PREVIOUS EVENING. FIND ENCLOSED A FAX FROM WEIDE.

LOVE —— K

This must have closed a very significant door on Kurt's *Slaughter-house-Five* experience, and I was sorry I hadn't been there to talk with him about it.

Because I returned in late June from an extended visit in Turkey, I also had to miss the California wedding of our mutual friend, Bob Weide to Linda Bates, as did Kurt. He said he had, however, written them to say he "hoped the wedding night went about as well as could be expected." By then Bob had completed work on his documentary, *Lenny Bruce: Swear To Tell the Truth*, which would receive an Academy Award nomination for best feature documentary, and later an Emmy.

Kurt had been enjoying summer visits from his kids but had also written several magazine pieces, including a feature on the year 2000 for *Playboy*. The latter would appear as "Last Words for a Century" in the January 1999 issue, and he capitalized on a favorite family memory of his father's silly exuberance during the Depression, when their Studebaker's odometer at a 999,999.9 was about to turn and wipe out all those nines! He included his late brother's slyly off-scale story about a Native American tribe called the "Fuh-kar-wee," a culture "driven off their ancestral lands by pioneers, peace treaties, and the United States Cavalry." As the tribe's chief was dying, he had mournfully cried out "Where the fuh-kar-wee?" In Kurt's view, this was an appropriate question for the end of 1999.

The approaching end of the century also finalized his Dresden experience when he made his last trip there in October to speak. He wrote that he had gone "down again into the cellar where O'Hare and the rest of us survived. Only then did I realize that we had seen an Atlantis—before it sank forever beneath the waves." Following his seventy-sixth birthday, he wrote to celebrate the achievements of his seven children, including son Mark's forthcoming new marriage to "an ideal mate for him." His letter concluded

> When I was in Dresden, I lectured to a crowd of Dresdeners, and I had this thought: "I have seen Dresden, and you have not."
> Love as always—

Box 27 Sagaponack NY 11962 August 29 2002

Dearest Student --

Tiger gotta hunt, bird gotta fly,
Loree gotta sit and wonder why, why, why?
Tiger gotta sleep, bird gotta land,
Loree gotta tell herself she understand.

I read your essay for the Supper Club at once. What a respectable detective you are, indefatigably collecting clues at the scene of the crime, which is to say our planet.

As a psychology major you surely know that those you will be addressing, being old academics, have been teaching the same old tried and true stories in their fields for decades by now, and so are apt to feel insulted if anyone tells them, as you are about to do, that it is time they learned a new one. But do it anyway. A few will sparkle in response, and fall in love with you, and want to know more.

Louis Pasteur earned the hatred of the medical profession of his time with his germ theory of diseases.   My brother Bernie had the same experience with the United States Weather Bureau when he told them the truth about what made it snow and rain, and what thunder and lightning were all about. They said in effect, "Get out of here!"

I will read the books you have recommended.

Love as always --

10

Northampton Transfer, 1999–2000

Bagombo Snuff Box

About the time of Kurt's seventy-sixth birthday in November of 1998, he told me he was taking time out to write an introduction to a "new book." Actually, it was a new collection compiled by Peter Reed of some of Kurt's old short stories published years ago in magazines like *Colliers* and *Saturday Evening Post*. Titled *Bagombo Snuff Box*, some narratives drew on his war experiences while others questioned benefits of 1950s' science and technology. Peter observes in the preface that some "demonstrate that burdensome expectations that can be placed on women in a man's world" (p. xvi). He adds, "It seemed obvious that these scattered tales deserved a proper home of their own, just as those [collected] in . . . *Welcome to the Monkey House*" (p. xviii).

Kurt's introduction expressed gratitude to Peter, but Kurt was less kind about the stories themselves. When the book came out the following spring, he inscribed page proofs to me as "the worst of my worst"—and later wrote that in reading the stories he had "wanted to fix every one of them. . . . They are to be presented as charming antiques" (3/4/99).

It had been earlier in February that he'd called with the sad news that our dear friend Andre Dubus had died (2/24/99), apparently of a heart attack. I regretted it had been nearly two years since I'd last spoken with Andre—a call to congratulate him for his wonderful new short story collection I'd just read, *Dancing after Hours*, published in 1996. At the time he'd been struggling out of depression, and that book was proof of how horrendous pain had honed his already fine writing. Andre's personal generosity and the deep ethical power and compassion of his work had touched many including his writing students.

When Kurt phoned about Andre, he also anguished about growing warfare in the Yugoslavian provinces of Croatia and Bosnia and violent rebellion escalating in Kosovo. In March, NATO began launching the form of warfare Kurt most detested: air strikes wreaking totally unfair odds against helpless victims.

So the injustice and arrogance of war was once again on his mind. But so was science, which he deemed just as arrogant. A few days later he sent a copy of a rushed essay he'd just completed for a biotechnology issue of *Forbes* magazine. In it, he reminisced about geniuses in the late 1940s' Research Laboratory at General Electric when he was a publicist there. Noting how these "gifted, self-enraptured people" had made a lot of money for the company, he revealed that one of those famous scientists, Nobel Laureate Irving Langmuir, had been his model for Felix Hoenikker, the absent-minded inventor of *ice nine* in his novel, *Cat's Cradle*. He stressed that he'd written "a *portrait* of Dr. Langmuir, not a caricature," to emphasize his current warning that like *ice nine*, scientific advances such as cloning may have unintended consequences.

One of those consequences was human pride in the face of life's absurdity: "It is now revealed that the destiny of Earthlings is to become the means of an insensate Universe to know itself." By this he satirically referred to the so-called "anthropic principle," the controversial cosmological view that implies the evolving purpose of the universe is humanity. That is, the universe *is* because *we* are. Kurt was highly skeptical that the very existence of self-aware biological creatures like us had placed constraints on the kind of universe we can inhabit, thus lending cosmic significance to the very fact of human existence.

Kurt's friend, John Updike, had taken his own skeptical spin with the anthropic principle in his 1986 novel, *Roger's Version*. Another friend, paleontologist Stephen Jay Gould, had likewise taken a critical view in his 1987 collection of essays, *The Flamingo's Smile*, asserting that once life starts, evolution could take many paths to a variety of forms of intelligence other than that of human consciousness.

This was not the first time Kurt and Gould had found similar conclusions about evolution, Kurt's *Galapagos* being a case in point. That spring of 1999, however, Kurt forwarded me a copy of the March 6 letter to Gould he'd just written, after running into him at an occasion the night before. Like Kurt, Gould believed it was oversimplified to suggest natural selection is the *single* cause accounting for all complexity and variation of life on the planet. Rather, he theorized the importance of what he called "punctuated equilibrium" in life's development, marked by abrupt periods or spurts of evolutionary change, perhaps triggered by such unpredictable events as sudden climate change or the impact of a comet.

Given his "obsession with human beings' place in the Universe," Kurt wondered satirically in his letter to Gould about rattlesnakes and lightning bugs:

> Only a completely humorless person could believe that such preposterously elaborate Dr. Seuss creatures could be the result of judicious shopping in the marriage market, so to speak. I have the same problem with the Big Bang Theory. Anybody with a sense of humor *has* to laugh.

He observed that "nerds and dweebs" at Rockefeller University a few blocks from his house were

> playing and winning ever fancier games with genetic materials. That such games have been played elsewhere in the Universe, even in our own Milky Way, is a sure thing, wouldn't you say? We can't be the only biologically CREATIVE animals. . . . Eons ago . . . CREATORS like us in space ships or the fifth dimension . . . played some games with animals which had already EVOLVED

here . . . introducing lizards . . .to the joys and heartbreaks
of aviation, and making snakes with hypodermic syringes in
their mouths and doorbells on their tails, and so on. And
lightning bugs.

He'd enclosed one of his favorite bumper stickers (*Our planet's immune system is trying to destroy us!*) as a special gift to Gould, explaining its statement was "lifted from my essay on the year 2000 in the
January 1999 *Playboy.*"

Kurt was fascinated by evolution and serious about his often-
repeated question, "What are people for?" He truly believed playfulness was a value much less likely to harm the planet, despite its failure
to add to the gross national product. Meanwhile, his own questioning
of life's purpose was often as grim as that of his beloved mentor, Mark
Twain, who (he continued to remind me) believed humanity was created by Satan. Kurt's own most profound, if bleak, observation was
that "LIFE IS NO WAY TO TREAT AN ANIMAL." This is the
statement emblazoned on his drawing of a gravestone, one of his favorite screenprints, and what he told me was his "Einsteinian insight," his own "E = mc squared."

I had one more letter just before he was to arrive back in Iowa to
visit Cedar Falls for a two-day speaking engagement on April 19 and
20, for UNI's Department of Modern Languages. It contained a
statement he'd addressed April 14, 1999, to the editor of the *New
York Times* about ethnic cleansing in Kosovo. I found no evidence it
was published, but it chastised NATO for its inability to resist

the nearly irresistible temptation to be entertainers on
television, to compete with movies by blowing up bridges and
police stations and so on. . . .

. . .The homicidal paranoia and schizophrenia of ethnic
cleansing does its worst quickly now, almost instantly . . . in
Rwanda and now Kosovo, and who knows where else. The disease
used to take years.

Kosovo was still on his mind when he reached Cedar Falls to speak on "Language and Society" and to meet with student classes and faculty. But first he took a little time to relax at my home with my daughter Leslie and her kids, who had driven down from Minneapolis to join us for dinner. I'd invited Jerry Klinkowitz and his wife, Julie, as well, so we could toast Peter Reed's devotion to the *Bagombo* project and to his substantial history of critical work with and for Kurt.

Taking all this in was my eleven-year-old grandson, Austen, a budding young artist at the time, who'd admired the abundant Vonnegut drawings and prints in my home. He'd brought along his sketch book, hoping Kurt might give him some pointers. We were just finishing dinner when Kurt and Austen slipped away from the table and soon were bent over Austen's sketchbook in the living room. Later all were duly impressed with his new pencil drawing with a baseball theme. The proud grin on Austen's face said everything about that experience for him, and I thought at the time, how typical it was of Kurt's generosity with people he hardly knew, even kids. (He'd last seen Austen when he was a toddler.)

This was Kurt's fourth visit to the UNI campus, the first being thirty-two years earlier, in April of 1967, when he was a forty-five-year-old author with an underground following, and *Slaughterhouse-Five* was still taking workable shape in his mind. We spoke briefly the next morning, just as he was about to enter a student symposium and a full schedule of presentations. That evening I joined a capacity crowd at the Strayer-Wood Theatre for his lecture on "Language and Society." Hundreds more overflowed into a nearby building to witness by simulcast this seventy-six-year-old literary superstar amble onto the stage to wild acclaim.

His message began with a criticism of the "show business" television industry luring people away from language and the experiences of hearing and reading and creating literature. He blamed NATO for exploiting TV to get into the news, and drew from the *Times* piece he'd just written to talk about the plight of Kosovo and other countries like Rwanda, also being subjected to ethnic cleansing at the hands of arrogant leaders who cared nothing for their cultural gifts and values.

"You've been raised by TV and movies to be picture people, not language people," he said, suggesting the audience had been betrayed by TV and newspapers to believe the only reason for doing something was to make money and have power. Using one of his favorite lines, he asserted, "That's not what the arts are about. The arts make your soul grow. . . . If you want to hurt your parents and you don't have the guts to be a homosexual, go into the arts!" Bemoaning the fact that many languages are actually dying, and that poetry is dying as well, he insisted, "The payoff for writing poetry is the actual writing of the poem." He charmed this audience who testified with a wild standing ovation.

The next day, Jon Ericson of the local *Waterloo-Cedar Falls Courier* said of his appearance, "In some ways, it resembled the final tours of the Grateful Dead. People had promised themselves they would someday go see the band before Jerry Garcia died. Those people fighting to see . . . Kurt Vonnegut wanted to experience in person an artist who changed their view of the world"(4/20/99).

Indeed, when Kurt left the hall he was mobbed by admirers and well-wishers at an outdoor reception and stood with his back against the building for at least half an hour in the mild springtime dusk, listening intently, answering questions, making jokes, and laughing. I heard at least two women tell him they had named a child after him. He was high on the crowd, and I think he could have stayed another hour. Finally, when I saw no sign of a faculty member poised to rescue him, I kept my promise to provide a getaway and signaled a previously arranged friend waiting nearby with a splendid old Lincoln Continental as limo service. It felt rather like a Mafia kidnap, but it worked, and he was ready to unwind with a drink at the motel bar.

The next morning he was buoyant when I picked him up for a quick breakfast at my house. With a fully packed day ahead, culminating in a final speech that evening, he was ready to get on with it. When I told him he was a real trooper, he just grinned, lit a cigarette and wondered where the coffee was.

We had only a little time to talk, but I hoped to hear about his plans for the summer. His darling Lily, now sixteen, would be spending some time with him and Jill in Sagaponack, and he would continue searching for a new high school for her fall term. She was still interested in music and drama, but it was tough to find a program the whole family liked. He obviously felt some concern about this, but since it was a family matter, neither of us pursued it. Instead, I hoped he would manage to relax and have some quality playtime that summer. Fat chance, I thought—not with his attention span. He might like afternoon naps, but extended leisure was not his style.

Summer was a long way off, though, and first, he said he'd likely be seeing Peter and Maggie Reed in Minneapolis the next month when he lectured there, and then a few other speaking gigs, including one in Georgia. When I drove him to the campus, we said goodbye, knowing his speech that night would be mobbed and he'd have an early flight out in the morning.

Indeed, his presentation that evening was to another packed house and simulcast. He was still buoyant. The culmination had to be his rap performance of the "Prologue" to Chaucer's *Canterbury Tales*, complete with finger snapping and (somewhat shuffled) hops, in celebration of Middle English language and rhythms ("WHAN that a-PRIL-le with its SHOUers SOO-te, The DROU-te of MAR-che hath PIER-ced to the ROO-te"). It was a pretty cool rap for an old geezer approaching eighty. The crowd screamed with delight. He loved hamming it up as much as they did. If this was his last visit to Cedar Falls, as many who had driven miles surmised, it had been a delightful celebration of language and the humane enchantment of literature his audiences would not forget.

So, he headed back East again, called a couple of times later that spring, and in late May sent a spiral-bound manuscript of the graduation address he'd presented May 15 at Agnes Scott College in Atlanta, Georgia. His speech began "Hello. I hope you are all wearing sunscreen." It was the first time I knew of his playfulness with the famous sunscreen hoax—presumably a commencement address he'd presented at MIT and widely circulated on the Internet, but actually a newspaper column written by Mary Schmich for the *Chicago Tribune* two years earlier, in June of 1997. Every English-speaking computer user knew by now about the hoax, and it doubtless drew a laugh at Agnes Scott in the year 1999.

It was a few months later in early August when Kurt called from "the country," to alert me to watch for a package from him, a gift that had given him the nostalgic illusion he was "gazing back into his childhood." It arrived poorly wrapped, containing a sculpture—a large, clear plastic box, enclosing white, wooden miniatures of a swing, a slide, and a delicate fence, all forming a playground scene with an almost magical quality.

He called again, sounding rather troubled, to ask what I thought of the sculpture. He'd bought it impulsively at the opening of an East Hampton exhibition, having been taken with its freshness. I agreed, charmed by his childlike delight, but I puzzled when he asked about "the love letter." When I said I'd seen none, he said he meant the videotape. There had been no videotape in the package.

This remained an unresolved mystery but left me very uneasy about his state of mind. I hoped his upcoming visit with his daughter Nanny and family in Northampton would give him a lift. She'd been investigating a local school that might be of interest to Lily. Kurt's vacation stop there had taken place before I heard from Nanny about the "catastrophe."

Kurt, staying at local Northampton hotel, had gone out one evening to a nearby restaurant. Walking through the dark parking lot behind the hotel, he had tripped and banged himself up rather substantially, so returned to his room instead. When the manager saw him, he phoned Nanny, who immediately took him to emergency care.

It seemed clear to all, including Kurt, that he was considerably shaken by the accident but perhaps equally shocked by his temporary dependency. Nonetheless, Nanny and her family and friends had delighted in indulging him back to health with an abundance of TLC. This accomplished, and Jill apparently having discovered a previously unknown attractive school for Lily only a few blocks from their home in Manhattan, the status quo would be resumed. Kurt returned to the City by train, much to the disappointment of his Northampton family.

Kurt celebrated his seventy-seventh birthday that November and a week later sent a postcard: "I used to call my chainsmoking an 'honorable suicide,' but I've just had a chest X-ray and my lungs are clear. *Merde!*"

I teased him, suggesting his lungs must be leather by now and would probably be preserved in the Smithsonian after his death. As the twenty-first millennium dawned in January, he sent the *New York Times* obituary of Adam Yarmolinsky, Jane Vonnegut's second husband who had recently died of leukemia at age seventy-seven in Washington, DC. Kurt's exact age.

And then, by the end of that first month of the year 2000, Kurt himself would be hospitalized in critical condition—from smoke inhalation. A stray cigarette in his Manhattan home had caused a fire, and in his effort to put it out, he'd nearly succumbed. Fortunately both Jill and Lily were present to summon a rescue squad that administered immediate aid, but it was another one of those turning points.

Kurt was in a dangerously weakened state. Increasing tensions grew about preferable therapeutic treatments, with his Massachusetts families believing he needed extended family care instead of institutional rehabilitation. Eventually, Kurt did move to Northampton, where Nanny found a nearby apartment for his privacy but close enough to see to his daily nourishment and therapy. Jill and Lily remained in Manhattan.

It seemed to work reasonably well, and Kurt continued to regain strength and dignity, although in March he called to say his situation reminded him of "a doctor friend of [the French author] Celine's, who wanted more than anything a death which would be dignified. He died in convulsions under a grand piano."

*   *   *

In April, Kurt made a trip from Northampton back to New York City to read a memorial tribute to his dear friend, Joseph Heller, who had died of a heart attack the previous December, following a rare neurological disease. The memorial was held at a members-only meeting at the American Academy of Arts and Letters, on April 4, 2000. In his statement, Kurt spoke of Joe's humble beginnings, his military service as a bombardier and of how he and Joe had both taught at City College. He praised his brilliant literary insight into the absurdity of life, something he said Heller's novels had elevated to new significance.

In this tribute Kurt told me he shared the anecdote about attending a multibillionaire's party with Heller, at which Kurt asked how it made him feel "to know that our host, only yesterday, probably made more money than *Catch-22*, one of the most popular novels of the century, has earned world-wide." Joe's reply was, "The knowledge that I've got enough."

Kurt told this story many times. It's a story that expressed his profound regard for Joe's humility but at the same time masked his own significant ambivalence about affluence, something I believe he carried through much of his life. Joe Heller was born the son of a Coney Island truck driver who died when Joe was five. Kurt, on the other hand, was born the son of a wealthy architect who, as he reported numerous times, lost everything during the Great Depression. I know Kurt deeply honored Joe Heller's humane ability to tolerate the absurdity of life, even though it sometimes made him "grumpy."

I am less sure that Kurt himself was ever amused in the least about poverty. He reflected in speeches and in print the pain his parents manifested in their loss of the family fortune, even though as a youngster he had felt its personal significance to be minor. But during the years of his early writing career, with a growing family to support, poverty was an experience verging on desperation, one that drove him into odd jobs that deprived him of writing time, especially after his sister's death and his and Jane's decision to add three more children to their family. It would be hard to ignore its impact upon his life and that of his family. He even had often expressed his concern about *my* financial challenges and believed single mothers faced particularly daunting odds.

* * *

I teased Kurt occasionally about his affluence, given that when I first knew him in Iowa City, he was broke, but at the same time, happily embedded in a similarly impoverished and beloved writing community. To see him later, tuxedo clad, boarding a limo in Manhattan, or on the front page of *People* magazine seemed totally uncharacteristic of the man we all knew and loved back in Iowa. There is no doubt of his generosity and kindness to those in need, then or ever. On the other hand, he almost apologetically acknowledged to me that he appreciated being able to "pay for the services of others." I'm not sure he ever quite transcended anxiety about poverty, or, like Joe Heller, was satisfied he had enough. Nor do I think he regretted his ability to hang out with the rich and famous on occasion.

Be that as it may, in the spring of 2000, living alone in a Northampton apartment at age seventy-seven, Kurt may well have hit one of the darker times of his life. In early April, about the time he would have been composing his tribute to Heller, he sent me a copy of Oscar Wilde's stunning essay, *De Profundis*, written from prison in the depths of despair and dishonor. On the cover, dated April 3, he wrote that Nanny's husband Scott had given him a copy of the work, hoping it might help him through a rough spot. "It turned out to be a tremendous piece of romantic music which, for the moment, restored my soul." The essay is, aside from a manifestation of Wilde's profound anguish, a passionate expression of his need to find *meaning* in his suffering. That gift had come to him only when he found "something hidden away in my nature, like a treasure in a field," namely, Humility. Through this he was able to seek a "fresh mode of self-realization," which led him to recognize he must free himself from "any possible bitterness of feeling against the world." No matter that he was penniless and homeless, the external things of life were unimportant, so long as he would "be able to recreate my creative faculty" and find peace and comfort in the natural world.

Kurt probably never fully found peace and comfort, but he surely recognized he had less to recover from than Wilde. On April 7, he wrote that he was going ahead with a divorce from his wife.

My first reaction was relief, especially because he had the loving support of his daughter and her family and friends who adored him. His ambivalence about his challenged marriage had drained his energy for some time, and I could envision the intellectual and cultural community of Northampton providing him with refreshing new creative stimulation as well as warm esteem. Certainly the natural environment was beautiful and healing.

Nanny was quick to find him a more spacious apartment, one with a view, and to furnish it with the equipment he needed to do his art and to write comfortably. Smith College invited him to teach a course in creative writing in the fall which would be open to applicants that he could select from several colleges in the surrounding area. In short, the community welcomed him with open arms. He even was preparing for an invited art show sponsored by the R. Michelson Galleries in October.

Pleased with what seemed a suitable, if not perfect solution for my old friend, in June I departed Iowa with my daughter, Leslie, for a long-anticipated, shaman-guided tour of sacred Inca sites in Peru. It would be a life-changing trip for both of us and especially for me, considering my next birthday would be my seventieth. It was time.

When we returned in late June, I wrote Kurt about some of our experiences, anticipating an account of his pleasant new life in Northampton. I heard nothing until mid-September. The reason he hadn't replied earlier? He'd been playing the role of "a lugubrious clown in a ponderously plotted soap opera with insoluble problems." In short, he had decided *not* to proceed with what a divorce would require but instead was living a de facto separation.

By October, it seemed that his innate charm and sense of humor had kicked in again, and soon he was sending me copies of his memos to students and an occasional story that had touched him. Local newspaper clippings sent by others revealed he had given his "How To Get a Job Like Mine" speech to a delighted Northampton audience. Another reported a local brewery's creation of a ten-barrel batch of "Kurt's Valley Malt" based on the family recipe of his grandfather Lieber's prize-winning brew. The brew master, Chris O'Connor, of the Northampton 11 Brewster Court brew house, had chosen one of Kurt's pictures ("Tralfamadore #1") to be reproduced for the label. The beer would be served at the opening of Kurt's show at the Northampton Gallery later that month. It didn't surprise me the town was falling in love with Kurt Vonnegut.

Then came November and the stunning news Kurt received the day before his seventy-eighth birthday from the mother of a brilliant young Czech theater director, Petr Lébl, who had died of suicide. This was a man who, Kurt told me, "is said to have revived theater in Prague single-handedly" and whom Kurt had befriended with great affection some years earlier in Czechoslovakia, through his friendship with Vaclav Havel. Lébl had been a devout fan of Kurt's work and had recently produced an adaptation of *Slapstick*. Another friend of Lébl had translated the letter written by the young man's grief-stricken mother, Eva Léblová, and had also sent a videotape of a memorial documenting the work of this thirty-four-year-old artistic director of Prague's Balustrade Theatre. Apparently suffering from a bipolar disorder, he had hanged himself in his own theater.

Needless to say, it was a tragic birthday "celebration" to cap off Kurt's turbulent year. Mrs. Léblová's letter spoke of her son's "spiritual bond" with him, beginning with the young director's staging of Kurt's *Grotesques* in 1985 "(which had begun his full and artistic career)" until the last moments when Petr had still kept Kurt's photograph close by. Her son had named Kurt "an angel of his time" in the dedication of his production of Chekhov's *The Seagull*.

Kurt sent me a copy of his return message to her that explained the coincidence of receiving her letter and the video memorial on the eve of his own seventy-eighth birthday, and how he had felt like the old man in Beckett's *Krapp's Last Tape*, interacting with a machine rather than a human being as he witnessed the video account of Lébl's brilliant career. Kurt spoke of himself as an old man at the "requiem for a young genius killed by beauty so intense as to have become unbearable, whose clinical name is depression." He saw the documentary as "a perfect requiem, leaving nothing more for me to say or think about the gorgeous and harrowing romance of your dear son's life, nor about the appalling dignity of his death." He concluded by identifying her son as "a martyred saint of the arts."

I have never heard anyone articulate celebratory remorse so profoundly.

Obviously Kurt was stunned by the terrible beauty of the talented young man's death and called me several times to discuss it. Having suffered my own husband's suicide, I was deeply moved by his compassion. He told me how the videotape tribute began with quotations from *Darkness Visible* by Kurt's old friend, Bill Styron, about his own struggle with horrendous depression. Lébl's favorite playwright had been Chekhov, whose *Ivanov* he had directed on a Saturday evening, only a few hours before hanging himself in the early hours of Sunday morning. A special guest performance had been performed in the theater Sunday evening, with Lébl's body not being discovered until after the final curtain. His controversial and gifted career as both a designer and director had only a six-year tenure in the Balustrade, the same theater in which Vaclav Havel had staged his early successes in the 1960s.

Kurt had always loved the theater and delighted in having his own works performed. He also occasionally participated in amateur performances himself and was thrilled that his daughter Lily seemed attracted toward a stage career. But Kurt felt the paradox of young Lébl's last performance underlined the bizarre richness of drama's capacity to portray life's profound ambiguities, something he, like most artists, held in awe if not reverence.

Fortunately, there were some lighter moments of life Kurt could celebrate with his Northampton family and friends as well. A few months later, he performed as a guest scat-singer with his grandson Max Prior's band in the annual Northampton benefit talent show (the "Really Big Show") held at the Northampton's Academy of Music on February 25, 2001. Co-guest performer with Max's group ("Special K and His Crew") was Jon Fishman of the wildly popular Phish musical group.

How the Fishman-Vonnegut appearance brought the house down was a tribute to the entrepreneurial expertise of the Vonnegut-Prior family: Max had learned some time earlier, from reading in an *Entertainment Weekly* magazine, that the favorite book of his favorite performer, John Fishman, was Kurt Vonnegut's novel, *Cat's Cradle*. Max's mom had colluded in the plan to take Max to a Phish performance in New York City with an autographed copy of this book. That began the family friendship.

When Nanny and Max invited Fishman to appear with Kurt and Max's band for a surprise performance, the ensemble came to include Fishman himself "performing" on the hose of an old vacuum cleaner Nanny had found in their basement. Kurt opened with his Chaucer rap and then "dueled" scat-style, with Phish rocking on the vacuum hose, backed by Max on guitar along with three of his high school buddies. (Max was quoted later as saying on behalf of his group, "It was truly one of the happiest ten minutes of our lives.") As it turns out, John Fishman would compose musical versions of some of the Bokonon poems from Kurt's *Cat's Cradle*. Later, Nanny created a splendid work of art based on Bokonon sayings in honor of her dad's eighty-fourth birthday, both characteristic of the kind of creative inspiration that grew out of Kurt's stay in Northampton.

Later that spring, because I had a meeting on the East Coast, I spoke with Nanny about the possibility of a stopover visit for a couple days with the family on my way home. I'd been in more frequent touch with her by phone because of the special circumstances of Kurt's life there and felt increasingly close. Of course I'd spend some time with Kurt, as well, agreeing it might be helpful to both of us to discuss his situation more directly.

It was an especially sweet time to share with Nanny and her likewise gifted husband, Scott Prior, who was at the time working on a huge painting—an exquisitely haunting landscape of an abandoned amusement park, a site familiar to him during his youth in Maine. Scott works in precise representative detail in his small studio next to their home, and Nanny has a similar attached workspace where she does her paintings, drawings, and crafts.

Her paintings often suggest a narrative, perhaps somewhat reminiscent of her father's wry sense of humor. I was struck once again at how she embodied a fascinating combination of her parents. Scott is quiet and warmly consistent, a solid family base. Nanny was doing everything she could to make Kurt's life in Northampton comfortable enough that he might consider it a viable move. With typical Vonnegut humor, she joked that doing Kurt's laundry might even give her the chance to make a fortune selling his shorts to Max's girlfriends.

Nanny and I took one day for a memorable road trip to Hartford to tour Mark Twain's magnificent house, now a historic museum. Being in that space was almost magically eerie—making it easy to become submerged into Twain's life and what seemed its parallels with Kurt's—their love for storytelling and art, struggles with depression, love of humor, concern about money and politics. And coping with tragic loss.

Kurt's apartment was walking distance from the Prior home, as well as from the Smith campus and the commercial district of Northampton. When Nanny drove me over for our lunch date, he was sitting on a couch hunched over a laptop computer on a coffee table in a roomy, high-ceilinged living room area overlooking the foothills. An electric piano keyboard, a desk, and a stereo system were nearby.

Kurt was fit and cheerful as he rose to give us both a hug.

Later he and I walked to a downtown restaurant for lunch, where he was greeted by name with welcoming smiles. When the hostess approached us, he gestured toward a table in the back. "We're not married," he teased with a grin.

After lunch we did a brief tour of the downtown. First, the brewery where Kurt's grandfather's lager recipe had been re-created. The owner cheerfully guided us around the huge vats, explaining the mixing and aging procedures with obvious enthusiasm. Then there was a brief stop for Pall Malls at the little grocery where Kurt shopped, and a walk through a scented garden and flower shop on the way toward the Smith campus.

He acknowledged he was still in a state of astonishment about how lacking in interest the Smith girls were about makeup or any efforts to enhance their feminine attractiveness, something he'd written to me about, with near disbelief. I assured him it was good that he finally was broadening his insights into feminist values. We ambled through the crowded bookstore where he picked up envelopes and stamps.

"See what I mean?" he said as we pushed out into the afternoon sunshine. "No 'babes' here!"

I suggested he just try to relax and appreciate it.

He pointed out the hall where he met his students twice a week. Then he spoke softly, as though revealing a secret: "You know? Not one person on the English faculty speaks to me?" He was half joking, but I knew he was serious.

I suddenly recognized he truly felt he had no "gang" here. And it *did* seem like intellectual elitism, although he may have exaggerated. I just shook my head and took his arm, hating that he felt so lonely. And furious that his rich intelligence and humane generosity were apparently being shunned by his colleagues. It comforted me to know his own students loved him. He had sent me some of their touching statements of gratitude for his help and their hesitant awe until being charmed by his kindness and humor. I could understand why he was miserable, but it was a mutual loss if he was being avoided by his colleagues.

We entered a warm and humid greenhouse on the campus, a site he frequented. His spirits lifted some as he identified his favorite exotic plants. I couldn't come up with much additional cheer but felt even worse as he talked about his intention to return to Manhattan when the spring semester was over: Lily needed him. He was getting too old to change things, too old to live alone. Too old to endure a no-win divorce.

I understood. But it was painful to see him this low, and I did my best to engage him with stories about the magic of Machu Picchu and how moved Leslie and I had been by our Peru trip. I insisted he consider making a visit to Iowa in the summer, when all my kids would be coming back to help celebrate my seventieth birthday. Of course,

I knew that wouldn't happen, but it gave me a chance to remind him how much they all still loved him.

Later, we both went to Nanny and Scott's for dinner, a cheerful time of joshing with his grandsons and teasing darling Nellie, who obviously adored her grandpa, as they all did.

I spent the next day at Kurt's apartment again, prior to my departure. When I arrived he was elated he had just received a box of CD recordings of a new musical composition for his earlier *Requiem* text, created by his friend Seymour Barab. We listened to the beautiful new settings of *Cosmos Cantata,* with vocal selections backed by the Manhattan Chamber Orchestra—to my ears a more pleasing performance than the first recorded rendition.

He wanted me to see his working studio where he did his drawings on acetate before sending them on to Joe for screen printing. It was generous space, with a skylighted worktable, combined with guest bedroom.

"Lily stays here when she visits," he explained. Again I thought how perfect the apartment was for his creative efforts. Quiet, private, and near a loving family. I wished that kind of family joy would have been enough to sustain him in Northampton, but it obviously wasn't. And I also knew quiet and private space, no matter how pleasant or productive, were not necessarily enough for Kurt. He needed his extended gang of peers in Manhattan and very likely he also needed the vibrant intellectual and cultural life of the City.

I spied the bound page proofs of Gail Godwin's new book, *Heart,* and picked it up. She'd been a student in Kurt's Iowa City Workshop and had remained a good friend. "How's Gail's book?"

"See what you think," he said, grinning. "I'll work for a while." I curled up with her book for the next hour or so while Kurt bent over his laptop on the coffee table in his living room.

Emerging a bit droopy-eyed, after skimming the book, I found him still crouched over that machine, and thought to myself, how can that not completely wreck his back? He'd *always* worked in such positions, ever since Iowa City where he usually had hunched over a portable typewriter on a wide window sill, or on an upside-down wastebasket in his Workshop office.

"How'd you like the book?" he asked.

I had to confess I hadn't been gripped—"I guess I like her fiction better. So how's *yours*? You have a great title!" This was, as he had told me, *If God Were Alive Today*.

"Pretty slow," he acknowledged. "But it goes better when I have company. So play something," he said, gesturing toward the keyboard.

"You know I can't really play," I said, fiddling with the keys. "Don't you have some sheet music?" He only played by ear, and somehow had always insisted I did, too. Which was definitely not the case. I turned on some of the electronic buttons and experimented with keys—this machine could reproduce a complete orchestra.

Finally he closed his computer.

"It really does help when I'm not alone," he grinned. He started picking out CDs he wanted me to hear while I made some coffee in the kitchen: the "Ukulele Dick" performer who had sent him a recording he was crazy about . . . his favorite Beethoven . . . dance tunes from the fifties . . . "Nice music," he said, pulling me to my feet for a slow turn round the room.

Finally, it was time for Nanny to arrive to chauffeur Kurt off to his student office hours. It was getting pretty dark outside as he fumbled in the closet for an umbrella.

"Take something from the shelf before you leave," he said, motioning to the divider wall holding knickknacks and sculptures, one of a naked lion-headed male carrying a man's head on a tray.

"Magnificent!" I grimaced, holding it up.

He pointed to the head on the tray. "That's me!" Then he handed me a metal frog sculpture he'd picked up at the flower shop we'd visited the day before. "This is nice . . . for your garden, maybe?"

"I know where you got this," I teased, pointing to the shiny stone I'd sent shortly after he moved to Northampton, from my trip to Peru.

"I'm keeping that."

* * *

Outdoors, it was suddenly very chilly. When we pulled up to his classroom building, he stepped out of the car and leaned through the open window: "Give us a kiss," he said quietly, then turned and walked slowly up the walk toward the building. Those drooping shoulders—no one else could ever look so melancholy. I think both Nanny and I had tears in our eyes as we drove away. I tried not to doubt I if would ever see him again.

Kurt did leave Northampton and Smith College at the end of that spring semester and spent the summer in Sagaponack before return-ing to his Manhattan home and life with his wife and their daughter.

In early June, I made a road trip to Tennessee to help celebrate the home my son had built on a lovely, wooded acreage south of Nashville. On the way back to Iowa, I took a Kentucky side trip to the Lexington studio of Joe Petro. He was underway with his project to restore with vivid silkscreen artistry the fading magic marker draw-ings Kurt had given me so many years ago. And indeed, it *was* magic to see the transformations that looked exactly like the original draw-ings. Joe patiently explained the technology of this process, which I still don't understand completely. But I could comprehend the splen-dor of the plans he had for a large, silk-covered portfolio to contain them, a handmade wooden box lined with French marbling paper. The eight screen prints within would contain Kurt's own introduc-tion, as well as a tribute by the British illustrator, Ralph Steadman, some of whose work Joe was also screening. I agreed Steadman had written a stunning celebration of Kurt's work, which read in part:

These pictures are the primeval marks from a man on a quest to surprise simply in line and color. Don't even look for form, or the odd inflection. His ART is as effective and pure as the vision of a child . . . ART . . . as specific as the meaning of life itself. ART as LIFE. LIFE as ART. . . . He is succeeding, and I think the cunning swine is going to take us all to the cleaners.

*   *   *

As an added treat while I was in Lexington, Joe had invited one of Kurt's old friends to join us for lunch, Ollie Lyon, from the General Electric days when he and Kurt had worked together in Schenectady. A delightful man who obviously loved Kurt, he had great compassion for what he'd been going through in his personal life. I was terribly pleased Joe had befriended him. Not long after, he drove Ollie to visit Kurt at Sagaponack.

*   *   *

I arrived home, with the days growing shorter and schools opening again for the fall term. Within the week a postcard from Kurt arrived:

> Dear Loree—Quite something, the synergy on my behalf between you and Joe Petro III. Did he tell you that the anticipated portfolio, at my suggestion, will be called *Enchanted IOU's?* "Magic Markers," get it? I can never begin to express, you warm person, how much I.O.U. K

I'm sure Joe wasn't old enough to have known that "Marker" is the old-fashioned word for an I.O.U. *MAGIC MARKERS*: get it?

"ABSOLUT VONNEGUT,"
Silkscreen by Kurt Vonnegut, © 1996
www.vonnegut.com

JAN. 31, '03

U.S. HISTORY TRIVIA:
THE MOST SANE, HUMANE,
ELOQUENT SPEECH EVER
DELIVERED BY AN AMER
ICAN WAS LINCOLN'S AT
GETTYSBURG IN 1865. THE
MOST SANE, HUMANE, ELO
QUENT LETTER EVER SENT
TO A REPRESENTATIVE
IN AN AMERICAN LEG
ISLATURE WAS WRITTEN
BY A WIDOW LIVING
ALONE IN CEDAR FALLS,
IOWA, IN 2003.

P.O.v. Lostcards, Box 9407, Newark, NJ 19.

LOREE
RACKSTRAW
2109 WALNUT
CEDAR FALLS
IA. 50613

NEW YORK NY 100
PM
JAN
03

LOVE 37 USA

11

War Yet Again, 2001–2004

A nd then came September 11 and the destruction of the World
Trade Center in New York City.

I was relieved to hear from Nanny that her dad and family were
safe in Manhattan. Kurt called shortly after that. Soon, he was among
those of us dismayed by President George Bush's decision to retaliate
with air strikes on Afghanistan.

That same month, residents of his Turtle Bay community gathered
for a candlelight ceremony, a night for remembrance in Dag Ham-
marskjöld Plaza. In November, he sent a copy of his remarks from the
Turtle Bay Newsletter. In it he recalled how, two years earlier, firefighters from this community had saved *him*, his house, and family. Now,
as "sort of a prayer," he named aloud "all those local firefighters who
had lost their lives in responding to the Towers attack from "Engine
Company 8, Ladder Company 2, Battalion 8." He concluded, "It is
daylight in Afghanistan. There are many unwelcome fires there, and
many, many human beings are trying to put them out." Anyone who
had read *Slaughterhouse-Five* would have recognized how the Dresden
firebombing haunted his statement.

That month he received the Carl Sandburg Literary Award in
Chicago from the Friends of the Chicago Public Library, and he sent
me his reception speech that recognized Sandburg as a fellow Midwestern artist who elevated "the self respect, the dignity and political

acumen of American wage earners, of our working class." Along with his favorite Indiana writers, Powers Hapgood and Eugene Debs, he celebrated Sandberg's Midwestern values that he said stemmed from the Sermon on the Mount. Beatitudinal compassion was on his mind, especially when his government was wreaking revenge for the September 11 attacks.

Like many of us, Kurt approached the end of 2001 with a mix of grief, outrage, and apprehension, but he seemed to find comfort in a November birthday greeting he'd received from Mrs. Léblová, the mother of that young Czech theater director who had hanged himself the previous year. I was visiting friends in California when he called to share Mrs. Léblová's new message. I understood her gratitude that Kurt respected what he called the "appalling dignity" of her son's extraordinary theatrical expression of tragedy.

His own ambivalence about life made its way into the tribute he forwarded early in January, for the forthcoming celebration of John Irving's sixtieth birthday. In it, Kurt acknowledged that although he and Irving were said to be humorists, "I wouldn't know how to kid him now about his sixtieth birthday. What's so funny?"

Nonetheless, he continued,

> If you laugh instead of cry, there is less cleaning up to do afterwards. . . . John could . . . make me and anybody else with half a brain bust out with the most therapeutic variety of laughter, which is about how beautiful but grotesquely absurd it is to be a human being.

About that time, Kurt also credited his partnership with Joe Petro as giving him a new lease on life, especially since he felt himself so bogged down by work on his new novel. On January 5, 2002, he wrote that he was "still having a heck of a time putting *If God Were Alive Today* on its feet so it can go somewhere." Without creative involvement, his own chronic battle with depression grew more burdensome. He continued to send occasional new screen prints in postcard form, but his correspondence became more often limited to phone calls or brief notes. In February he sent, without comment, a copy of a moving documentary tribute to his brother by Duncan Blanchard, a longtime professional colleague of Bernie's.

It was the next month that he left a phone message regarding the grave illness of my first Iowa Workshop mentor, Verlin Cassill. Verlin's wife, Kay, confirmed his lengthy illness and hospitalization when I called. I was grateful to catch up with the lives of the Cassill family, whose children had been my kids' playmates, and to remind Kay how important Verlin had been to me and my teaching career. A week later, she let me know she'd conveyed my message to Verlin before his death at eighty-two. It was eerie to feel that loss—both he and Dick Yates had been World War II veterans, just as Kurt was. Kurt would be eighty on his next birthday. I couldn't, or at least *wouldn't* imagine his not being alive.

In April, I received a message Kurt had penned at the bottom of a note that he'd received from someone else:

Dearest Loree—

This morning, April 19, 2002, I was in the airport at Detroit, on my way home to NYC, having lectured at Albion College, Albion, Michigan, the night before. A nice looking young man, maybe in his thirties, spoke to me by name, and we talked some about teaching literature to learning disabled kids. He was doing it near Saratoga, NY. I used to do it on Cape Cod. En route to New York, I received this note from him, delivered by a flight attendant. I would never see him again.

Love—

K

The touching note explained the writer's gratitude for his conversation with Kurt, especially following his recent experience of life's brutality: his baby had died and his wife had left him. He'd tried finding others who "understood life's cruelty," but only after reading five

228 • LOVE AS ALWAYS, KURT

of Kurt's last six books had he found the perspective he needed. He wanted to say "thank you!"

A few days later Kurt sent a copy of the warm preface he'd written for his son Mark's new edition of *Eden Express*. It was good to know Kurt had eased back into the writing and speaking responsibilities that charged his days and kept him productive and involved. But I knew he would suffer when, on May 20, his good friend Stephen J. Gould died at age sixty after a long struggle with cancer.

Gould had by then completed his master opus, *The Structure of Evolutionary Theory*, some twenty years in the making. He had been one of the few scientists I knew of with whom Kurt could banter about flaws he perceived in natural selection. Big brains eager to invent systems successful enough to threaten the entire planet was no way to treat *any* animal.

*   *   *

Much more compatible with Kurt's hope for human potential was the ability to play and create things of beauty. So he was happy to help out with a benefit exhibition at a Northampton gallery to help raise funds for a skate park for kids. After his grandson Ezra and pals' love for skateboarding had been frustrated by local laws, he joined Nanny's family in contributing a "new suite of four prints" to kick off the fund-raising.

But such generosity is not to overlook Kurt's copious ability to express outrage at injustice, arrogance, and stupidity, particularly when it came to politicians, including testimony before government bodies in defense of social justice or the arts. In 2002, with his eightieth birthday some two months away, he spoke on the first anniversary of the 9/11 attacks at Saint Marks on the Bowery:

> The world will little note nor long remember what we say here.
> This is because we are powerless.
> Peace has no representatives in Washington, DC.
> Why not?
> Peace is not entertaining.

A day later, he faxed the following message to the editors of the *New York Times:*

> It may give us some comfort in these worrisome times to know that in all of history only one country has actually been crazy enough to detonate atomic weapons in the midst of civilian populations, turning unarmed men, women, and children into radioactive soot and bone meal. And that was a long, long time ago now.

While I never saw his message printed in the *Times*, he clipped a couple letters by others, one who complained about a request for heroically militant books to be sent to American troops abroad. The alternatives? Vonnegut's *Slaughterhouse-Five* and Heller's *Catch-22*.

And he hadn't given up on his reluctant novel, *If God Were Alive Today*. He sent a new preface along with a note that he was "starting all over again!" (9/22/02). Although lighter in tone than what I'd seen earlier, it explicitly acknowledged the genius central to his (and Charlie Chaplin's) own life and work as: "How much it hurts to be a human being."

Kurt's response to life was not to elevate his characters above a recognition of pain by creating tragic figures like Odysseus or Hamlet to die heroically with noble courage and elegance (often taking a lot of others with them), but rather to invent clownish heroes like Billy Pilgrim to muddle clumsily through, sustained by music or silly jokes or moments of humble awe or fantasies of sexual bliss. The power of this human comedic trait is a gentle but sustaining one, and not so likely to result in worldwide wars or holocausts. That its literary expression seems beneath the dignity or wisdom of some literary pedants in famous universities or political leaders of powerful countries or religious institutions is perhaps worthy of circumspection.

On the other hand, it always surprised me that Kurt never became jaded about enthusiastic responses to his work. I never saw him other than humbly grateful for positive response to his playfulness as a speaker or writer. And perhaps it made him even more appreciative when someone also recognized the subtle intellectual depth of his insight or performance. Because he often addressed college or university audiences, the opportunities for such interaction may have been more ample.

For example, on November 5, 2002, a few days before his eightieth birthday, he spoke at Tufts University. After his presentation of "How To Get a Job Like Mine," he was handed written messages by at least three different people who wanted to express at considerable length their gratitude and admiration. He was charmed and amused by these messages, which were obviously carefully prepared in advance.

One admirer had handed him a postcard photograph of the famous statue in Rome of Giordano Bruno, the Dominican monk and astronomer burned at the stake by the Inquisition. The admirer's note described an Italian-speaking lunatic asserting scornfully to some French tourists that *Voltaire* had never come to Rome because he was afraid of the Pope. Thus, the writer thanked Kurt for books that had taught him the importance of questioning and studying "even the forbidden night sky."

A second was a two-page, single-spaced letter from the founder of a scholarly institute studying synchronicity, who had first recognized this phenomenon in Kurt's *Cat's Cradle*. He hoped for an appointment to discuss further insights in Kurt's work.

A third person handed him a music CD composed by a Berklee College of Music student, recorded simultaneously with Kurt's reading from *Slaughterhouse-Five* (of Billy Pilgrim telling the story "backwards" of bombers over Dresden sucking up the firestorm and replanting bombing materials back into the earth). A note from composer Simon Heselev's professor explained the salience of the recording "at this present time." Kurt told me he had asked for and received twenty more copies of the CD, one of which was included, along with a copy of a later communication from Heselev asking permission to make the work commercially available. (The CD is available as a single under the title *Tock Tick* by Wall Lizard Music.)

He sent these notes on his eightieth birthday and included a copy of a touching letter "from my sister's oldest boy," an endearing greeting that thanked Kurt for taking him and his two brothers in over half a century ago.

I knew others around the country, including myself, had worked on creative greetings to celebrate this special birthday, with most never expecting he would make it to this anniversary, given his incessant, lifelong chain smoking. Various press reports provided some details about the actual New York City celebration, and he later sent a copy of the invitation to his black tie "Surprise Dinner Party" at the Swedish Embassy, "hosted by the Consul General of Sweden and his wife, together with Mrs. Jill Krementz." The celebrity guest list was generous. A proclamation from Mayor Michael R. Bloomberg acknowledged himself as a Kilgore Trout devotee and proclaimed November 11, 2002, as "KURT VONNEGUT, JR. DAY." (He also mentioned he knew Kurt was receiving gifts of cigarettes from Kentucky, which had virtually no tax on tobacco.)

A second celebration took place a few days later in Kurt's hometown of Indianapolis, where he appeared, with comedian Will Shriner and filmmaker Bob Weide, for "A Gathering of Wits," a fund-raising celebration for the 1894 Society of Athenaeum Foundation. As keynoter, Kurt helped build the restoration fund for the Athenaeum building designed by his architect grandfather. Shriner contributed a film of his father, Herb, the legendary Hoosier humorist. The event had been staged by Kurt's dear childhood friend, Majie Failey, in part as an excuse for his hometown to pay respect to Kurt and his family.

In the remaining days of 2002, Kurt completed an introduction for a new collection of what he called "anti-war, anti-Bush posters . . . by Micah Ian Wright . . . reminiscent in spirit of works by artists like Kathe Kollwitz and George Grosz."

His Christmas greeting was a Vonnegut/Petro screen print of an empty golden birdcage with an open door, along with a copy of an article (embossed by his penned "NOEL!" salutation) and entitled "Where Science Meets Theology" from the current *This Week* magazine. A thoughtful piece by Gregg Easterbrook, it propounded the incongruity that the more science discovers about the nature of the universe and its origin, the greater the mystery of how something, the universe, could have been made out of nothing. Kurt had scribbled on the copy: "The big mistake has to be in our language."

That our language itself limits or shapes what we perceive to be true reflected his anthropologist's recognition of how cultural perceptions and values shape our capacity for awareness and comprehension. A phone discussion about this time convinced me that Kurt gave some credence to "intelligent design," especially because of his insistence that the mammalian eye could not have evolved by natural selection. I sent him biologist Paul Shepard's *Man in the Landscape*, that suggests different landscapes play a large role on the early biological development of how and what the eye can see, but he sent it back telling me he was more interested in my marginal notes. In short, I was intrigued by Kurt's "view" of evolution, but finally decided maybe neither one of us knew enough to have an intelligent discussion.

Of course the year 2003 was darkened by the onset of the Iraqi war and the long-threatened "Shock and Awe" assault on Baghdad beginning that March, understandably a distinct influence on everyone's perceptions about then. Kurt was frustrated that the *Times* wasn't printing his editorial letters. And then came a lucky compensation: He began writing for a Chicago-based biweekly news magazine called *In These Times*. Editor Joel Bleifuss had interviewed Kurt for a two-page story critical of the Bush policy, which began his long-term relationship with the journal. It was founded in 1976 to "identify and clarify the struggles against corporate power now multiplying in American society." The journal's masthead soon listed Kurt's name as a senior editor, with its Web site quote by him: "If it weren't for *In These Times*, I'd be a man without a country."

Indeed, it just may have given Kurt a new reason to live to have this venue for his outrage and grief about what was happening to the country. His articles provided a vent for his despair about the corporate powers of institutions, from Enron and WorldCom to television and the government, running roughshod and without conscience over average fellow humans here and abroad. It was, I believe, the first time Kurt could fully articulate his growing insight about why these institutions had become so heartless in their treatment of American citizens. That insight had begun in Northampton when he read a fascinating book by Dr. Hervey Cleckley titled *The Mask of Sanity*, which he called "the classical medical text on the psychopathic personality." It identifies those with "PP" as presentable, intelligent, decisive people whose pathological flaw is their complete lack of conscience. They are incapable of caring or of doubting their cruel decisions about the fate of those less powerful. Kurt saw this malady in the "corporate cruelty" of institutions like Enron, and believed it had made its way into the politics of the day, since his own government seemed utterly bereft of compassion for the Iraqi citizenry defenseless against "shock and awe" weaponry.

When his *In These Times* interview was first posted on the Web, it resulted in hundreds of online responses from gratified readers and soon expanded the journal's *online* accounts into what editor Bleifuss called "one of the most popular sites on the Internet." It actually *was* something of a digital miracle: born-again Luddite Kurt Vonnegut's online Web posting dialog with readers! This phenomenon (it was well known Kurt did *not* use the Internet) occurred because he could reply immediately by fax to questions sent by fax to him from the magazines' host page by Bleifuss, who instantly put his replies online. Readers wrote increasingly thoughtful observations and questions in this popular "dialogue." Kurt eventually bundled the printed dialogue with spiral binding to distribute to friends. So even though he wasn't writing books any more, at least he could share his creative concerns in a different venue.

Ironically, the Internet made Kurt's ongoing communication more readily available worldwide, to institution heads as well as average readers, which resulted in even more requests for his words of support. One such was the International Peace Foundation, to whom Kurt faxed on February 8, 2003, the following:

Those Americans determined to make war on Iraq, a tyranny already quite effectively neutered by the United Nations, and one which has never threatened us, intend to divert us and themselves from America's local and immediate problems, which are profoundly disturbing, with a truly thrilling TV show.

He honored a similar request from The Bertrand Russell Peace Foundation in England. In April he faxed managing editor Will Dana at *Rolling Stone* magazine a statement declaring "George W. Bush to be a truly primitive human being." And he insisted that Americans had not been hated for their "liberty and justice," as Bush would have it, but rather hated "because our corporations have long been the principal deliverers and imposers of new technologies and economic schemes which wreck the self-respect, the cultures of men, women and children in so many other countries."

In several phone calls, Kurt seemed increasingly energized by his new public dialogue about our inept government's cowboy arrogance, even though it was impossible not to be depressed by it as well. On March 19, the eve of the bombing of Baghdad, he called again, wondering disconsolately if I had read Mark Twain's novel *The Mysterious Stranger*. I hadn't.

"He believed Satan created the world. It's very convincing," he said quietly.

I tried cheering him up, but it was hard to be jovial in light of the horror we'd soon witness of the new Bush TV spectacular. I agreed that Twain might have been right about people like Bush and his satanic ambition in launching "The New American Century." We commiserated about the horror of what was inevitably to come, with the impotent rage and remorse that millions of others were undoubtedly feeling that night. It was agonizingly difficult to recognize how anyone could feel otherwise.

He asked if I had received the page proofs he'd sent of the new Blake Bailey biography of Dick Yates, to which we both had contributed. That mammoth book hadn't added cheer to my week, given its profound assessment of the pain-filled life of our mutual friend, although it included a decent recognition of the power of his work as a writer.

It was only later that I managed to read Twain's *The Mysterious Stranger*, and understood why Kurt had been so darkly affected by its prophetic power. I never told him when I did read it, nor have I ever recommended it, so moved was I by its mesmeric darkness. By comparison, *Life on the Mississippi* and most other Mark Twain books seemed written by a totally different author.

* * *

Early in April, Kurt forwarded a letter he'd received from John Vincent Boyer, executive director of The Mark Twain House in Hartford, Connecticut, thanking him for agreeing to present the annual Samuel Clemens Lecture later that month. (That perhaps explained why he was earlier reading *The Mysterious Stranger*, one of Twain's lesser known works.)

While I was not present for Kurt's April 30 speech, it was evident from the video he sent that it was a smashing success. His daughter Nanny, who attended, agreed. While celebrating the writer at the same time he managed to show how Mark Twain's ideals of humaneness and humor presciently condemned the present day criminal greed of corporations and the militant arrogance of our federal government.

A quote from the grateful Twain House director's letter to Kurt summed it up: "The town is still reeling, wincing, laughing, reflecting, and savoring your wonderful exposition on the frailty of man, the duplicity of Washington, the vacuity of our hubris, and the fragility of our affections." I know Kurt regarded it as one of his most important speeches, and it seemed to me, when he phoned to report, it was one he felt most honored to give. (Earlier I had passed along a somewhat off-key political joke, which he enthusiastically reported he'd used, allowing him to express how unpleasant it was to be "living under a government run by Bush, Dick, and Colin.")

236 • LOVE AS ALWAYS, KURT

In the videotape, his physical resemblance at age eighty to Twain was marked, even though he made clear his mustache was reminiscent of his father and brother, not of Mark Twain. He'd lost weight and looked considerably frailer than when I'd last seen him, three years earlier in Northampton. It was wrenching not to be close enough to give him a hug of appreciation. He seemed so alone.

An archived copy of the *Hartford Courant* enthusiastically covered a previous Mark Twain Memorial speech by Kurt in May 1979, marking the kick-off for a million-dollar fund-raising project to preserve the nineteenth-century home. The story, by Michael Regan, began by saying "With the curly hair, mustache, and irreverent wit, it could have been Samuel L. Clemens himself standing at the podium." On that occasion, Kurt had been fifty-six years old.

The physical parallels between Twain and Kurt have been noted by many, but there were other similarities, as well. Of course each had a mutual gift for and love of storytelling and enjoyed the generous use of humor and satire. Both worried about money early on and were later able to accumulate considerable wealth, although Twain suffered financially in his later years. Each followed politics closely and were often critical of government and especially social injustice. And both were given to darkness of moods, increasingly so as they aged.

As comparisons go, I found it an interesting twenty-first-century perspective, when the July 2003 issue of *Vanity Fair* spotlighted a dramatic full-page photograph of three aging literary icons: Kurt, Gore Vidal, and Norman Mailer, describing them as "The last three lions of the World War II novel . . . who are all veterans of that war." The article asserted they "have distinguished themselves this year by taking strong stands against America's latest war."

Kurt phoned a couple times during that summer, once to hear how I liked the "work in progress" version of Bob Weide's filmed documentary, titled *Kurt Vonnegut: American Made.* He and Kurt had been present for its screening in New York late that spring, and Bob had sent me a video copy, his special appreciation of Kurt's stand-up comedy richly captured. I was eager to see the finished product and hopeful he would be as eager to complete the needed editing.

Later that fall I reconnected with Vance Bourjaily's former wife, Tina, who was visiting in Iowa City. She and I paid a call on her (and Kurt's) old friend, Frank Conroy, still the Workshop's director who by then was in frail health. I'd determined to gift the Workshop a portfolio of the silk-screen prints Joe had created from Kurt's magic marker drawings. It was a bit like reliving the sixties to chat with Frank, even though we were in the *new* Workshop headquarters—a restored, century-old home called the Dey House overlooking the Iowa River. It was a far cry from the shabby Quonset huts. And it was fun to see one of Kurt's large screen prints titled "The Formal Portrait of Kilgore Trout" hanging over the fireplace in Frank's office.

In September, Kurt was on the lecture circuit again, addressing an enthusiastic crowd at the University of Wisconsin. But later that month, he was among many shocked by the death of his dear friend George Plimpton at age seventy-six. They'd been friends since the sixties, when Kurt was still living in Barnstable and had been interviewed a number of times by Plimpton for his *Paris Review* journal. Kurt phoned to describe the October 14 memorial service, which ironically had replaced the previously scheduled fifty-year anniversary celebration of *Paris Review.* Instead, more than eight hundred of the country's most famous literati gathered to mourn the loss of this extraordinary man. Kurt had agreed earlier to present an anniversary toast but instead toasted his lost friend. He repeated his farewell benediction quietly for me over the phone with a quiver in his voice: "Goodnight, sweet prince. May flights of angels sing thee to thy rest." I ached for the palpable loss Kurt felt. He was heartsick to lose this most gentle, kind, and playful pal.

His mood was none cheerier when he called later that month— with continuing anguish about the approaching presidential campaign for George W. Bush's second term. I wondered, with sympathetic apprehension, that since my son Rob and I were about to take a long-planned getaway to the Galapagos Islands, did Kurt think it might be wise for us to investigate Ecuadorian immigration policies?

If I had difficulty imagining another four years of Bush as president, Kurt was beyond despair. In small compensation, he sent me his friend Lewis Lapham's new collection of *Harper's* essays for my equatorial holiday reading.

It seemed as though Kurt trudged into the year 2004 on the edge of weariness—obviously grieved by the political situation in Iraq as well as by the unceasing exploitation of the planet and its life potential. And perhaps by his own aging. My frustration at being so far away rose with my increasing concern for his welfare. From that time on, he wrote fewer letters, substituting phone calls or drawings or copies of essays with brief notes attached.

Early in January he sent, without explanation, a copy of a New Year's greeting he'd received from a young inmate of a state prison expressing gratitude for a book Kurt had sent him, but which had been withheld because it was "not from an authorized vendor."

Then, on January 20, 2004, George W. Bush, now a full-fledged war president and having been named "Man of the Year" by *Time* magazine, presented his upbeat State of the Union address to the nation. That speech inspired an urgent message from "Kilgore Trout" in the form of an *In These Times* interview with Kurt Vonnegut, following a so-called "Orange Alert." This spoof was tagged "Economic terrorist attack expected at 8 p.m. EST" and published under the title "State of the Asylum" in the March issue (pp. 18–19). The "interview" allowed Kurt to inform Kilgore Trout that our commander in chief was in a "made-for-TV movie," which is now our form of government. He further insisted the president was "sincere" when "he gave a tax cut to the rich because they could make wiser use of it than the government ever could." It concluded with the grim appraisal that "the planet's immune system is trying to get rid of us with AIDS . . . but not even *it* can keep George W. Bush from getting elected to a second term."

Of course he was grimly right, but at least he had a forum.

On Valentine's Day came another copy in my mail of his 1945 freed prisoner-of-war letter assuring his family he was alive, its tone an embryonic hint of what would become the Vonnegut style. The gesture of resending this letter in 2004, the fifty-ninth anniversary of the Dresden firebombing, clearly reflected Kurt's increasingly cynical despair about Iraq and the grim reality that now, nearly sixty years later, nothing had really changed. Major historic sites, cultures, and human beings were being destroyed, ironically again by American bombs. It was as though he felt utterly bereft of any new words to express his disappointment with humanity, perhaps with life itself.

It's obvious to Vonnegut aficionados, and it bears repeating, that he was one of the most patriotic Americans I ever knew, especially coming as he did from the proud heritage of German immigrants who, in the nineteenth century, gratefully celebrated this country's freedoms and opportunities. He was especially proud his German great grandfathers had fought on the Northern side in the Civil War.

Given Kurt's own World War II combat in the homeland of his ancestors, and nearly being killed by bombs from his own countrymen as a war prisoner—well, it *does* suggest a certain aspect of life's paradox had left an impression on his young psyche. I'm often reminded of his statement in *Slaughterhouse-Five* when, on a return visit twenty-two years *after* the firebombing, he quotes his Dresden taxi driver: "I hope that we'll meet again in a world of peace and freedom in the taxi cab *if the accident will*" (p. 2, emphasis added).

The powerful role of accidents in Kurt Vonnegut's war experience (and life) had begun then, when, in his view, the fluke of weather had sent British and American bombers to Dresden, rather than to a previously scheduled target. Clearly, that irony shaped his fiction as well as his life and worldview.

It was in his speech at Eastern Washington University in Spokane later that month, on April 17, that it seemed he had worked especially hard to temper his message of despair about our government with enough humor to keep himself, if not his audience, from giving up entirely.

I'd been away for a week about the same time and returned home, two days after his speech, to find his phone message in a hauntingly resigned voice on my machine:

> Hi Loree, this is Kurt. I'm in Spokane, I don't know quite why. I love the name of the paper here which is *Spokesman*, isn't that cute? Anyway, oh shit. Faced a lot of people again tonight, and I wish you were here. Bye.

And the next day, when my held mail was delivered, I found the several drafts of his speech sent on successive days the previous week. My heart fell. How many years our wonderful, long-distance friendship had gone on—all those years sustained by the U.S. mail and hit-or-miss phone calls. And now, it seemed he was feeling less sure of himself, with each of those several drafts containing minute editorial changes. He'd worked meticulously on it. Later he sent a videotape. Even more moving was how he had taken pains to assure that the grimness of his remarks was balanced by a charming new conclusion—the addition of waltz music to which he whimsically danced off stage.

It was a work of art. First a "message of hope" to offset his satirical opener (his audience need not "worry about our soldiers overseas: They are none of your business. Soldiers are what rich kids get for Christmas, and they can do anything they want with them.") His offsetting message of hope was that no matter how corrupt and heartless society and organizations become, "music will still be perfectly wonderful." Then he announced he had "arranged for a Strauss waltz to be played as you depart, so you can waltz the heck out of here when it is time to go." He spoke from the heart: It truly was dancing that helped lighten his own dark moments or celebrate times of elation. Since his usual message was painful, he wanted to soften it with a sweet, if silly, promise of cheerful music and dance.

Thus, following his chalkboard lesson on literature, and his story about his Uncle Alex reminding folks, "If this isn't nice, I don't know what is," the perfectly timed Strauss waltz filled the huge auditorium.

With a smile on his face, Kurt then began slowly turning three-step pirouettes around the chalkboard and out of sight offstage.

The audience roared to its feet for a long ovation. He did not make a curtain call.

About a week later, the revelations of Abu Ghraib prison became headline news, adding to his challenge to offer what he called comforting stories: cheerful admonitions to engage in creative activities and acts of kindness. It was here that he repeated again what his son Mark had told him years before about life's purpose: "to help each other get through this thing, whatever it is."

Kurt's creative work *was* a comfort he practiced, as did his kids and forbears. The Vonnegut family's artistic abilities being of special significance in Indianapolis, that July he sent a copy of the Indianapolis Art Center announcement of an August exhibition of the work of four generations of Vonneguts, beginning with Kurt's architect grandfather Bernard, who had designed nineteenth-century landmark Indianapolis structures. The signature Art Deco building for Indiana Bell designed by Kurt's father was among his others in the city. Finally, Vonnegut-Petro screen prints would complete the August show, along with paintings by Mark and Edie.

I hoped it would also cheer him that summer to be putting together a new book—a collection of his speeches. Later he said Joe was gathering a portfolio of his statements entitled "STUFF I SAID'" to silkscreen in poster fashion. So as the Democrats and Republicans were in the process of selecting the next candidates for president, Kurt was trying to keep himself out of the blues by being "creative."

He did a powerful piece for the August 2 *In These Times* titled "I Love You, Madame Librarian" celebrating the courage of librarians to resist removing books from shelves or revealing names of borrowers when threatened by "anti-democratic bullies" or "thought police." His conclusion? "The America I love still exists at the front desks of our public libraries." But he still despaired bitterly of the fact that we Americans "now present ourselves to the rest of the world as proud, grinning, jet-jawed, pitiless war lovers, with appallingly powerful weaponry, and unopposed. In case you haven't noticed, we are now almost as feared and hated all over the world as the Nazis were" (p. 30). He was not amused in any way by the behavior of our government: "Our president is a Christian? So was Adolph Hitler, only he was elected." Tough words for an incensed and grievously disappointed American icon.

The November presidential election was nearing, but Kurt's fine piece entitled "Preface" appeared in the late October *In These Times*. He'd sent me several revisions a couple months earlier, and his refined point was that no matter how the election turned out,

> Both candidates were and still are members of the exclusive secret society at Yale, called "Skull and Bones." That means that, no matter which one wins, we will have a Skull and Bones President at a time when entire vertebrate species, because of how we have poisoned the topsoil, the waters and the atmosphere, are becoming, *hey presto*, nothing but skulls and bones. Poetry!

In fact, Kurt so despaired of both Kerry and Bush as candidates that the outcome of the election finally was inconsequential to the gloom he felt. Instead, on November 13, he sent, without comment, an H. L. Mencken quote sent to him by his friend Howard Zinn and his wife Rosalyn:

> As Democracy is perfected, the office of the president represents, more and more closely, the inner soul of the people. On some great and glorious day the plain folks of the land will reach their heart's desire at last and the white House will be adorned by a downright moron. (H. L. Mencken 1880–1956)

It's not likely I was as depressed as Kurt after the Bush election, but looking back on our correspondence I realize I may not have been far behind. The last message I received from him that year was what he called the "final version" of a poem, titled "American Christmas Card 2004," faxed to *In These Times* (and me) on December 20, 2004. It had to do with the narrator meeting a man in Nigeria years ago: An Ibo, with three hundred relatives he knew by name, was traveling with his wife on foot during wartime to introduce their child to its family. The poem's narrator asks "Wouldn't you like to have been such a famous baby?" . . . and then wishes he could magically give every lost American the love and comfort of an extended family. He closed with the following:

Just two people and a babe in the manger,
given a heartless Government,
is no survival scheme.

DEAR LOREE — ·

REMARKS BY KURT VONNEGUT TO BE DELIVERED AT ST. MARKS ON THE BOWERY ON THE NIGHT OF SEPTEMBER ELEVENTH, 2002

The world will little note nor long remember what we say here.
This is because we are powerless.
Peace has no representatives in Washington DC.
Why not?
Peace is not entertaining.

LOVE AS ALWAYS —

K

12

Poetry as Survival, 2005–2007

A Man Without a Country

The deep sadness into which Kurt seemed to have descended really
worried me as the politically miserable year of 2004 came to an
end. I knew he really *needed* to write in order to stay alive. Fiction
wasn't working for him, and he'd said just about everything he could
as an essayist or columnist for *In These Times*. But something happened to get him going again: a *genre* shift! He began to get a second
wind and really have some fun with poetry.

A month earlier he'd sent his poetic celebration of his late pal,
Joseph Heller, to the *New Yorker* and was thrilled when it was accepted. Elated, he called to celebrate. Sure enough, in January 2005
he sent a proof of his poem as it would eventually appear in the magazine, with a note that he was "on pins and needles" about seeing it
actually in print. And what followed in the coming year was a growing accumulation of drafts, portfolios, and publications of *poetry* by
Kurt Vonnegut.

His poems, plus the huge acclaim that followed the October 2005
publication of his essay/poetry/art collection titled *A Man Without a
Country* seemed to turn the tide for him personally. If the poems were
not profound literary gems, they were nonetheless rich distillations of
deeply felt themes that often turned on irony or satire. To be engaged

in a creative effort with language always made him feel useful and lifted his spirits. Publication was icing on the cake.

In my view, one of his best was called "Requiem," which appeared in gold type over a stunning color photograph (of an exploding star) on the cover of the *Spokesman*, the Bertrand Russell Peace Foundation publication in England. This issue (No. 85) marked the fiftieth anniversary of the Albert Einstein, Bertrand Russell *Manifesto* against thermo-nuclear weapons.

Kurt did not forego writing new essays or editorial comments for *In These Times*, however. One of these was a "Letter to the Editor" response to a long and thoughtful lead article, "How to Turn Your Red State Blue," by Christopher Hayes (3/22/05). Hayes' piece pondered why liberal issues like better schools and health insurance and social security had failed to sway conservatives in the last election. He wondered which deeply felt progressive ideologies could possibly compete with strong evangelical appeals like banning abortion or gay marriage, which apparently had blinded the majority of voters to more desperately needed social and economic changes offered by the Democrats.

Kurt's editorial answer came directly to the point. "Progressives represent . . . an attack on patriarchy . . . the fundamental certainty . . . that women are men's property. That is the 'value' George W. Bush, like the late Pope, celebrates in both his manners and his religion." As an anthropologist, Kurt said he found it "unsurprising that nearly half of voting American human beings . . . voted with utmost passion for him. To them, all other issues, war or peace, prosperity or economic collapse . . . are by comparison flatulence in a typhoon, so to speak" (5/23/05, *In These Times*, p. 4).

He took considerable delight in the fact that, after forwarding this editorial letter to the head of the department of anthropology at his alma mater, the University of Chicago, he had received an affirming reply from none other than the department chair, "fellow anthropologist, Alan L. Kolata." (When he sent me a copy of this letter and an explanation, he added, "What a humane reply this is!")

This is not to say that all his energy was invested in the vigor of fighting the good fight that spring. Kurt lost two friends who were important to him. The first was playwright Arthur Miller, who died in February at age eighty-nine, nearly seven years Kurt's senior, and like Kurt, an important voice of American conscience, both in his artistic endeavors and his political assertions. Kurt phoned after his memorial, held May 9 at the Majestic Theater in New York City, to reflect on Miller's importance—to the world and to himself. "I knew him," Kurt said quietly, with evident reverence. He mentioned some of the people who had paid tribute that day. "I cried when Estelle Parson read the Linda Loman speech from *Death of a Salesman*," he said. (I, of course, also wept after hearing his description of that tribute from Miller's widow.)

The other longtime friend he lost that April was Frank Conroy, the Iowa Writers' Workshop director. In fact, Kurt knew about his death before I did and said he'd already spoken with Frank's wife when he called me to see if there'd been significant press reports. The next day I sent clippings from the Iowa City and Des Moines papers and told him about the memorial service scheduled for April 22, when John Irving was to be among those celebrating Frank's life. Again, it especially grieved him when friends of Frank's age died, almost as though he were being abandoned to yet another dose of extended life when younger pals had been freed.

But this time he didn't seem so weighed down, I think perhaps because he had poetry to play with. In the May 16 issue of the *New Yorker*, his poem titled "Joe Heller" appeared at the top of page 38, right in the middle of "Talk of the Town" section. He was downright elated when he phoned to celebrate.

Later that month he sent a new poem called "Algren Meets Donoso," his old reminiscence of his favorite Workshop anecdote, when Nelson Algren had observed to José Donoso how interesting it must have been to live in a country so long and narrow as Chile. I asked Kurt if he might be willing to let David Hamilton, the editor of the *Iowa Review* literary magazine at the University of Iowa, consider the poem for publication. When he assented, I called David, who was delighted, with the happy result that he published the poem. Kurt and I had a fun correspondence about this, with me acting as his agent and letting him know his poem would earn a grand sum of twenty-five bucks, plus two free copies of the magazine. For this, Kurt assured me of the agent's commission of ten percent, and forthwith sent a check for $2.50 to the "Loree Rackstraw Agency."

Later that summer, he scored with another poetry publication—this time three of his poems, in fact, which were published in volume No. 85 of the *Spokesman,* the same Bertrand Russell Peace Foundation journal that had published his "Requiem" earlier that year. These were considerably more lighthearted poems, titled "Song of the Flaming Neuter" (about his own aging sexual experience), "Intelligent Design" (his complaint about Darwinian adaptation theory), and "Neocons" (satirizing Yale's contributions to presidential candidates).

To cap it off, he sent a new CD of tunes by "Ukulele Dick," which he insisted was "a sure cure for depression." It's a bubbling and bouncy compilation of pre-1950s' tunes performed by one Rick McKee, a Santa Cruz musician, along with twenty or so other actors and musicians. Kurt was right: one couldn't help smiling along with the songs. (I could imagine his grin, and maybe a dance step or two, as he listened.)

So the summer of 2005 seemed a reasonably decent time for an eighty-two-year-old who had long claimed he was tired of living. In July he sent the proofs of a new book by young Colby Buzzell for which Kurt was writing the following promotional blurb: "Nothing less than the soul of an extremely interesting human being fighting in Iraq on our behalf." *My War: Killing Time in Iraq* was a gripping narrative by a bright kid who was more interested in skateboarding than college, who had enlisted out of boredom in 2003, and who had become a gunner in a Stryker armored vehicle running reconnaissance in the Sunni Triangle area. The narrative is a remarkably vivid account from the young man's journals and blogs written during his active service there.

When we talked about the book after I read it, Kurt acknowledged he had been taken by the author's total engagement in his battle experience and recognized his passion as something common to fighters in war, himself included. I was a bit taken aback at first when he said quietly, "I wouldn't have given up my experience as a soldier for anything." I heard him say something similar on a couple of public radio interviews in the following months, and I think it added a valuable insight and complexity to antiwar commitments, especially his. As I ruminated on this seeming contradiction, it made some sense that given Kurt's lifelong chronic depression (and his almost insistent habit of laughter whenever possible), that the stressful concentration of courage, fear, and achievement in battle could have been a unique adrenalin high that ironically was a lift for him. Did he, then, love war or look forward to it? Of course not. But this particular "reconciliation" about war surely added at least another layer of complexity to his fascination with human awareness.

He phoned in late July to reminisce about some of his past literary ventures in Russia, just a few days before I was to leave on a long-anticipated trip to that country. He seemed delighted I'd be having considerable immersion into the art and culture of St. Petersburg, a city he still thought of as Leningrad, with memories of the incredible suffering its citizens endured during the Nazi siege of World War II. He gave me an ironic minutia of history and suggested I ask my guide whether this was common knowledge: *Stalin and Prokofiev both died on the same day—and Stalin had banned his music!* (Neither of the two Russian guides I queried had known this curious fact. Who but Kurt Vonnegut *would* have had such information?)

When I returned home in August, a copy of Kurt's new book, *A Man Without a Country* was waiting for me, with the inscription "Welcome home, dear Loree." It was, I thought, a total delight and handsomely laid out with poems, personal reminiscences, political protests, and excerpts from his speeches or *In These Times* articles interspersed with his "sayings" that Joe and he had been putting together into poster format. Published in hardback by Seven Stories

Press, it had been deftly edited by the Press's editor and founder, Daniel Simon, who had likewise published Kurt's *God Bless You, Dr. Kevorkian*, as well as *Like Shaking Hands with God*, a compelling bookstore conversation between Kurt and author Lee Stringer in 1998. This new, slim volume landed immediately on the *New York Times* nonfiction best-seller list and stayed there for several months.

Kurt sent a copy of the favorable *New York Times Book Review* critique by A. O. Scott on October 9 but phoned later to talk rather disconsolately about response to his book. Scott had summarized Kurt's remarkable literary career and noted his centrality among the emerging postmodern writers of the sixties and seventies. But Kurt had particularly focused on Scott's insightful comments about how Kurt's work had never required "a scholarly concordance or an interpretive apparatus to figure out what Vonnegut means," suggesting to Kurt the painful irony that his "*transparency . . . has diminished his utility in the academy, where literary reputations are made and preserved*" (p. 31). Kurt reminded me of his teaching experience at Smith College and said quietly, "I looked in the library catalog, and they didn't have any of my books. Academics had no respect for my work." (A later check indicated the Smith Library *did* include a substantial Vonnegut collection, but apparently not when he taught there, at least to Kurt's knowledge.)

It was no consolation, of course, to remind him of the many scholars we both knew who deeply respected his work. Indeed, when the *Washington Post* gave him a two-page spread at the top of its arts section a couple days later, staff writer Bob Thompson had relied substantially upon an interview with Peter Reed, then emeritus chair of the University of Minnesota Department of English and, as noted before, a longtime serious scholar of Vonnegut's work. Nonetheless, Thompson perhaps crassly concluded, "Kurt Vonnegut Jr. has made a life's work of being unhappy with the world." Even so, his story did undertake a serious review of Kurt's opus, and recognized the high rank of *Slaughterhouse-Five* on the Modern Library list of the top twentieth-century books, along with master critic Harold Bloom's designation of his work as part of the "Western canon."

If Kurt was not overly pleased with critical press response to *A Man Without a Country*, he had some real fun with it on cable television. He called me the night of his appearance on the HBO's *Real Time with Bill Maher*, which aired live on September 9. Half serious, he said, "I hope I don't fuck it up." I told him to "loosen up—only half the continent will be watching." His was to be the remote interview done by the caustic Maher—a favorite political critic and comic, but someone capable of biting satire. Because Maher and his guests ran overtime in their initial discussion of the Bush failure to cope with the Hurricane Katrina disaster, Kurt's remote appearance was somewhat formal and out of context. Nonetheless he segued smoothly with his ready harangue of other screw-ups in American history by politicians and their hubris. When I spoke to him the next day, I marveled at his ability to have come on cold like that and pull it off. I could tell he was pleased with his performance.

The following week he had a live appearance on Comedy Central's *The Daily Show with Jon Stewart*. At first I was again a bit taken aback by seeing how Kurt had aged since I'd last seen him, which was four years ago in Northampton, mostly by his slow gait onto the platform. After Stewart credited Kurt's books with helping him survive adolescence, Kurt plunged into his anti-establishment repartee. It was a total success, and the audience screamed with delight when Stewart shook hands with him and quipped, "I'm very sorry to see you've lost your edge." I think (and hope) Kurt must have grinned all the way home.

I would have given almost anything to have been there to congratulate him that night, but at the same time, I told myself I had to start getting prepared for the possibility that he wouldn't always be around. I thought long into the night about the paradoxical gift of his strangely intimate "presence" in my life throughout these many years, intimacy mostly through language—his voice over the phone, which I often was poised to pick up before it even rang; in his frequent letters, which I still miss every time I reach into my mailbox; and through his books, which comfort me from their place on my shelves and compel me with their actual reading. The rooms of my home are animated by his whimsical artworks and "sayings" that insist upon smiles. What a strange and wonderful friendship.

A Man Without a Country continued to ride the best-seller lists for another eight weeks, with printings eventually topping three hundred thousand copies and going into paperback. On October 7, Kurt was featured on the PBS program *Now* with David Brancaccio, which was a solid twenty-minute interview with plenty of time to even discuss the Bush administration's failure to help the victims of Katrina in the hurricane disaster and aftermath.

By the end of 2005, the *New Yorker* reported that Kurt was serving as a commentator for the Swarthmore College's student run *War News Radio* program that was being podcast with live telephone interviews to Iraq. Not bad for an aging old fart who was trying to be a good sport about being so old. Among the last written words I had from him that year was a Noel greeting attached to a copy of a letter he had written as an addendum to *The Daily Show* appearance and hadn't had time to articulate on the air. It was later published by *In These Times* and then republished in the British *Spokesman*. The addendum included five admonitions he'd taken from the *Holy Bible*, which he thought had been trashed by righteous Americans. It ended with the Biblical "You cannot serve both God and Mammon," followed by Kurt's reference, "Look at Pat Robertson! He's as happy as a hog up to its ears in excrement!"

The *Man Without a Country* celebration continued into the next year and so, alas, did the war in Iraq. Kurt apparently was hearing from G.I.s stationed in the Middle East. He sent, without comment, a letter from a bored but witty G.I. who was awaiting orders in Kuwait and who'd asked him to please write back to him in longhand. (Later Kurt told me he *had* answered the twenty-year-old as requested.) Kurt and I both knew his energy was waning, and I was moved by his determination to take the time and effort to write out a personal note to soldiers who would have a handwritten letter to brag about. And I was astonished to learn in February that he was out on the speaking circuit again, in Hartford, Connecticut, where he appeared with Joyce Carol

Oates and Jennifer Weiner on The Connecticut Forum's *Evening with Our Favorite Writers* at the Bushnell Center.

Then in March he addressed a packed crowd of two thousand at Ohio State University in Columbus, the biggest gathering for a speaker at the Ohio Union since Michael Moore's appearance there a decade earlier. After announcing this would be his last speech given for money, which drew moans of protest from his audience, he gained his first roars of laughter and applause with his recent favorite, "The only difference between Bush and Hitler is that Hitler was elected."

Covering his speech in the March 5 *Ohio Free Press* online, Harvey Wasserman reported that Kurt's message of dystopia about politics was relieved somewhat by his suggestion that music always helped to cheer him up. He said Kurt even broke into a "tender rendition of 'Stardust Memories,'" which turned the crowd reverential if not tearful. He spoke of the importance of kindness and of being alert to good times. His speech was, as always, deftly crafted with serious concerns balanced by humor and lightness—and with humble appreciation for his ability as a writer and for "the knowledge that I have enough." This latter, I think, was a significant closure of possible concerns in his past.

Kurt continued to be a bit contentious about negative overreactions by evolutionists to the idea of "intelligent design," since for him, widely accepted evolutionary theory seemed to suggest a failure to fully understand certain puzzling biological characteristics. We had a phone discussion about this sometime in April, after which he sent me one of his new posters bearing the following statement: "There are organizing principles in the universe which we can no more understand than my dog can." This statement may have been as close as Kurt came to a direct articulation of a kind of mysticism. He had long believed human awareness was sacred, but he insisted it was shaped at least in part by the *accidents* of evolution, including that of our very language and syntax.

Certainly his own fiction, first and most profoundly expressed in the erratic structure of *Slaughterhouse-Five*, was one of his earliest efforts at suggesting the irrationality of the universe and humanity's oversimplification of causality. He had always been sensitive to what he saw as the malevolent capriciousness of nature, to say nothing of the naïveté of belief in a caring, rational deity.

Then in June came wafting through the mail a copy of the invitation for him to present the annual Marian McFadden Memorial Lecture as the centerpiece of the City of Indianapolis designation of the coming year 2007 as the "Year of Vonnegut." Throughout the entire period, monthly celebrations of the Vonnegut family's contributions to the arts would be offered to the public by state and local organizations. These would include recognition of a number of major Indianapolis and state buildings designed by his paternal grandfather and father, as well as lectures, films, concerts, and exhibits. Local citizens would be invited to suggest their favorite Vonnegut book, the winner of which would then be placed in the time capsule of the newly transformed Central Library scheduled to reopen in 2007. That book would become the focus of the City's "One Book, One City" initiative. And henceforth, an annual lecture would be named in his honor. The whole thing was an invitation Kurt said left him "thunderstruck."

But the summer of 2006 held even more Vonnegut celebrations: He appeared on the cover of issue No. 27, "Ode to the Midwest" of *STOPSMILING: The Magazine for High-Minded Lowlifes*, an elegantly slick journal published in Chicago. Inside was an eighteen-page color feature titled "The Melancholia of Everything Completed" and included photographs of Kurt by his daughter Edie and her son Buck Squibb, a scattering of Kurt's poems, an excerpt from one of his short stories from the recent *Bagombo Snuff Box* collection, along with a number of reproductions of his posters and screenprints. Highlighting the feature was a long interview with Kurt about his career and reminiscences of his family and life in the Midwest.

He was also featured in a four-page article titled "Vonnegut's Apocalypse" by Douglas Brinkley in the August 24 issue of *Rolling Stone*. I suggested he had doubtless enjoyed the magazine's pinup girl cover reminiscent of the 1940s' *Playboy* covers, this one of a gorgeous, saluting blonde in a very brief U.S. Navy uniform. The Vonnegut article began with an advisory that warned: "He survived being captured by the Nazis and the suicide of his mother to write some of the funniest, darkest novels of our time, but it took George W. Bush to break him."

It was a slick feature that detailed Kurt's apocalyptic view of the worldwide dilemma stemming from addiction to petroleum and corrupt political leadership in the United States, but it also offered an insightful overview of his life and work. One of the highlights was a boldface Vonnegut quote on the last page: "Evolution is a mistake. Humans are a mistake. We've destroyed our planet." It was the vision that haunted him, one reflecting Mark Twain's view at the end of his life, but had come much closer to reality since that time. Indeed, it reflected Kurt's early and oft-repeated (and serious) question in his fiction and conversation: "What are people *for?*" At least he had some satisfaction in demonstrating through his writing and speeches that humanist values of decency and kindness are what sustained life for him, and could make life's challenges less painful for all concerned.

Meanwhile, even young writers do not cease their toil. Evidence of this was the elegant new archives and library structure newly added to the Writers' Workshop Dey House on the University of Iowa campus spanning the Iowa River, where Kurt and I first met. By 2006, a former student of the late Frank Conroy, Lan Samantha Chang, was heading the program. To help celebrate the October dedication of that new structure, I was able to present the Kurt Vonnegut/Joe Petro portfolio of *Enchanted IOUs* transformed from the original magic marker drawings Kurt had given me years earlier. I attended the dedication and reception for the new building, experiencing a twang of sentimentality about "coming full circle," especially when I saw two of those Vonnegut screen prints on exhibit in the new Conroy Library. I had a flashback on the time, more than forty years earlier, when I had visited Kurt's office in the old Quonset hut Workshop, lugging a folio of drawings on the way from class, never realizing, of course, what a large role art would play in his life. Or what a huge role *he* would play in mine.

I was pleased that Kurt's two years of teaching at the Workshop would have some representation on the premises and would reflect his long friendship and regard for Frank Conroy. Nonetheless, the splendid ambience of the whole scene was jarringly, if elegantly in contrast to the comforting memory of the old Workshop housed in the rickety aluminum Quonset barracks all those many years ago. These darling, well-dressed young students now posted at classroom doors to politely guide visitors were babies! Inside were elegantly structured round wooden tables about which they would gather to discuss each other's stories or poems in beautifully lighted rooms, overlooking the Iowa River. It was a gorgeously brave new world, even if it seemed such elegance was totally incongruent with conditions most writers I knew had struggled.

More power to them, I thought, wishing I felt more enthusiastic for their future. And the planet's.

I duly reported on the celebration to Kurt, along with a birthday greeting marking his eighty-fourth year of life on November 11. I knew he would have been saddened by the death earlier that month of his friend, novelist William Styron, at age eighty-one. Old age was not a condition he was suffering gladly, no matter how he lightened that burden by joking about celibacy and parallel parking challenges.

So it made me sad that he had to suffer yet another downer in the form of correspondence he shared with me from one Andrey Filipov, a young Bulgarian playwright who had adapted Kurt's novel, *Timequake,* for the stage. The play had had a successful premiere that spring, with one of the actors playing the role of Kurt. But a few days before his birthday, Kurt had received a grief-stricken letter from Andrey, whose young wife and sister had been killed in a car accident by a "drunken madman" after a joyful autumn outing in the mountains. His mother had survived the accident but was dreadfully injured. Struggling with depression, the youthful playwright was now writing to ask Kurt if he could suggest anyone in the States who might be interested in his *Timequake* as a play or script.

I never learned the outcome of his hopes, although a recent Google search suggests an Albany University professor in New York has worked with Filipov on an English translation of his *Timequake* play as recently as March 2007. One wonders how many young artists in the world have been touched by Kurt's inspiration and will continue to pursue the creative visions he inspired. I knew Kurt was warmed by affirmations of that possibility.

It was just a few days after his eighty-fourth birthday, when Kurt phoned to reminisce about the Workshop days: "We were so lucky to all be together back then." He recalled how he and his daughter Edie used to love watching the first *Batman* programs on Andre Dubus's old television set on Saturday afternoons: "The guy who played him always had a bit of a tummy hanging over his belt." Laughing until he coughed, he recalled the story Workshop director Paul Engle had told about John Gerber who headed the English Department at Iowa: "You know? That man is a *smiler*. Put him in a closet and lock the door, and a week later he's still smiling!"

Smiles meant a lot to Kurt. Somehow, his reminiscences from the past seemed to suggest his own quiet summation of cheerful times in his life, and I was grateful he wanted to share those times in his slowing drift toward the end.

It was my delight that he also took considerable pleasure from the happy news of my daughter Leslie's forthcoming marriage. She had written him a detailed letter about her fiancé and her feelings about being married a second time: aspirations about their children, and about making a difference as partners in the world. Because Kurt had always worried about single moms, I knew he meant it when he phoned to tell me of his joy for her. I mentioned how kind he and Jane had been to Leslie and her brother, Rob, back in Iowa City when we all were young. And he reminded me how he had enjoyed having lunch with Rob when he was in town for a visit the previous summer.

So as 2007 dawned, Kurt was focusing his efforts on preparation for the Indianapolis "Year of Vonnegut" at which he was scheduled for a major speech. His presentation of the "Marian McFadden Memorial Lecture" would be the crowning event for an elaborate series of cultural presentations and tours throughout the year. The speech had been a major challenge, he confided in a phone call as he was struggling over it, but a few days later, he'd had a breakthrough. He was finally confident everything would be OK. It was evident he was truly awed and honored by the event and by the tributes being bestowed on him and his family heritage. He had always been proud of certain parts of his Indiana legacy and had publicly celebrated his German free-thinker ancestry innumerable times in previous speeches.

As much as I would have loved to be present, when I discussed this possibility with Kurt, I knew I would not be there. Especially when he said, "I can't take care of you," I knew he meant that this event was going to take all the energy he had to bring off. He promised he would see that I received a videotape. Free tickets were available, and I had no doubt the Butler University venue would be packed.

On March 9, he sent a copy of a news feature from the *Philadelphia Inquirer* (2/25/07) by one Sandy Bauers about new audio recordings of Kurt's novels, as well as a new Caedmon CD called *Essential Vonnegut* that includes three excellent interviews with Kurt by Walter James Miller of New York University, a scholar especially able at raising key questions to facilitate lively discussion. It's a charming dialogue that reveals significant maturing in both men spanning three decades. The author of this news feature also referenced other recent CD recordings of Kurt's novels and concluded by quoting a fictional hotel clerk's observation about Kilgore Trout, the artist in *Breakfast of Champions*. The clerk sees Trout as "a man who is terribly wounded because he has dared to pass through the fires of truth to the other side." Bauers says, "For me, Trout is Vonnegut."

It was a discerning observation, and I believe Kurt thought so, too. At the top of the *Inquirer* copy, he had penned this statement, dated

3/9/07: "Dear Loree—if this isn't nice, I don't know what is. Love, KV." It comforted me to know he was pleased that he'd not be forgotten, that his work would perhaps even be regarded with continuing celebration in the years to come, even if he was no longer present.

Five days later, Joe Petro phoned Kurt to discuss a business question, but received no answer. In a couple more days, he called me to see if I knew why no one was answering the phone at Kurt's house. Within a few hours we both had connected with a different family member who trusted us with the confidential and chilling news of his accidental fall on the cement steps leading up to his brownstone on East 48th Street. He had not regained consciousness and was being treated at Bellevue.

As the days of waiting began, a few members of the small *karass* that had formed years ago at Kurt's two-day speaking marathon in the Quad Cities began a telephone and e-mail group vigil to help sustain morale and give comfort. Marc Leeds, the compiler of *The Vonnegut Encyclopedia*, was devastated that he had to depart the next day on a long-planned European tour and would leave before the outcome was known. Peter Reed in Minneapolis maintained his comforting quixotic concern throughout. Joe in Kentucky and I in Iowa conversed several times daily, and we both kept in regular touch with Vonnegut siblings and with Asa Pieratt, the now retired university librarian in Rhode Island. I spoke once or twice with Bob Weide in London, who stayed in regular phone communication with the family.

Kurt's wife Jill understandably wanted confidentiality and no publicity and was spending most of her time at the hospital with Kurt. Everyone respected that, and of course, all shared her concern silently from various distances. But the news was not optimistic. Kurt was on life support and had not shown any sign of awareness since the accident. Mark, Kurt's physician son, counseled his sisters about the grim medical realities.

One by one the Vonnegut offspring made their last visits to their dad and were somewhat comforted by the knowledge that he was in no pain. It was clear he would not regain sentience. He died the night of April 11, 2007. His obituary appeared on the *New York Times* Web page that night before I went to bed, numb with grief.

I was awakened before dawn the next morning by a phone call from a sobbing friend in Chile, before I had even had time to notify my own children. Similar calls persisted throughout the day, from all parts of the country. A number of friends still in the teaching profession reported their students weeping in the halls and classrooms of their universities. Strangers comforted each other on buses and in coffee shops worldwide.

On the Official Kurt Vonnegut Web site, Mark Vonnegut described Kurt's limited memorial service that he arranged in accord with his father's wishes at the Algonquin Hotel on April 21, which was attended by family and immediate friends. I did not attend. That was hard but the right thing to do. With limited space and so many others wanting to be there, undue pressure on family members was definitely not needed. I doubt Madison Square Garden could have accommodated everyone who wanted to say goodbye.

So Kurt would not be present to receive the honors Indianapolis had wished to grant him on April 27. His son Mark took his place to read his father's mostly whimsical and irreverent speech that chided Indiana somewhat for its past history of conservative politics and racism, while it honored Kurt's Indiana heroes, Hapgood and Debs. It was a brave thing for Mark to do, especially because Kurt's statement also honored Mark's own achievements as a humane writer and physician, even as it paid tribute to the architectural and other accomplishments of his own father and grandfather. Other family members were present to celebrate Mark's presentation as well as to help honor the achievements of past Vonneguts.

Many of them I'd seen and heard about over the forty years I'd known Kurt and his family. Among Kurt's was his ability to show that awareness makes life sacred—not perfect, but sacred. To him, that meant life needed and deserved kindness.

He was not a perfect human being, but one of his intentions as a writer and a person was that kindness to others should be central to life, including kindness to those who were themselves unkind. One of the curious and perhaps sacred things I observed about him was the self-generating joy his kindness made possible, a joy that seemed very much like love.

Even so, accidents could always turn life itself on its ear. It always made him feel better to laugh when that happened. Unfortunately, the last accident he experienced didn't appear to give him time to laugh. But then, he always tried to tell us that time wasn't what we thought it was. And after all, the "will of accident" may have been stronger than time that day and perhaps even kind to *him*, if not to us.

It helps me feel better to think he was OK with that.

finis

Kurt and Loree, Cedar Falls, Iowa, 1989.

AFTERWORD

It is forty-three years to the month since I walked into the Workshop classroom to meet this unknown writer who would be my mentor for the next year. I remember how awed he was then with existence itself. We had talked some about his bewilderment as a twenty-year-old kid coming out of that underground meat locker in Dresden to witness an elegant city transformed into a radiant holocaust of death and ash. He had found it daunting to process the paradox of his own country-men wreaking mass slaughter on defenseless people—people from whose stock his own family members had come. It seemed the use of traditional narrative for expressing rational thought was insufficient, if not contradictory, to making sense out of his experience.

During our long friendship, I continued to learn from Kurt—from his letters and phone calls, from my exploration of his books and their richness, from sharing some hilarious celebrations as well as dark de-spairs, and from our occasional reunions. He was on my mind almost every day.

I hope my memories might benefit others who chance to read them. They have been a way of grieving his absence as well as cele-brating his life.

Most of all, I hope his readers will keep passing his books on to others. His books are important. If you read them, you may hear birds talking, perhaps even celebrating.

If that isn't nice, what is?

"Poo-tee-weet?"

INDEX

Weiner, Jennifer, 253

Welcome to the Monkey House, 33, 161, 203

Wicker, Tom, 97

Wilde, Oscar, 213

Williams, Joy, 2, 177

Williams, Tennessee, 118, 173

Wilson, Leslie, 6, 14, 15, 20, 43, 46, 51, 172, 187, 190, 207, 214, 219, 257

Wilson, Rob, 14, 15, 43, 46, 51, 69, 187, 237, 257

Wilson, Robley, 49, 119

Wilson, Austen, 207

Wood, Grant, 9

The World According to Garp, 76

World War II, 4–6, 27, 30, 64, 120, 124, 132, 135–136, 167–168, 177, 182, 183, 199, 227, 236, 249; and Dresden, 4–5, 29–30, 55, 134, 135, 170, 191, 197, 239, 263; *See also Slaughterhouse-Five*

Wright, Micah Ian, 231

Wurst, Dennis, 197

Y

Yarmolinsky, Adam, 7, 75, 106, 111, 128, 129, 211

Yates, Richard, 31, 111; biography of, 234–235; in Boston, 81, 91; and *Cold Spring Harbor*, 126–127; death of, 172–173, 227; and declining health and finances, 141, 161–162; and Dick Rackstraw's death, 50; and Dubus accident, 126; and *The Easter Parade*, 61–62, 162; and Iowa Writers' Workshop, 26–28, 29; psychological problems of, 27, 62–63, 116; and Vonnegut's sixtieth birthday, 97–98, 99, 100; and *Young Hearts Crying*, 112

Young, Ida, 126

Yugoslavia, 204, 206–220

Z

Zinn, Howard, 242

Zinn, Rosalyn, 242